Studies in the History of Law and Justice

Volume 10

The purpose of this book series is to publish high quality volumes on the history of law and justice.

Legal history can be a deeply provocative and influential field, as illustrated by the growth of the European universities and the *ius commune*, the French Revolution, the American Revolution, and indeed all the great movements for national liberation through law. The study of history gives scholars and reformers the models and courage to question entrenched injustices, by demonstrating the contingency of law and other social arrangements.

Yet legal history today finds itself diminished in the universities and legal academy. Too often scholarship betrays no knowledge of what went before, or why legal institutions took the shape they did. This series seeks to remedy that deficiency.

Studies in the History of Law and Justice will be theoretical and reflective. Volumes will address the history of law and justice from a critical and comparative viewpoint. The studies in this series will be strong bold narratives of the development of law and justice. Some will be suitable for a very broad readership.

Contributions to this series will come from scholars on every continent and in every legal system. Volumes will promote international comparisons and dialogue. The purpose will be to provide the next generation of lawyers with the models and narratives needed to understand and improve the law and justice of their own era.

The series includes monographs focusing on a specific topic, as well as collections of articles covering a theme or collections of article by one author.

More information about this series at http://www.springer.com/series/11794

José María Beneyto · Justo Corti Varela
Editors

At the Origins of Modernity

Francisco de Vitoria and the Discovery of International Law

Springer

Editors
José María Beneyto
Institute for European Studies
CEU San Pablo University
Madrid
Spain

Justo Corti Varela
Institute for European Studies
CEU San Pablo University
Madrid
Spain

ISSN 2198-9842 ISSN 2198-9850 (electronic)
Studies in the History of Law and Justice
ISBN 978-3-319-62997-1 ISBN 978-3-319-62998-8 (eBook)
DOI 10.1007/978-3-319-62998-8

Library of Congress Control Number: 2017947443

Printed on acid-free paper

This Springer imprint is published by Springer Nature
The registered company is Springer International Publishing AG
The registered company address is: Gewerbestrasse 11, 6330 Cham, Switzerland

Contents

Chapter 1
Introduction: Francisco de Vitoria and the Origins of the Modern Global Order

Anthony Pagden

Abstract This Introduction seeks to demonstrate how the various contributions to the volume relate to one another. It seeks, also, to locate them in the context of Francisco de Vitoria's attempt to create a new supra-national juridical order. This, although it was clearly intended to offer some degree of legitimacy for the Spanish occupation of the Americas, was also conceived as a "law of nations" that, while grounded ultimately upon natural law, would be, in essence, a positive law derived from the presumed consensus of a hypothetical international community.

In 1951, the German jurist (and former Nazi) Carl Schmitt began his attempt to describe the new international global order which was slowly emerging from the destruction of the Second World by declaring that "for four hundred years from the sixteenth to the twentieth centuries the structure of European international law (*Völkerrecht*)" had been "determined by a fundamental course of events, conquest of a new world." It was this "legendary and unforeseen… and unrepeatable historical event," he claimed, which had given rise to what he called "the traditional Eurocentric order of international law."

Above all, he went on, it was "the famous *relectiones* of Francisco de Vitoria [which] given the intellectual courage these lectures exhibited in formulating questions, and given the perfection of their scholastic method… influenced and dominated all further discussions of the problem."[1]

From an historiographical point of view, this must seem an irredeemable anachronism. Modern international law, as it has evolved since the nineteenth century, is very far removed, both in the normative claims it wishes to make and in its objectives, from Vitoria's "law of nations." There may, however, be another way of understanding Vitoria's achievement which makes it no less remarkable. To speak of Vitoria (or the School of Salamanca more broadly) in terms of "founders"

[1]Schmitt 2003, 39, 69.

A. Pagden (✉)
University of California, Los Angeles, California, US
e-mail: pagden@polisci.ucla.edu

J.M. Beneyto and J. Corti Varela (eds.), *At the Origins of Modernity*,
Studies in the History of Law and Justice 10, DOI 10.1007/978-3-319-62998-8_1

or "fathers" is to suggest that he, and they, had devised the basic conceptions on which modern international law is based. And that they clearly did not do. All of the terms Vitoria uses—even those most immediately identifiable as legal—derive from the neo-Aristotelian philosophical and theological traditions (Schmitt's "scholastic methods") in which he had been schooled. What, however, Vitoria did do, as Schmitt had seen, was to adapt an already familiar vocabulary, drawn from the conventional scholastic interpretation of the natural law, and the Roman legal framing of the civil law, in which to redescribe the relationship between Europe and a group of peoples whom he described as "previously unknown to our world." Vitoria's impact on subsequent theorists of the "laws of nations," in particular, on Alberico Gentili, and Hugo Grotius, was as Franco Todescan insists here considerable. As Todescan's essay demonstrates, however, Vitoria's influence on later generations cannot be captured by a summary of citations, important though these clearly were. For what Vitoria could have been said to have bequeathed to his immediate heirs, and they in their turn to a succession of later writers—most notably Samuel Pufendorf, Christian Wolf, and Emer de Vattel—was the possibility of a language, and what would eventually become an entire philosophical-legal genre, summed up in phrase "the law of nature and of nations," in which to recast what had really become a new global order.

This would perish, along with the natural law itself, with Kant, and Hegel. But some part of it was resurrected in the mid-nineteenth century as what we today would be prepared to recognize as the basis of modern international law—that is, as an essentially positive law, arrived at by a process (real in this case, not hypothetical) of consent among nations based upon a shared understanding of a universal rule of justice.

The problem for later generations with Vitoria's framing of the problem was that it presupposed the existence of the very thing—a universal rule of justice—which it was attempting to define. It also left the content of the law itself unspecified. Or to put it differently, while it insisted that the *ius gentium* must have the force of law—*lex*—it failed to state just how those *leges* were to be arrived at. Gentili's solution was to make the law of nations identical with the Roman law (a strategy followed later by Vico and Gravina).[2] Grotius equated it with what he called the "unwritten Civil Law" which was similarly arrived at by the "continual Use, and the Testimony of Men skilled in the Laws."[3] In the nineteenth century, and in the absence of a belief in a natural or divine law underpinning all legal norms, the law of nations became, in effect, the law which governed the relationship between the "civilized" peoples of the world—the only ones, in effect, to have "Men skilled in the Laws." "Barbarians" who did not by definition live in civil, or law-governed communities, lay outside it. Even today, although the word "barbarian" has dropped out of use, the International Court of Justice lists among those principles it seeks to apply to

[2]See Pagden 2015.

[3]Grotius 2005, I, 163.

"such disputes as are submitted to it": "the general principles of law recognized by civilized nations."[4]

That, however, was precisely what Vitoria had denied. His view of the law of nations was uncompromisingly universalistic, and it was precisely this aspect of his thought that determined the ways his work has been interpreted by later generations. As Andrew Fitzmaurice explains in his essay, ever since the seventeenth century Vitoria and his successors have often been portrayed as combatants in a struggle against the settlers and the agents of the Crown, if not the Crown itself, for justice in the Americas. "I love the university of Salamanca', enthused, Samuel Johnson, in 1763, "for when the Spaniards were in doubt as to the lawfulness of their conquering America, the University of Salamanca gave it as their opinion that it was not lawful."[5] The fact that the Spanish authorities had listened to the Salamancan theologians rather than "their Christian friends and relations" claimed John Stuart Mill, a century later, had led them to "side" with "the Pagans" and to do their best to "protect the natives."[6] Without the moral interference of the "divines of Salamanca," the consequences of the Spanish conquest would, he argued, have been far more deadly than they were. Among most of the liberal international jurists of the nineteenth century, and in particular those associated with the highly influential *Institut de droit international*, the "School" and Vitoria in particular were also closely associated with a supposedly anti-imperialist discourse.

It is also this aspect of Vitoria which has often led him to be hailed, in the twentieth century as the "founder" or "father" of "international law." As Yolanda Gamarra explains here, although attempts to establish a genealogy for modern "international law" may now look quaintly antiquarian, it was a designation which played a significant role in the attempt by a Spanish legal elite with strong international ties, both in Europe and in the USA in the period from 1918 until the outbreak of the Spanish Civil War, to establish a new, humanistic, and, in some broader sense, modernistic interpretation of the legacy of the Spanish empire. Vitoria and his successors were cast as the ancestors of a mode of liberal international legal thinking which offered a counterbalance to the notorious "Black Legend" of relentless Spanish atrocities across the entire reach of the empire from the Netherlands to Peru.

More recently, however, they, and Vitoria in particular, have been seen less as courageous moralists, than as the earliest in a long line of apologists for a blatant form of Christian imperialism, a process which Pablo Zapatero describes in his contribution to this volume.[7] Historically neither image is entirely correct. Vitoria himself, as we know from his correspondence, was sincerely outraged by the behavior of those to whom he referred as the "Peruleros," which, he said, "freezes

[4]Article 39 of the *Statute of the International Court of Justice*.

[5]Boswell 1934, I, 45.

[6]*Considerations on Representative Government*, [1861] in Mill 1984, xix.

[7]See, e.g., Anghie 2005.

the blood in my veins."[8] Yet his discussion of the legitimacy of the conquest, a subject which he had begun, as Schmitt had seen in "an astonishingly objective manner," nevertheless, ends, in Schmitt's words "with the claim that the Spanish are waging a just war, and therefore may annex Indian lands if the Indians resist free *commercium* (not only 'trade') and the free mission of Christianity."[9] The first of these claims is not quite right, and the second is simply false. But it is true that for all his objectivity and indignation, Vitoria's concern was not with the morality or the legitimacy of the Spanish settlers' behavior in the Indies. Nor was he much interested in the ultimate fate of the Indians. His declared objective was rather to establish a legal basis for a situation which already existed and which he believed (or at least claimed to believe) had to be morally acceptable a priori because the Catholic Monarchs were clearly beyond reproach in this as were their successors. Since, as Zapatero notes, "the discovery of an entire continent populated by *infidels* [had] made the old paradigms unworkable," Vitoria was confronted with the need to recast those paradigms in such a way as to make them applicable to, in Zapatero's words "the reality of a larger World in which the Old Continent was a mere unit of the aggregate whole."

The debate over Vitoria's true objectives, and the significance of his contributions to the history of what might be described as the international legal order, has tended to focus on a very small part of his work, although as Simona Langella in this volume, has demonstrated, a great deal still needs to be done on Vitoria's other scattered writings, in particular his substantial accounts of the natural and civil law to be found in his commentaries on St. Thomas Aquinas Since, however, Vitoria has been taken up largely by jurists and historians of political thought most attention has been focused on two of Vitoria's *relectiones* "On the Newly Discovered Indians" (*De Indis recenter inventis*)—henceforth "On the American Indians"—and "On the Law of War" (*De iure belli*), both delivered in 1539. The first of these, the one which would make Vitoria celebrated, was concerned with the highly contentious question: "by what right were the barbarians subjected to Spanish rule?"[10]

Vitoria was not, of course, the first to ask this question. But he was the first to do so at length in public. *Relectiones* were essentially public lectures on topics of wider interest than most university lectures; and if contemporary accounts may be even half believed Vitoria attracted listeners by their hundreds from all across the university. He began by insisting in "On the American Indians" that his lecture was "demonstrative"—that is intended not to argue about the truth but to explain it. "Are we to suppose," he asked, that Ferdinand and Isabella, "most Catholic Monarchs" and Charles V, officially entitled "most righteous and Christian prince" might have failed "to make the most careful and meticulous inquiries" into a matter of such concern to both their security and their conscience? "Of course not:

[8]"Letter to Miguel de Arcos," 8 November 1534, in Vitoria 1991, 331.
[9]Schmitt 2003, 92.
[10]"On the American Indians" Vitoria 1991, 233.

further cavils are unnecessary, and even insolent."[11] By the time he had finished, however, it must have been clear to his audience that the Spanish Crown could make only the slimmest of claims to exercise what we today would call sovereignty and property rights—and what he called "private and public *dominium*"—in the Americas. Certainly, Charles V himself seems to have thought so since shortly afterward he issued a rebuke to the prior of San Esteban for having allowed his charges to "discuss and treat in their sermons and *relectiones*, the right that we have in the Indies, Islands and *Tierra Firma* of the Ocean Sea.... For to discuss such matter without our knowledge and without first informing us is most prejudicial and scandalous."[12]

Although it was for supposedly having denied the legitimacy of the Spanish conquests that Vitoria subsequently became famous outside Spain, it was not this which ultimately made his arguments so important for later generations. It was, instead, that in his attempt to answer the question "by what right were the barbarians subjected to Spanish rule?" he initiated a re-evaluation of the ancient concept of the law of nations—the Roman *ius gentium*—in a way which led to a fundamental re-evaluation of what Schmitt called the "*nomos* of the earth." His significance for the subsequent development of what was to become "international law" was not, that he had bequeathed to later generation a number of augments capable of grounding European claims to occupy non-European territories, or subjugate non-European peoples; it was that he had transformed what had hitherto been a body of normative moral arguments into a set of legal rights. The law of nations, therefore, became, as Niklas Luhman and others have pointed out, the sole instrument with which to recreate an order in a world that both the discoveries and the Reformation had effectively dismantled.[13]

Initially, the *ius gentium* had been the law used by the Romans in their dealing with non-Roman citizens, and it covered such universal, but non-natural institutions as slavery (defined in the *Digest* as "an institution of the *ius gentium*, whereby someone is made subject to the ownership of another, against nature").[14] Like all law, it had its origins in the *most maiorum* or the customs of the majority, for as Cicero had observed: "There is a fellowship that is extremely widespread shared by all with all."[15] This Vitoria recast as a form of positive law which, as he phrased it "is not equitable of itself [that is not identical with the natural law] but has been established by human statute grounded in reason." As Simona Langella points out, "in his commentary to the II-II, q. 57, a. 3, of 1535, Vitoria included the *ius gentium* in the positive right [*ius*]." And, as he phrased it in "On the American Indians," "the consent of the greater part of the world is enough to make it binding, especially

[11] *Ibid.*, 233–4.

[12] Printed in Getino 1930, 150–1.

[13] Luhman 2004, 440.

[14] *Digest* I. 5. IV.

[15] *De Officis*, III 69.

when it is for the common good of all men."[16] As André Azevedo Alves argues in this volume, "The *ius gentium* as Vitoria conceived it was thus common to all mankind and could be recognized by reason even though it was not created through the deliberate will of any human legislator."

What this implied was that the law of nations should be understood as that law which *could* have been agreed upon by "the consent of the greater part of the world" had anyone been in a position to discover what its collective reasoning might be. Such a law did not, however, actually require, as Vitoria's pupil and successor, Domingo De Soto put it, "a meeting of all men in one place" to decide what this was, because "reason dictates what are its particularities."[17] It was then enacted, if only *ex hypothesi*, by what Vitoria famously called the *respublica totius orbis*—"the republic of the whole world." Although this conception, as Johannes Thumfart points out in his essay in this volume, "is mainly a metaphor that Vitoria employs in one episode of the [*relectio*] *De Potestate civili*," it clearly operates, "to make the point that the undivided state of an interconnected world is more natural than the divided one and therefore ontologically and juridically precedes the latter as a stronger claim." What Vitoria had suggested was that there might exist a species of legal authority not merely between states (as the Roman *ius gentium* had been conceived) but also over all—to use Thumfart's language—the "commons" of the world. Vitoria's objective, as Franco Todescan points out here, was to avoid "the dangers implicit in individualistic and voluntaristic theories [of natural law] .... by setting up a *jus gentium* that would allow sovereign states to go beyond their contractual ties and form an organic community that would come together naturally." For Vitoria, this world *respublica* takes the form of a single legal person, with, *de iure* at least, full powers of enactment—the *vis legis*—so that, in Vitoria's words, "the law of nations does not have the force merely of pacts or agreements between men, but has the force of a positive enactment (*lex*)."[18]

By giving the "world" a juridical personality and by insisting that the law of nations was not a natural but a positive law, Vitoria was making two very striking claims. The first was that as the *respublica* of all humanity takes precedence over the nation, so the *ius gentium* must take precedence over the local legislative practices of individual states, which implies that in cases of conflict it must trump local domestic law. For no "kingdom may chose to ignore this law of nations."[19] As Francisco Castilla Urbano writes here, what Vitoria was in effect attempting to do was to transform:

> a Law of Peoples, which subjects human beings to its provisions, into a ius inter gentes, which makes of nations the main players. If the consent of the republics is the basis of the rules underlying the international order, the original dependence of the ius gentium on the

---

[16]Vitoria 1991, 281.

[17]Soto 1556, 197.

[18]"On Civil Power," Vitoria 1991, 40. For a more detailed account of how this operates see Deckers 1991, 345–94.

[19]*Ibid.*

nations cannot be denied; however that does not militate against its ontological priority with regard to the nations, not only because the pacts are incumbent on the parties, but also because their goal is to protect that totality which, in so far as it is composed of moral beings, constituted humanity before any nations came into being.

It was, and remains, of course, a highly controversial argument. It was rejected by some of Vitoria's own colleagues and by most of the great modern theorists of the law of nations in the seventeenth and eighteenth centuries. It is also, for instance, precisely in denial of the claim that an international court can take precedence over a domestic one that the USA (among other states) has refused to allow itself to be bound by the International Criminal Court because that "would allow the trial of American citizens for crimes committed on American soil, which are otherwise entirely within the judicial power of the USA." Similar objections have been raised against such international agreements as the Ottawa treaty on land mines and the Kyoto Protocol against climate change. Nevertheless, as Vitoria had seen, if any international law is to be a true *law* and not a simple set of moral injunctions it cannot be brushed aside by domestic law.

The second of Vitoria's claims was that if the law of nations was truly universal, if it really did constitute the rulings of the world *respublica* it must then apply to all peoples everywhere. The Indians could not—as Mauro Mantovani reminds us in his essay—be deprived of their goods or their land (their private *dominium*) nor of their sovereignty (their public *dominium*) merely because they were unbelievers, for *dominium*, in Simona Langella's words, was a faculty which conferred upon its bearers the "capacity to use things." It therefore constituted an inalienable right, which derived from natural law not grace, and consequently applied to all peoples everywhere no matter what their religious beliefs. Human nature, and the rights and duties which derived from it, were the same in all parts of the world. In the much-cited verse of St. Mathew: "He causes his sun to rise on the evil and the good, and sends rain on the righteous and unrighteous". (4:45) To suggest otherwise was the heresy into which the Calvinists (and in particular the English colonists in America) had fallen. For a Catholic, therefore, there could exist no distinction *in law* between Christians and non-Christians, "civilized" nations and "barbarous" ones. This, argued Schmitt, meant that "he [Vitoria] no longer recognized the spatial order of the medieval *respublica Christiana* with its distinction between the territory of Christian peoples and that of heathens and non-believers."[20]

It is this formulation of the law of nations which provided Vitoria with the only legitimate grounds on which to base a claim that the wars waged by the Spanish in America against its native inhabitants might have been just ones.[21] In Question 3 of "On the American Indians" he described eight titles which might be held to be just by such criteria. The only ones to which he seems to have been prepared to give any credence, however, are Articles 1 and 5. They are also the ones most pertinent to the subject of this volume and those that played the most significant roles in Vitoria's

[20]Schmitt 2003, 107.

[21]"On the American Indians," Vitoria 1991, 264.

attempt to forge a language which might be capable of sustaining a claim to the existence of universal juridical norms.[22]

The first is what he famously called "the right of natural partnership and communication" (*ius naturalis societas et communicationis*). This, as Thumfart phrases it, serves "as anthropological, customary (*communicatio*) and material (*commons*) underpinnings of international political collaboration."[23] It is a complex set of claims divided into five propositions. At the core, however, lies an allusion to the ancient obligation to offer hospitality to strangers. For "Nature" claimed Vitoria, quoting the *Digest* "has decreed a certain kinship between men (*Digest* I.i. 3)... Man is not a 'wolf to his fellow men' - *homo homini lupus* - as the comedian [Plautus] says, but a fellow."[24] All of this brings with it an obligation to friendship for "amity between men is part of the natural law." "In the beginning of the world," he continued:

> when all things were held in common, everyone was allowed to visit and travel through any land he wished. This right was clearly not taken away by the division of property; it was never the intention of nations to prevent men's free mutual intercourse with one another by its division.

This allowed Vitoria to transform the ancient concept of hospitality—the authority he cites is Virgil—into a right under the law of nations and the natural law.[25] "Among all nations," he wrote, "it is considered inhuman to treat travelers badly without some special cause, humane and dutiful to behave hospitably to strangers." As Thumfart says, "In this way, the commons are also the base of Vitoria's strongest just title in favor of conquest."

Expressed as a right under the terms both of the natural law and of the *ius gentium*, this was an original—if also highly debatable—claim. In making it, however, Vitoria was drawing on a long ancient and humanist tradition, which, like the natural law itself, is Stoic in origin. Clearly individuals, no matter how rude and barbarous they might be, had an inalienable right to communicate with their fellow beings, since communication constituted an essential part of their humanity. The fact that such communication was also perceived as a means of civilizing the barbarian in no way altered its standing as a right.

This, of course, meant that the Indians could not, "lawfully bar them [the Spaniards] from their homeland without due cause."[26] If they attempted to do so, then a just war might be waged against them. Of course, this would only apply if

---

[22]For a more extensive account see Pagden 2015.

[23]"On the American Indians," Vitoria 1991, 278. As he defines it, this seems to have been Vitoria's own creation. St. Augustine had suggested that denial of a right of passage might be sufficient *injuria* for a just war. But this has none of the structure of Vitoria's argument (*Quaestiones in Heptateuchum*, IV. 44; *Decretum* C.23. 2.3).

[24]"On the American Indians," Vitoria 1991, 280.

[25]*Ibid*., p. 278, citing Justinian *Institutes* I.2.1, "what natural reason has established among all nations is called the law of nations." See note above.

[26]*Ibid*., 279.

"these travels of the Spaniards are… neither harmful nor detrimental to the barbarians" something about which Vitoria remained evasive saying only that he "supposed it to be" (*ut supponimus*).[27] This assertion set in motion a prolonged debate over the limits and extent of what today is called "freedom of movement." (This is certainly not now held to be a universal right as Vitoria had argued; it is the case, however, that limited "freedom of movement" is considered to be a right (no 13) under the Universal Declaration of Human Rights of 1948 and that, of course, ever since the article 48 of the Treaty of Rome of 1957, it has been one of main guiding principles of the European Union.)

Vitoria extended the same argument to commerce. The natural right of communication delivers a right under the law of nations for all travelers (*peregrini*) to engage in trade with whosever they please "so long as they do not harm the citizens" of the lands through which they are traveling. Therefore, he added, "they [the Spaniards] may import the commodities which they [the Indians] lack and export the gold and silver and other things which they have in abundance." As André Azevedo Alves points out:

> The vigor of Vitoria's defense of the ius communicationis as a binding restriction on the legitimate power of states and empires can be illustrated by the fact that Grotius to a large extent built his own defense of the positions of the Dutch Republic in its conflict with Portugal and Spain in Asia by resorting to Vitoria's authority and to his reasoning in defense of free trade and open access to markets.

Indeed, at the very end of his lecture, Vitoria reminded his audience that the Portuguese had done just as well out of a licit trade "with similar sorts of people," without conquering them, as the Spaniards had done by possibly illicit occupation. Something which, he tentatively suggested, the Spanish crown might think of emulating.[28]

The transition from passage to trade was, however, at best, a shaky one since the right of passage, as a *natural* right could only be understood as both a "prefect" (one that is which is binding in all possible circumstances) and negative one: in that every individual has a natural right *not* to be hindered. The right to free trade, by contrast, comes our looking very much like an "imperfect" obligation. As the eighteenth-century Swiss diplomat, Emer de Vattel said of it later,—and he clearly had Vitoria in mind—"the obligation of trading with other nations is in itself an imperfect obligation, and gives them only an imperfect right…. When the Spaniards attacked the Americans under a pretence that those people refused to traffic with them, they only endeavored to throw a colourable veil over their own insatiable avarice."[29]

Furthermore, Vitoria is insistent throughout that the *ius gentium* is a body of law which must apply to all peoples equally; and this meant that if the Indians could not deny the Spanish right of free passage (and more contentiously settlement) in their

[27] *Ibid.*, 278.
[28] *Ibid.*, 291-2.
[29] Vattel 2008, 275.

territories so long as they made no attempt to violate the sovereignty (public *dominium*) of local rulers, neither could the Spanish deny such access to, say, the French. "It would not be lawful for the French to prohibit Spaniards from travelling or even living in France, or vice versa, so long as it caused no sort of harm to themselves."[30]

There were, however, serious problems with Vitoria's formulation of the argument. In 1546, the theologian, and another of Vitoria's close associates, Melchor Cano, remarked that although the Spaniards might have natural rights as travelers, or even as ambassadors, they had gone to America as neither. They had gone as conquerors. "We would not," he concluded dryly, "be prepared to describe Alexander the Great as a *peregrinus*"[31] As the Saxon jurist and historian, Samuel Pufendorf pointed out, in 1672, Vitoria's understanding of the right of hospitality confused transit, with property. This "natural communication," he wrote scathingly, "cannot prevent a property holder from having the final decision on the question, whether he wishes to share with others the use of his property." It was also, in Pufendorf's view, "crude indeed" to claim that everyone possessed such a right, irrespective of "the numbers in which they had come" or "their purpose in coming".[32]

For Pufendorf, however, the key issue was precisely the degree to which the law of nations, if it was a positive law with an international reach, could really override the civil laws of individual states. If it had been created by a consensus among nations, and not among single individuals in the state of nature relying solely upon their natural reason, then it was clear to Pufendorf that it could not, as Vitoria insisted it should, take precedence over other forms of positive law. It would, as Cano had argued, clearly be absurd to suggest that there might exist a law which would forbid a prince from controlling the passage of foreigners over his own territories. Vitoria's claim that the French could not lawfully "prevent the Spaniards from traveling to or even living in France and vice versa" would have given the French as perfect a right to wage war against Charles V as he had to make war on the Indians.

Any such right would in fact, however, be contrary to actual practice and a violation of the civil laws of Castile. Did it mean, then, that the civil laws of Castile were in some sense in violation of the common wisdom of the commonwealth of the world? Cleary the answer could only be no. In Vitoria's account, it would appear that rights that derived from the *ius gentium* must trump any laws derived from a purely civil code, since, as we have seen for Vitoria, the *respublica totius orbis* is prior to, and must take precedent over, any individual state. For Pufendorf, however, there simply could exist no right which had somehow survived the *divisio rerum*, because this had been precisely the moment in history in which the *ius gentium* itself had come into being. And this meant that the *ius gentium* was what

[30]"On the American Indians," Vitoria 1991, 278.

[31]"nisi vocetur Alexander peregrinus," *De Dominio indorum*, in Pereña 1956, 142.

[32]Pufendorf 1934, II, 364–6.

its name claimed it to be: a law which governed the relationships between states (and peoples), not a universal law governing the behavior of individuals in a hypothetical stateless condition. As Pufendorf understood it, Vitoria's assertion that any prince might possess the right to force the rulers of states "to abstain from harming others" came down to the claim that what were, in fact, private rights—such as the *ius peregrinandi*—could be used not merely to trump the rights of states, but also to legitimate wars in their defense which could of necessity, and by right, only be waged *by* states. "Most writers" concluded Pufendorf "feel that the safest reply to make is this: Every state may reach a decision, according to its own usage, on the admission of foreigners who come to it for other reasons than are necessary and deserving of sympathy." Refugees clearly possessed some kind of claim to permanent settlement, if only on the grounds of charity. But refugees had no right to behave as conquerors, and they certainly did not have any prior claim over any portion of their land of adoption. "Such persons," he concluded, "must recognize the established government of that country and so adapt themselves to it so that they may be the source of no conspiracies and revolts."[33] The Spanish had obviously not come to America as "refugees" and certainly had not recognized the established government of the Indians. Therefore, they had no right to be there at all.

The basic principle to which Vitoria was appealing, however, was the necessary universality of any law of nations. In general, the two analogous claims of the nineteenth-century-French jurist Gaston Jèze—as described here by Andrew Fitzmaurice—are broadly true: that "civilized powers have no more right to seize the territories of savages than savages have to occupy the European continent. The law of nations does not admit any distinction between the barbarians and the so-called civilized: men of all races, white or black, yellow or red, however unequal they are in fact have to be considered equal in the law." This is not to deny the accusation made by some post-colonial theorists that Vitoria's claims were often read by later generations to imply the direct opposite. But then no writer can be held accountable for the subsequent misuses made of their texts.

Merchants, furthermore, were not the only class of person to possess a right to travel. So, too, and far more problematically, were missionaries, who on Vitoria's account have a natural right to "teach them [the Indians] the truth if they are willing to hear."[34] It is this, perhaps more than any other claim, which has given rise to the post-colonial argument supposition that under the guise of universality, Vitoria was, in fact, arguing for the right of the Church to assert its authority over non-Christians.[35] But despite Vitoria's evocation of St. Mark "Go ye into the world and preach the gospel to every creature" the only *right*, Vitoria, in fact, invokes here

[33]*Ibid.*

[34]"On the American Indians," Vitoria 1991, 284.

[35]Antony Anghie, for instance claims, that "Vitoria bases his conclusion that the Indians are not sovereign on the simple assertion that they are pagan" Anghie 2005, 29. Cf. Sharon Korman who infers from Vitoria's claim that non-Christian rulers were bound to admit Christian missionaries under the *ius peregrinandi* implied that non-Christian states did not possess the same legal standing as Christian ones. Korman 1996, 53.

is an appeal to what was known as the "Law of Vicinage" and the "defence of the innocent" (to which I shall return). For "brotherly correction is as much part of the natural law as brotherly love" and the non-Christian is always, by definition, in need of correction.[36] But although the Indians may be, by the terms of the *ius communicationis*, under an obligation to allow the Christians to be *heard*, they are under no obligation to listen, much less, of course to believe what they hear. Vitoria was prepared to accept that if the Indian princes were actively to oppose the conversion of their subjects by force they might be resisted since this would constitute a harm inflicted by the rulers on the ruled. In that case: "the Spaniards could wage war on behalf of their [i.e., the Indians'] subjects for the oppression and wrongs they were suffering, especially in such important matters."[37] Then again, however, what applied to the Americans would also have to apply to the rest of the world. There is nothing in the logic of Vitoria's argument which could justify, for instance, denying admission of non-Christian missionaries to *Spain*. He did not, of course, say so, but it was surely such implications which led Charles V's advisors to condemn the *relectio* as "most prejudicial and scandalous."

The second of Vitoria's "just titles" (although it is, in fact, the fifth) is a remote ancestor of what in modern international law comes under the general heading of the "responsibility to protect." This, which was finally adopted by the United Nations in the General Assembly of the World Summit Outcome in 2005, has subsequently become what one analyst has called "the accepted international reflex in principle."[38] Vitoria calls it the "defence of the innocent against tyranny." The Spanish might, he wrote—and only *might*—have a right to intervene in the Americas, "either on account of the personal tyranny of the barbarians' masters towards their subjects or because of their tyrannical and oppressive laws against the innocent." As in Vitoria's words "the Spaniards are the barbarians' neighbors, as is shown by the parable of the Samaritan (Luke 10: 29-37); .... the barbarians are obliged to love their neighbors as themselves," and vice versa.[39] Under the terms of what was often called the "Roman Law of Vicinity," neighbors also have a corresponding duty to assist each other in times of crisis. Now as the rulers of individual states have an unassailable right to "punish those of its own members who are intent on harming it with execution or other penalties," it clearly follows that: "If the commonwealth has these powers against its own members, there can be no doubt that the whole world has the same powers against any harmful and evil men."[40]

But although, as we have seen, the world *respublica* does possess *de iure* the "power to enact laws" (*potestas ferendi leges*), there clearly exists no institutions

[36]"On the American Indians," Vitoria 1991, 284.

[37]*Ibid.* 285.

[38]Evans 2008, 53.

[39]*Ibid.* 287–8.

[40]"On the Law of War" Vitoria 1991, 305.

that could transform this into a de facto authority.[41] The question then arises: who, in the absence of some analogue of the United Nations, has the right to do the job for "the whole world"? Vitoria's answer is "the prince," by which he apparently means any legally established ruler, capable of assuming the legislative authority of the entire world for "these powers can only exist if exercised though the princes of the commonwealth":

> The prince has the authority not only over his own people but also over foreigners to force them to abstain from harming others; this is his right by the law of nations and the authority of the whole world. Indeed, it seems he has this right by natural law: the world could not exist unless some men had the power and authority to deter the wicked by force from doing harm to the good and the innocent.[42]

On Vitoria's account, under the appropriate conditions, the sovereign of any one state could draw upon the authority of the law of nations in order to act on behalf of the world *respublica*. In doing so, however, he was not exercising the purely private right that "any person even a private citizen may declare and wage a defensive war"—since he had not himself been harmed by the behavior of the "barbarians."[43] He was instead assuming the legislative authority of the *respublica totius orbis*, and in doing so, as Francisco Castilla Urbano explains here, he was constrained to act *only* for the sole and exclusive good of the world commonwealth. In the case of the Americas, then, the Spanish are merely the instruments of a putative international community. They are in America by historical contingency, and the task of defending the innocent has thus fallen to them. But it could just as easily have been assumed by any other ruler, Christian or—since unbelievers have just as much right to "public *dominium*" as Christians—non-Christian. The entire argument is, however, at best problematical, since it implies that the authority to act on behalf of one legal entity—the international community—can only derive from another which is, historically, a subsequent creation.

The principal evidence Vitoria used to support his claim that the American Indians were being forced to live under "tyrannical and oppressive laws against the innocent" was human sacrifice and cannibalism. Although Vitoria accepts that there is no prohibition against cannibalism "in divine or civil law" and that it is not, therefore, a mortal sin "provided that it is not against charity to God or one's neighbor" (although it is hard to know who one is going to eat if not one's neighbor); it is clearly contrary to the *ius gentium* since it "is held in abomination by all nations who have a civil and human life."[44] Human sacrifice is more tricky if only because the biblical stories of Abraham and Jephthah seemed to imply that

---

[41] "On Civil Power," Vitoria 1991, 40 and see Miaja de la Muela 1965. Vitoria like most scholastics, accepted the traditional distinction between *potestas* and *auctoritas* (on which Hobbes heaped such scorn). On this issue see, Wagner 2011 who describes *potestas* as a "factual power reflexively embedded in a legal order."

[42] "On the Law of War," Vitoria 1991, 305.

[43] *Ibid.*, 299.

[44] "On Dietary Laws," Vitoria 1991, 209.

God—or at least the God of the Old Testament—was not averse to human sacrifice at least in principle. But that, too, is finally dismissed on the grounds that no man may "deliver himself up to execution" (unless justly convicted of a crime), for the same reason that he may not commit suicide, because possession in his own body (*dominium corporis suuis*) belongs not to him, but to God.[45]

It is important to note, however, that although human sacrifice, at least, constitutes a violation of the law of nature, it is not that which, in Vitoria's view, might justify intervention, any more than a Christian prince might legitimately make war on another Christian prince because his subjects are "adulterers or fornicators, perjurers or thieves because these things are against natural law."[46] As Francisco Suárez observed later, it was not man's task to vindicate the Almighty. If God wishes to take revenge upon the pagans for their sins, he remarked acidly, "he is capable of doing so for himself."[47] The difference between "unnatural" activities practiced among individuals in Christian states and the cannibalism and human sacrifice practiced in the Americas is that whereas the former are forbidden by law, the latter were sanctioned by the state. They are, that is, a part of the civil law. It is this which makes them tyrannical. The *harm* which the rulers of the barbarian are prepared to inflict upon their own subjects in this way clearly constitutes a breach not of the natural law but of the *ius gentium*. And it because of this, not because of the gruesome nature of the practices themselves, that the human community may intervene to prevent them.

It is also the case, Vitoria insisted, that: "It makes no difference that all the barbarians consent to these kinds of laws and sacrifices, or that they refuse to accept the Spaniards as their liberators in this matter." For as Soto phrased it, "that which nature teaches is not within the reach of everyone, but only those who have serene reason and are free from all obscurity (*nebula*)."[48] Prolonged habit is capable of distorting every human being's understanding of the natural law and by implicating the law of nations. "For sometimes," wrote Suárez, "due to bad customs, and in those who have fallen profoundly into evil, the knowledge of the natural law may be changed."[49] Clearly, then, if the rulers of the "barbarians" refuse to abandon their crimes against their own peoples: "their masters may be changed and new princes set up."[50]

It is worth noting, however, that neither the "defence of the innocence" nor "the responsibility to protect" is able to create sovereignty. In other words, although Vitoria does not say on what grounds the "new prince" would be created, there is nothing to suggest that it should be a Spanish one. Indeed, he was quite explicit that: "If necessity and the requirements of war demand that the greater part of

[45]*Ibid.*, 215.

[46]*Ibid.*, 1.5 218.

[47]Suárez 1954, 149–152.

[48]Soto 1556, 195.

[49]Suárez 1965, 94.

[50]"On the American Indians," Vitoria 1991, 287–8.

enemy territory, or a large number of cities be occupied in this way, they ought to be returned once the war is over and peace has been made."[51] Although this was not written in the American context, it would seem to suggest that indeed the new prince would have to be a native one.

Vitoria's conception of war "in defence of the innocent," in common with all attempts to justify armed intervention in the interests of "others," fails, of course, to specify very clearly what would count as "tyranny" and "oppressive laws" outside the two specific—and extreme—cases he cites. It was, too, an innovative move since, in general, theories of the "just war" avoided claims made on behalf of third parties, unless these were, specifically, involved as "allies" (*socii*). The Indians might for instance have sought the assistance of the Europeans in their (legitimate) struggles against other Indians. This had indeed, as Vitoria pointed out, happened in the case of the Tlaxcalans who—at least in Hernán Cortés' account of events—had sought Spanish aid in their struggle against the Aztecs. But no subsequent writer on the laws of war was prepared to accept that one ruler had the authority to decide what constitutes an "offence against the innocent" in another state, nor to intervene on their behalf. Intervention was only licit if the actions of that state also in some way constituted a clear and direct threat to the belligerent.

It was also the case that "defence of the innocent" constituted, in effect, the intervention by a *state* in defense of the rights of *individuals*. It might well—indeed most certainly would—involve substantial damage to non-combatants,—a subject explored in detail in Jörg Alejandro Tellkamp's essay—most especially, if as Vitoria insisted, the "innocents" in question do not need to recognize the fact that they *are* victims. Furthermore, as Tellkamp points out (although in the context of a rather different moral issue), "because the moral action has to be evaluated in its entirety and not only with regard to the intended end," it could well be argued that the disruption of the state, which in other instances (see the account by André Azevedo Alves) Vitoria viewed as the greatest possible harm, would far outweigh the good that might pertain to individuals threatened by either human sacrifice or cannibalism.

It had to wait until something which clearly resembled an international community which possessed some sense of itself—however vague—as a political order —that is to say it had to wait until first the creation of the League of Nations in 1920 and then the creation of the United Nations in 1945, before it became possible to think of Vitoria's "just title" as what it has now subsequently become: namely the principal legal ground for the intervention of one state in the affairs of another. It had to wait, that is, until the "international community" began to look upon itself as something resembling Vitoria's *respublica totius orbis*, and the "law of nations" became accepted, in principle at least, as a universally binding law which could not be simply overruled by domestic legislation.

We still, of course, have a long way to go. But Vitoria's *relectiones* set in train a series of debates, which have by no means ceased, about what the international

[51]"On the Law of War," Vitoria 1991, 324.

community actually is; about what rights individuals might have to move and live where they chose; about what responsibility the more powerful, or, as they came to be called in the nineteenth century, more "civilized', nations of the world should bear the for protecting the peoples of what are now dubbed "failed states." As the English jurist Sir Travers Twiss put it in 1856: "These were the early streaks of dawn, the earnest of the coming day." It would perhaps be overstating the case to say, as Thumfart does here, that "Vitoria foresees the kind of close post-Westphalian international collaboration that is working more or less well today in agreements such as The Hague Conventions, UN, international trade treaties, the EU, and, also, the Convention on Cybercrime." He could hardly have "foreseen" any of these things. But his attempt to sketch out the possible conditions for a *respublica totius orbis* was certainly one crucial component in a prolonged struggle to create a language it which it might be possible to frame the universal juridical order, to which all of these are dedicated.

It is for this reason that Vitoria appears (ironically, perhaps, with the features of James Brown Scott, the man who was perhaps most responsible for establishing Vitoria's reputation in the USA) in a gigantic garish fresco in the Ceremonial Hall of the US Department of Justice in Washington, in the company of inter alios Moses, Solon, Justinian, St. Thomas Aquinas, the signatories of Magna Carta, and the framers of the American Constitution, and standing between Socrates and Hugo Grotius.

References

Anghie A (2005) Imperialism, sovereignty and the making of international law. Cambridge University Press, Cambridge

Boswell J (1934) Boswell's life of Johnson. In: Hill GB (ed) Oxford University Press, Oxford

Deckers D (1991) Gerechtigkeit und Recht. Eine historisch-kritische Untersuchung der Gerechtigkeitslehre des Francisco de Vitoria (1483–1546). Universitätsverlag Freiburg, Freiburg

Evans G (2008) The responsibility to protect. Ending mass atrocity crimes once and for all. Brookings Institution Press, Washington DC

Getino Alonso (1930) El Maestro Fray Francisco de Vitoria. Imprenta católica, Madrid

Grotius H (2005) The rights of war and peace. In: Tuck R (ed) De Iure Pacis et Belli, 1625. Liberty Fund, Indianapolis

Korman S (1996) The Right of Conquest. The Acquisition of Territory by Force in International Law and Practice. Oxford: The Clarendon Press

Luhman Niklas (2004) Law as a social system. Oxford University Press, Oxford

Miaja de la Muela A (1965) El derecho *totius orbis* en el pensamiento de Francisco de Vitoria. Revista española de derecho internacional 18:341–52

Mill JS (1984) Essays on equality law and education. In: Robson JM (ed) Collected works of John Stuart Mill, vol 18. University of Toronto Press, Toronto

Pagden A (2015) The burdens of Empire 1539 to the present. Cambridge, Cambridge

Pufendorf S (1934) De iure naturae et gentium libri octo, [1672] (trans: Oldfather CH, Oldfather WA). Clarendon Press, Oxford

Schmitt C (2003) The nomos of the earth in the international law of the Jus Publicum Europaeum. Trans: Umen GL (ed) Telos Press, New York

Soto D de (1556) De iustitia et iure, libri decem, Salamanca

Suárez F (1954) Disputatio xii. De Bello, from Opus de triplice virtute theologica, fide spe et charitate [Paris, 1621], printed in vol. 2 of L. Pereña Vicente, Teoria de la guerra en Francisco Suárez, 2 vols, Madrid: C.S.I.C

Suárez F (1965) De legibus. Comentarios al tratado de la ley ed. and trans. Francisco Puy and Luís Núñez. Universidad de Granada, Granada

Vattel E de (2008) The law of nations or, principles of the law of nature. In: Kapossy B, Whatmore R (eds) Le droit des gens. Ou principes de la loi naturelle, 1797. Liberty Fund, Indianapolis

Vitoria F de (1991) Vitoria political writings. In: Pagden A, Lawrance J (trans and eds). Cambridge University Press, Cambridge

Wagner A (2011) Francisco de Vitoria and Alberico Gentili on the legal character of the global commonwealth. Oxford Journal of Legal Studies 31(3):565–582

Part I
Vitoria as the Father of International Law

Chapter 2
From the "*Imago Dei*" to the "*Bon Sauvage*": Francisco de Vitoria and the Natural Law School

Franco Todescan

Abstract The traditional interpretation of the doctrine on "nature" focusses particularly upon the relationship between the theories of Vitoria and Grotius, highlighting the differences in their lives and work, their spiritual affinities and doctrinal influence, particularly on *jus gentium*. It is important, both from a historical and from a theoretical perspective, to investigate to what extent the doctrine on "nature" developed by the "second scholastic" theologians (Vitoria, Vázquez, Suárez) has exerted an influence on their idea of natural law and, by extension, on the modern *Natural Law School.*

1 Introduction: A Triptych in the Manner of Ferdinando Gallego

Quare non multo incertior erit diffinitio, si ex naturalibus procedat, quam si ex sacris litteris argumentaremur.[1] According to Hans Thieme,[2] Francisco de Vitoria introduced the possibility of including the notion of *ratio naturalis* within divine revelation and the Sacred Scriptures, thus paving the way for the establishment of modern natural law. This presentation is based on the assumption that the way law is conceived is not so much dependent on the beliefs and intentions of those who manage to wield power in given areas of society, but rather on the familiarity thereof with the principles that provide the cultural foundation for a given historical era. Therefore, our endeavour is to investigate the secularisation of natural law,

Translation from Italian into English by Eleonora Harris.

[1]"For the definition will not be much more uncertain, whether we proceed from natural things, or whether we argue from the Sacred Scriptures".
[2]Thieme 1973, 15.

F. Todescan (✉)
University of Padua, Padua, Italy
e-mail: franco.todescan@unipd.it

J.M. Beneyto and J. Corti Varela (eds.), *At the Origins of Modernity*,
Studies in the History of Law and Justice 10, DOI 10.1007/978-3-319-62998-8_2

inasmuch as it allows for the creation of a stable bond among concepts pertaining to different cultural spheres, such as law, politics and scientific knowledge. To this end, we will examine a number of "strong ideas" that have a great deal of resonance and may have significant consequences, both in theory and in practice. In the modern era, these important ideas in the areas of law and politics have induced the belief that certain political institutions or legal clauses are necessary insofar as they are committed to a certain goal and are designed in a certain way; similarly, these important ideas have allowed for the success of conceptual apparatuses that are believed capable of producing unquestionable knowledge regarding the outside world in various fields of science.[3]

According to Ramón Hernández Martín's research,[4] Vitoria's influence is felt in the works of the most relevant lawyers and philosophers of the seventeenth and eighteenth centuries. Hugo Grotius, for example, cited Vitoria 68 times in the *De jure praedae* and 58 times in the *De jure belli ac pacis* and was in agreement with the latter as to the injustice of going to war on the basis of religious beliefs, thus legitimising the subjects' refusal to take part in the war itself.[5] Alberico Gentili referenced Vitoria to support the claim, expressed in his *De jure belli*, that the Spanish were justified in waging war against the native populations of the New World because the latter denied the former passage.[6] In his *De jure naturae et gentium*, Samuel Pufendorf explicitly mentioned Vitoria three times in order to disprove his reasoning on the topic of the Americas and affirm the right to hospitality.[7] In the first of the *Two Treatises of Civil Government*, John Locke vehemently confuted Robert Filmer's theory, and in doing so, he had to deal with the latter's frequent references to second scholasticism. Even though Locke's reasoning was concise and he thus avoided mentioning the authors in question directly, it is clear that he had them in mind, and many passages strongly hinted at Vitoria's doctrine, as reprised by Francisco Suárez and Roberto Bellarmino.[8] Moreover, he wrote about the wars in the Americas and received the testimonies of Garcilaso de la Vega and Fernando de Soto, among others. Another possible echo of Vitoria's doctrines can be found in Thomas Hobbes's works, according to the Dominican Scholar Guillermo Fraile, who studied the analogies between the political theorisations of the authors in question in his[9] essay *Hobbes y Rousseau con Vitoria al fondo*.

Our view is that the influences and the impact of Vitoria's theory on the modern theorisation of natural law can best be examined by keeping the theory itself in the rear-view mirror. The reader may note that our musings will be conducted in the

---

[3]Cavalla 2011, 161–162.

[4]Hernández Martín 1999, 87–112.

[5]See in particular on this topic: Puig Peña 1933, 543–606; 1934, 12–113; 213–314; Truyol Serra 1984, 17–27; see also Larequi 1929, 226–242.

[6]Gentili 1598, l. I, c. 19.

[7]Pufendorf 1727, l. III, c. 3, nn. 9 and 12.

[8]Locke 1690, First Treatise, ch. VI and VIII.

[9]Fraile 1964–1965, 45–62.

style of a triptych in the manner of part-Spanish, part-Flemish painter Ferdinando Gallego, some of whose artwork has been exhibited here in Salamanca. Like any true-to-form triptych, our dissertation is made up of a frame, a central panel and two side panels.

2 The Frame: The Historical and Political Coordinates of Modernity

The birth of the modern State In order to understand the modern age, two factors need to be taken into account. The first is that this period must be considered in the light of the progressive strengthening of an anthropocentric conception over a theocentric one. Therefore, the medieval theocentric perspective must be viewed as a kind of scenic background from which modern civilisation progressively detached itself through a slow process that is not apparent to the casual observer. The second is that the anthropocentric outlook in question constituted a reaction to a cultural and historical situation, full of divisions and readings. The universality principle implicit in medieval conceptions fell apart, and from a legal standpoint, this produced two consequences. The first was that modern national states had to establish their legal autonomy in order to establish their political autonomy; hence, they had to progressively distance themselves from the Empire and Roman law as *jus commune*. Just as Roman law had served as a unifying device in medieval times, it was now perceived as an obstacle to the establishment of national law. Therefore, legal methodology began to consider Roman law as a purely historical object of study. The second was broader in scope: the newly founded political communities, all affirming their sovereignty by no longer recognising the existence of a superior political authority, i.e. the Empire, generated international law issues.[10]

The discovery of the Americas The Emperor could no longer resolve conflicts of a legal nature, because the Empire had lost its universal reach and had become a state like any other. Moreover, international law issues were arising as a result of previously unheard-of situations, for example the discovery of new continents towards the end of the fifteenth century, which had the effect of broadening Europe's cultural horizons. In medieval Europe, there were two great categories from an anthropological standpoint: Christians and non-Christians or, more specifically, those against Christianity, for example the followers of Mohammed. The discovery of the Americas posed a sudden challenge to European culture, as it implied that there was a third category of people who, while similar in physical features, had never known Christianity, i.e. the Indios. New issues arose: was it justifiable to wage war against populations who had never attacked Europe? Could these lands legitimately be colonised? Was colonisation itself acceptable? Was it licit to establish international trade? The medieval world was ending, partly because

[10]See Cavanna 1982, 381–478.

of the decline of the Empire, but also partly because of the exponential widening of Europe's horizons.

The end of religious unity Religious unity came to an end. The Pope was not only the symbol of spiritual unity, but also symbol of potential political unity, a famous example of this duality being the controversy arising between Portugal and Spain over the division of the Atlantic Ocean that was mediated by the Pope. At the end of the fifteenth century, the Pope was an internationally recognised force, but he represented one of the last instances of the setting sun of universality. The sixteenth century brought about multiple intra-religion rifts and a varied European religious landscape: Henry VIII's schism; Luther's protestant revolution; Calvin's protestant revolution. While Spain and Italy remained faithful to the Catholic faith, Germany was profoundly divided, and France was also divided between Catholicism and Calvinism. The modern world rose out of divisiveness. From a legal and political viewpoint, Catholicism, Calvinism and Lutheranism not only represented fractures within Europe, but they also represented ideologies that transformed the cultural landscape and thus decisively influenced modern thinking.

3 The Central Panel: The Theoretical Coordinates of Modernity

The modern hermeneutical categories of the Natural Law School The *Natural Law School* can be placed on the dividing line between two civilisations, the theocentric medieval and the anthropocentric modern. Before its representatives are introduced, we will focus on the features that set it apart from the classical school. These can be enumerated as follows: (a) individualism; (b) rationalism; (c) secularisation. However, there can be a "school" only insofar as these features are present in its representatives, since there is no discipleship among these authors and no homogenous group of doctrines. The aforementioned features must be examined separately.

Individualism It is, in an ideological sense, the common element of all theories that consider the individual as the founding principle of the social and historical world. An individualistic civilisation does not need to justify the individual's existence within society, but rather the existence of society in relation to the individual.

Rationalism This feature is not limited to the belief that reason is more valuable than experience, but rather it is a stance that comes before either and identifies reason as man's ability to know the truth in all of its manifestations. It follows that reason is seen as greater than truth: modern rationalism posits that reason is the measure of truth, not the other way around. To quote Protagoras's motto, we could say that in the modern era man strives to be "the measure of all things".

Secularisation This is the most crucial, albeit difficult, concept. It is a strictly legal term, consisting of the dispossessing of ecclesiastical properties conducted by modern states, starting with the Westphalia Treaties. Nevertheless, the term in

question has taken on a cultural meaning, signifying the act perpetrated by modern thinking, which amounts to ridding religious theories of their contents to an extensive degree, and turning the latter into secular models and mind frames. For this reason alone, secularisation is held in particular regard as a means of interpreting the passage from the medieval to the modern era: secularisation is the process by which every stance is subverted, while the façade remains intact.

Cultural secularisation can be further divided into two subcategories: secularisation by separation and secularisation by transformation.[11] The former proposes to keep the categories of sacred and profane radically distinct. In particular, sacred secularisation consists of exalting the value and purity of the sacred by expunging any connection with the profane sphere, whereas profane secularisation occurs when the sacred sphere is set apart from the profane sphere in order to preserve the latter's "purity". These two perspectives differ greatly, but at the same time, they are profoundly similar. They differ in intent: sacred secularisation aims to protect and give value to everything that is considered sacred, just as profane secularisation aims to devalue it in order to affirm worldly values. They are similar in effect: both conceptions posit a separation between the two spheres in question. It is a paradox of modern culture.

The second subcategory is harder to define, albeit more interesting. Secularisation by transformation occurs when the theocentric culture is slowly eroded from the inside, and its terminology, concepts and images, while formally maintained intact, are emptied of their contents, which in turn are replaced by secular contents. Once the contents have been radically transformed, getting rid of the superfluous facade becomes a formality.

4 The First Side Panel: Vitoria, the Jurists and the Natural Law

Vitoria In Vitoria's works, the thomistic approach to natural law is not significantly altered and the perspective on human nature is essentially in line with thomistic ideals.[12] According to Vitoria, man is a paradoxical being who yearns for infinity, and yet is unable to obtain it on his own. Natural law is thus the guiding norm for human privation, and it must be taken into account within the confines of this anthropological perspective, in the light of the all-encompassing vision on human nature descending from divine revelation-inspired critical thinking.

> Conclusio est affirmativa quia licet proprie in Deo sit lex et regula tamquam in regulante, notitia tamen quae derivatur ad nos tamquam effectus regulae divinae vocatur etiam regula et lex. Ex hoc articulo potestis habere quod iudicium quod habemus et notitia qua ego dicto

[11]See Auer 1964, 253–254.

[12]See Todescan 2014c, 41–123.

hoc esse faciendum, non obligat de se, nisi inquantum derivatur a lege aeterna. Omnia alia sunt clare.[13]

As a matter of fact, Vitoria deals with natural law in the genuinely thomistic context of the *exitus-reditus*, that is to say the idea that man is created by God and given a place in the universe, while remaining congenitally propelled to return to the House of the Lord.[14] Vitoria's musings on natural law are conducted from the perspective of the divine, reflecting on what it means to be human, and the mysterious role man is called upon to play in the universe by providential design: according to this view, God does not call man to him extrinsically, but rather by providing him with an inclination that drives him to the realisation of his divine goals as a beatification-oriented return. The link that Vitoria establishes between natural law and blessedness attests to the intimate nature of man, which is seen as dynamic and filled with purpose, and to the measure by which man was conceived. Therefore, natural law must be interpreted in the light of man's inclination towards the evolution of human nature, and not as a blind endeavour, but rather as the aspiration to realise God's plan with God's help.

Natural law and natura rationalis: Vázquez Gabriel Vázquez's theory is especially relevant because of the new interpretation it attributes to the thomistic doctrine of natural law, an interpretation that sets it apart from the School of Salamanca.[15] As a matter of fact, while both Vitoria and Soto had recognised that moral values had an objective standing, they had never gone so far as attempting to separate natural law from divine reason, nor had they drawn any radical conclusions. Divine law remained the lynchpin of the doctrine established by the School of Salamanca, expressing God's providential and mysterious design for the universe. On the contrary, Vázquez concentrates his efforts on natural law as a distinct and autonomous concept: the ontological foundation of law is a rule based directly on nature, and not on anyone's will.

> Cumque omne bonum vel malum per ordinem ad regulam aliquam dicatur bonum vel malum, justum vel injustum, consequens fit ut ante omne imperium, ante omnem voluntatem, imo ante omne judicium sit regula quaedam harum actionum, quae suapte natura constet, sicut res omnes suapte natura contradictionem non implicant: haec autem non potest alia esse, quam ipsamet rationalis natura ex se non implicans contradictionem [...] Prima igitur lex naturalis in creatura rationali est ipsamet natura, quatenus rationalis, quia haec est prima regula boni et mali.[16]

---

[13]de Vitoria 2010a (1533–1534), q. 91, a. 2 (p. 163). "Aquinas replies in the affirmative, because although the rules of law are in God as in the thing which is the rule, the knowledge of them which is channelled into us an effect of the divine rule is also called a rule and measure. From this article you may deduce that our judgment and knowledge, which I rely upon when I dictate that such and such is to be done, does not oblige per se, but only insofar as it derives from eternal law. All the rest is clear".

[14]See in parallel Mongillo 1970, 103–123.

[15]See Todescan 2014a, 240–251.

[16]Vázquez 1605, d. 150, c. 3, n. 23. "Whenever each good or bad action—according to some rule—is judged good or bad, just or unjust, it happens that, as a consequence, before any order,

Some actions are so intrinsically evil that their malicious nature cannot be dependent on anyone's will, not even God's will; in fact, they precede divine judgement. Moreover, given that every action is qualified as good or bad in accordance with a rule, it follows that said rule, which is identified as rational nature (*natura rationalis*) and is informed by the principle of non-contradiction, comes before any command or judgement.

Natural law and ratio naturalis: Suárez In Suárez's works, nature is taken into consideration from two distinct points of view: on the one hand, it is regarded as pure nature, reachable through the employment of the natural reason; on the other hand, it is described as nature resulting from the infusion of God's grace within man, to the awareness of which faith lights the way.[17]

> Circa legem naturalem docet Theologia, hominem secundum duplicem naturam et duplex rationis lumen considerari posse. Primo secundum puram naturam, seu substantiam animae rationalis, et consequenter secundum rationis lumen illi connaturale; secundo juxta naturam gratiae desuper homini infusae, et secundum divinum, ac supernaturale lumen fidei, per quod pro statu viae regitur et gubernatur […] Et juxta haec duo principia distinguit duplicem legem naturalem: aliam simpliciter naturalem respectu hominis; aliam, quae licet supernaturalis sit respectu hominis (quia totus ordo gratiae illi supernaturalis est) nihilominus naturalis dici potest respectu gratiae, quia etiam gratia habet suam propriam essentiam et naturam, cui connaturale est lumen infusum […] Sic ergo lex naturalis duplex distingui potest, una pure naturalis, alia simpliciter supernaturalis, naturalis autem respective, per comparationem ad gratiam.[18]

Nature stands in relation to divine grace as reason stands in relation to faith from a theoretical viewpoint. An obvious consequence of this distinction is that all values pertaining to the relationship between man and God are considered as separate from a "purely natural" set of values, and while the two sets of values are not in conflict with each other, the idea of separateness prevails and Saint Thomas's unitary perspective disappears, despite Soto's attempt to maintain it (and not without

(Footnote 16 continued)

before any will, and even before any judgment, there is a certain rule for such actions, so that it naturally follows that no action is in contradiction with itself: this, however, happens on account of its very rational nature, which cannot be opposed to itself […] In short, the first natural law in a rational creature is its very nature, as rational, because this is the first rule of good and evil".

[17]See Todescan 2014a, 251–269.

[18]Suárez 1612, 1. I, c. 3, n. 11. "As regards the natural law, Theology teaches us that man can be considered according to a dual nature and according to a dual light of reason. Firstly, according to a pure nature, that is, the substance of a rational soul and, consequently, in accordance with the light of reason that is innate in him. Secondly, according to the nature of the Grace infused from above into man, and conforming to the divine and supernatural light of Faith, through which—also on the basis of his state of life—he is guided and governed. Alongside these two principles [Theology] distinguishes a twofold natural law, namely: a simply natural one, related to man, as opposed to the other, supernatural with regard to man (since all the order of Grace is, for him, supernatural), which, however, can be considered natural according to Grace, for Grace too has its own essence and nature, to which is connatural an infused light […] So the natural law can be considered of a dual nature, of which one being purely natural, and the other simply supernatural, or even natural, through a comparison with Grace".

difficulties, we might add). By suppressing the hypothesis of a divine order, nature retains its autonomous existence, as is suggested by Suárez's postulation of intrinsic bounty or maliciousness of human actions (*intrinseca honestas vel malitia actuum*).

At this point, every argument is consistent with a dual logic. Every notion encapsulates diverging paths: there is a law for mankind in its "pure nature" status (*lex pura naturalis*); there is a law that is "natural" with respect to divine grace, albeit supernatural in relation to mankind, as its mission is to direct men towards eternal salvation by doing away with the obscure and error-prone "pure" natural law (*lex connaturalis gratiae*).

According to Suárez, natural law is hypothetically self-supporting and enclosed within the pure nature order; it is thus possible to smoothly redirect mankind's yearning for the Absolute towards theological speculation with no bearing on philosophy, that is to say extrinsically superordinate divine grace, while preserving "purely" natural law as a distinct topic of study—the *Doctor Eximius*'s preferred topic.

Grotius and the etiamsi daremus The young Grotius's main concern in the *De jure praedae* was *jus gentium*. As Peter Haggenmacher observed, the sources of law in Chapter II serve as reference for *jus gentium primarium*. In this chapter, Grotius defined a series of sources of law by identifying the rule to which each source owed its existence and validity. The creation process itself is always the same: it starts and ends with a single will that forms an intricate pattern and fashions itself "comme les cascades d'une fontaine baroque". The primary source is represented by God's will, from which natural law, the universal law of all creation, is derived. Through the collective will of men, who are perceived as rational beings, secondary natural law (or *jus gentium primarium*) is established, as well as a series of subordinate hybrid norms pertaining both to *jus civile* and *jus gentium* and, even lower in this hierarchy, *jus gentium secundarium*, stemming from the will of all secular states. Finally, there are contracts, which are derived from the will of single individuals and which, through a peculiar contract, i.e. the "social contract" that holds civil society and the State together, allow the latter, together with its judicial institutions, to establish civil law.

However, Grotius is recognised as the forefather of modern natural law because of his "*etiamsi daremus*" secular theorisation, which is contained in the masterpiece from his later years, *De jure belli ac pacis*. The traditional view is that the Dutch author founded secular natural law because he held that natural law would suffer no alteration even if it were not derived from God (literally, if God did not exist, *etiamsi daremus non esse Deum*). However, it is our view that the autonomous existence of natural law was not affirmed so abruptly, but rather in relation to Grotius's "system" of laws, and therefore, it makes no sense to isolate the famous phrase without explaining the systemic context surrounding it.[19]

(a) *Lex humana* Grotius went to great lengths to explain the notion of human law, and he afforded an extensive degree of autonomy to the product of the

[19]See Todescan 2014b, 91–139.

legislator's will, which was apparent where this law clashed with natural law. Grotius believed that there were instances of conducts that were allowed under human law, yet forbidden by natural law, just as there were conducts forbidden by human law and allowed by natural law; a conflict between the two legal orders was thus a real possibility. However, there was a way out of this conundrum, and it required always choosing the negative rule: if one conformed to the natural law forbidding a conduct allowed by a human law or vice versa, neither of the legal orders in question was breached. Nevertheless, if natural law explicitly prescribed a conduct that was forbidden by human law or vice versa, natural law had to prevail every time.

(b) *Lex divina* Natural law and divine law are supraordinate in relation to human law. However, Grotius's view of divine law was also based on will, in this case the will of God, and it distanced itself from those of Luther and Calvin, which sought to link natural law with divine law, in that it described divine law as a mechanism through which conducts were qualified as bad or good, not because of their intrinsic nature—that would have been natural law, but rather because of the very fact that they were forbidden or prescribed. He also noted that the Old Testament was exclusively applicable to the Jewish people of ancient times, just as the New Testament required the kind of spiritual generosity that could only be expected of Christians. At this point, Grotius cannot be defined as a "rationalist", given that his stances are still quite close to the views expressed in the *De jure praedae*.

(c) *Lex naturalis* What of the "*etiamsi daremus*" passage, then? First and foremost, Grotius seemed determined to break natural law free from the aura of sacredness that medieval theology had enshrined it in by forcing a connection with divine law. In Grotius's theoretical system, natural law shrugs off any residual trace of voluntarism and thus the affirmation of its validity *etiamsi daremus non esse Deum*.

> Et haec quidem quae jam diximus, locum "aliquem" haberent etiamsi daremus, quod sine summo scelere dari nequit, non esse Deum, aut non curari a beo negotia humana.[20]

It is because of this conviction, expressed in a hardly "secular" context, that Grotius is widely regarded as he who "secularised" the natural law. In particular, as we pointed out elsewhere, for Grotius, a man who lived within the historical context of Humanism and the Reform, faith is not superimposed on nature, it is isolated from it: the truths of faith belong exclusively to divine law, and it is not for the science of natural law to discuss them. It would not be accurate to hold that Grotius believed that secular natural law was opposed to Christian natural law; however, in accordance with the Reform, he did perceive them to be radically separate and independent. This separation operates on two distinct but important levels: firstly, a secularisation by which the sacred world of the New Testament is preserved in its

[20]Grotius 1925 (1625), Prolegomena, § 11. "What we have been saying would have a degree of validity even if we should concede, that which cannot be conceded without the utmost wickedness, that there is no God, or that the affairs of men are of no concern to Him".

pure state; secondly, a "profane" secularisation, guaranteeing the autonomy and perceptibility of the natural world and, conversely, of natural law.

(d) *Lex aeterna* Despite the fact that divine law was the traditional closing element of this system, in the *De iure belli ac pacis* there is no trace of it. Is this pure coincidence? Probably not, as one of the major philosophers of the eighteenth century—Leibniz—noted: *Meo iudicio recte Grotius doctrinam Scholasticorum de Lege Dei aeterna cum principio socialitatis coniunxit.*[21] Divine law was omitted for a theoretical reason: since in Grotius's theory the rational principle and the voluntary principle coexist, the system as a whole is set and comprehensible, as the "algebraic sum" of what *voluntas* (divine law) and *ratio* (natural law) prescribe. Consequently, there is no need for an ulterior law, like the mysterious and problematic law theorised in the thomistic system.

Pufendorf and the perseitas's critique In the *De jure naturae et gentium*, Pufendorf embarked on a critique of the perseity doctrine exemplified by Vázquez ([22]): that the thesis according to which theft, adultery, murder and so on are evil in themselves represented a baseless statement, devoid of any proof whatsoever, masked as rational intuition.

But to make the knowledge of the law of nature, of which we are not treating, and which includes all moral and civil doctrines that are genuine and solid, to make the knowledge, we say, fully come up to the measure and perfection of science, we do not think it necessary to assert, with some writers, that there are several things honest or dishonest of themselves (per se), and antecedent to all imposition, and so to make these things the object of our natural and perpetual law, in opposition to positive law, where matters are right or wrong, just as the lawgiver was pleas'd to make than either. For, since honesty (or moral necessity) and turpitude are affections of human deeds, arising from their agreeableness or disagreeableness to a rule, or a law, and since a law is the command of a superior, it does not appear how we can conceive any goodness or turpitude before all law and without the imposition of a superior.

> Ad hoc tamen, ut disciplina juris naturae, circa quam occupamur, et quae genuinam ac solidam doctrinam moralem et civilem absolvit, verae scientiae mensuram implere possit, haudquidquam necessarium arbitramur cum nonnullis statuere, quaedam per se citra omnem impositionem esse honesta aut turpia: et haec facere objectum juris naturalis et perpetui; cum illa, quae ideo honesta aut turpia sunt, quia legislator voluit, sub legum positivarum censum veniant. Cum enim honestas sive necessitas moralis et turpitudo sint affections actionum humanarum ortae ex convenientia aut disconvenientia a norma seu lege; lex vero sit jussum superioris; non apparet, quomodo honestas aut turpitudo intelligi possit ante legem, et citra superioris impositionem.[23]

---

[21]"In my judgement, Grotius was right in connecting the Scholastic doctrine of the eternal Law of God with the principle of sociability".

[22]See Todescan 2014b, 295–319.

[23]Pufendorf 1727 (1672), l. I, c. 2, n. 6 (p. 17). "But to make the knowledge of the law of nature, of which we are now treating, and which includes all moral and civil doctrines that are genuine and

The real struggle for philosophers of law was to investigate the reasons why some conducts are good or bad, but the supporters of perseity believed they were excused from providing evidence and were satisfied with what was commonly asserted. However, Pufendorf held that there was no such thing as intrinsically good or intrinsically bad, but rather good or bad with reference to a given law presiding over human nature. His adversaries objected that human nature was an eternal idea, and thus, its consequences also had to be regarded as eternal truths. Pufendorf argued that human nature was not unchangeable, but rather the product of a contingent exertion of divine will: since God willed the creation of a rational and sociable being, all actions consistent with said nature were just, but not insofar as they represented a logical necessity, given that they were the product of divine will.

5 The Second Side Panel: Vitoria, the Philosophers and the Natural Rights

The question of the state of nature The state of nature is usually treated as a new theoretical element associated with the *Natural Law School*. Influential scholars[24] have reasoned that the modern doctrine of natural law is a methodology that can be broken down into three distinct phases, in spite of its heterogeneous ideologies and contents: *state of nature, social contract* and *political state*. Therefore, the foundation of the political state occurs as a result of overcoming the state of nature through a social contract. Among the many issues relating to the theorisation of the state of nature, there are two in particular that we would like to focus on: the first concerns how the very notion of the state of nature came to be; the second, whether it is considered as having existed in history or as an abstract, logical hypothesis.[25] With regard to the first issue, it ought to be noted that the state of nature does not constitute a novelty, but rather the prosecution of a question that had been raised both in ancient and in medieval times, and was given a rather original answer in the sixteenth century by the second scholastics. Our view is that the modern doctrine of natural law represents a secularised version of the statuses' theory propounded by

(Footnote 23 continued)
solid, to make this knowledge, we say, fully come up to the measure and perfection of Science, we do not think it necessary to assert, with some writers, that there are several things honest or dishonest of themselves (per se) and antecedent to all imposition, and so to make these things the object of our natural and perpetual law, in opposition to positive law, where matters are right or wrong, just as the law-giver was pleased to make them either. For, since honesty (or moral necessity) and turpitude are affections of human deeds, arising from their agreeableness or disagreeableness to a rule, or a law, and since a law is the law command of a superior, it does not appear how we can conceive any goodness or turpitude before all law, and without the imposition of a superior".

[24]Opocher 1993, 101 ff.

[25]See Todescan 2001, 139–148.

Christian theologians ever since Patristic Theology, according to which the history of salvation (*historia salutis*) is comprised of three phases: *status naturae integrae*, *status naturae lapsae* and *status gratiae*. The first represents Adam and Eve's predicament from creation to original sin; the second concerns their descendants; and the third deals with humanity redeemed by the death and resurrection of Christ. However, it ought to be noted that while the *status naturae lapsae* follows the previous status diachronically, the *status gratiae* happens simultaneously with the former, because while grace can be attained through the sacraments, all men are born stained by original sin, which can only be erased by baptism. It has been noted, particularly by Henri de Lubac,[26] that fifteenth century scholastic theology brought about an innovation, more or less from Cajetan onwards. In the debate concerning *appetutus beatitudinis*—i.e. the yearning for maximum happiness *naturalis quoad appetitionem, supernaturalis vero quoad adsecutionem*,[27] to quote the traditional scholastic theology—Cajetan substituted the active natural *appetitus* for the supernatural with the passive *potentia oboedientialis*, and he then proceeded to modify the traditional theory of the three statuses by introducing a fourth status that was regarded as preceding the other three, the *status purae naturae*. Both second scholasticism and the contemporary critiques of the Lutheran and Baianist heresies are relevant to this modification.

Vitoria Evidently, Cajetan's doctrine concerning man's ultimate goal set itself so far apart from the thomistic anthropology that it could not pass unnoticed, nor avoid some form of opposition among the *Summa* commentators. Major resistance, accompanied by a systematic attempt to reaffirm the traditional theorisation, could be found at the University of Salamanca, where Vitoria had chosen to commentate Thomas Aquinus's *Summa theologicae* instead of the usual *Librum sententiarum*, as a result of his Paris-based education under Juan Fenario and Petrus Crockaert.

Vitoria's theory is not devoid of originality, and it brings about a certain measure of progress in the treatment of the supernatural. The natural yearning for the *visio Dei* that he supported in opposition to Cajetan does not share the same features as Soto's theorisation. According to the *Doctor Subtilis*, this yearning was essentially a *pondus naturae*, devised for the achievement of good *in particulari* and incapable of going beyond consciousness; on the contrary, Vitoria believed that this *appetitus* was prescribed by nature itself (*exercitatus ab ipsa natura*), but it was also comprised of conscious manifestations, for instance a patent yearning for good *in generali* or a constant dissatisfaction with earthly goods. This *appetitus* was not expected to find its own resolution, and yet it was not exerted in vain, since the natural aspiration was in itself sufficient, as was the possibility of achieving its goal either in the natural or in supernatural world.

[26]de Lubac 1978, 263 ff.

[27]"Natural with regard to the appetite, but supernatural with regard to the thing which is to be achieved".

Vitoria's theological teachings represent an important connection between this issue and human rights.[28] Striking such a balance was tricky at first: perfecting a notion of state that properly included independence, sovereignty and individual rights while setting the foundation for the establishment of a community of states was no small task. The dangers implicit in individualistic and voluntaristic theories had to be avoided by setting up a *jus gentium* that would allow sovereign states to go beyond their contractual ties and form an organic community that would come together naturally. This is, after all, what Vitoria, the "founder" of international law, is commonly praised for, and contemporary historiography has mostly focused on this "glaring" aspect of his work. Take, for example, this crucial passage regarding the rights and dignity of Native Americans:

> Creaturae irrationales non possunt habere dominium. Patet, quia dominium est jus, ut fatetur etiam Conradus. Sed creaturae irrationales non possunt habere jus. Ergo nec dominium. Probatur minor, quia non possunt pati inuriam; ergo non habent jus […] Et confirmatur propositio auctoritate S. Thomae: Sola creatura rationalis habet dominium sui actus, quia, ut ipse etiam dicit, per hoc aliquis est dominus suorum actuum, qua potest hoc vel illud eligere; unde etiam, ut ibidem dicit, appetitus circa ultimim finem non sumus domini. […] Non enim dicimus aliquem esse dominum, nisi eius quod situm est in sua facultate. Ita enim loquimur: non est in mea facultate, non est in mea potestate, quando non sum dominus. Bruta autem cum non moveant se, sed potius moveantur, ut S. Thomas ait, eadem ratione nec habent dominium.[29]

Three themes emerge from reading between the lines: (a) property (*dominium*), (b) freedom (*libertas*) and (c) yearning for the ultimate return (*appetitus beatitudinis*).

(a) *Property* The corrosive albeit stimulating cultural climate at the beginning of the sixteenth century strongly influenced Vitoria's formative years in Paris and informed the entire vision that the second scholastics had with regard to the relationship between man and property. The Parisian period is significant from a historical point of view, because the studies Vitoria conducted then had an

[28]See Todescan 2015, 71–110.

[29]de Vitoria 2010b (1538–1539), I, 20 (pp. 247–248). "Irrational creatures clearly cannot have any dominion, for dominion is a legal right (dominium est ius), as Conrad Summenhart himself admits. Irrational creatures cannot have legal rights; therefore, they cannot have any dominion. The minor premiss is proved by the fact that irrational creatures cannot be victims of an injustice (iniuria), and therefore cannot have legal rights […] This argument is confirmed by Aquinas: only rational creatures have mastery over their own actions (dominium sui actus), as Aquinas also shows in ST I. 82. 1 ad 3. [A person is master of his own actions insofar as he is able to make choices and another; hence, as Aquinas says in the same passage, we are not masters as regards our appetite for our own destiny, for example] […] We do not speak of anyone being 'the owner' of a thing (dominum esse) unless that thing lies within is control. We often say, for example: 'It is not in my control, it is not in my power', meaning I am not master or owner (dominus) of it. By this argument brutes, which do not move by their own will but are moved by some other, as Aquinas says, cannot have any dominion (dominium)".

impact in Spain, allowing young theology scholars to confront this cultural experience with a renewed interest in the thomistic doctrines.[30]

Vitoria often consulted Konrad Summenhart's *Tractatus septipartitus de contractibus*, where the latter, who had been educated in the same circumstances as the former, translated the general premises expressed by voluntaristic currents. He did so in order to construct his own autonomous system, and he found that the cultural world of the *recentiores* was congenial to his being a *homo novus*, a true man of his time, and the inventor of a theoretical system consistent with the contemporary world, rather than the theorist of a bygone age.

The Vitorian interpretation of *in rem* rights progressively translated into a dualistic vision of the world of individuals and phenomena, resulting in an attempt to construct a metaphysical theory that would allow property to be viewed through the lens of the individual as a projection of the latter's sovereignty. Because of the metaphysical detachment from property, the individual could be identified as *dominus*, and the legal order was considered as the sum of instances of dominance; *dominium*, regarded in strictly rigorous legal terms, became the interpretative mainstay of the whole system.

(b) *Freedom* Free will was regarded as the underlying premise of *dominium*, given that it was in itself *dominium*. Freedom and property were thus conceived as interchangeable. The individual's freedom coincided with their agency over themselves; their very existence as a free agent consisted of all expressions of dominance. The use of a strictly legal term to describe a psychological attitude may seem inappropriate, especially since in everyday language said attitude is described as "self-assuredness". However, there is nothing generic or psychological about the notion of *dominium sui*. Dominion over oneself and one's actions had a theological and legal significance; it was given by God to every rational being created in his likeness, and it was not that different from dominion over an object, which is why the *de dominio* treatise is a rigorously unitary block, and dominion over one's actions is discussed in the first chapter.

(c) *Imago Dei and appetitus beatitudinis* The foundation of the property principle lies with the notion of *imago Dei*, and it unites legal reasoning with theology.

> Hoc patet, quia [pueri] possunt pati iniuriam; ergo habent jus rerum; ergo est illis dominium, quod nihil aliud est quam jus. Item bona pupillorum non sunt in bonis tutorum, et habent dominos, et non alios; ergo pupillos. Item pupilli sunt heredes. Sed heres succedit in jus defuncti et est dominus hereditatis. Item diximus quod fundamentum dominii est imago Dei, quae adhuc est in pueris, et Apostolum eodem loco: Quanto tempore heres parvulis est, nihil differt a servo, cum sit dominus omnium.[31]

[30] See Grossi 1973, 121 ff.

[31] de Vitoria 2010b (1538–1539), I, 21 (p. 249). "Children before the age of reason can be masters. This is self-evident, first because a child can be the victim of an injustice (*iniuria*); therefore a child can have legal rights, therefore it can have a right of ownership (*dominium rerum*), which is a legal right. Again, the possessions of an orphan minor in guardianship are not the property of the guardians, and yet they must be the property of one of the two parties; a fortiori they are the

This train of thought refers to "younglings" and perhaps also to the mentally challenged. However, natives are far from mentally incapacitated; they simply make use of reason differently. It is apparent that they have their own legal order and institutional framework, including the institution of marriage, magistrates, lords, laws, industry, trade, all manifest exertions of reason. It follows that the same motivations apply to them.

> Sola creatura rationalis habet dominium sui actus, quia, ut ipse etiam dicit, per hoc aliquis est dominus suorum actuum, qua potest hoc vel illud eligere; unde etiam, ut ibidem dicit, appetitus circa ultimum finem non sumus domini. […] Non enim dicimus aliquem esse dominum, nisi eius quod situm est in sua facultate. Ita enim loquimur: non est in mea facultate, non est in mea potestate, quando non sum dominus. Bruta autem cum non moveant se, sed potius moveantur, ut S. Thomas ait, eadem ratione nec habent dominium.[32]

And so the third theme—i.e. *appetitus*, a strong yearning—emerges. It is the desire for grace, the *appetitus beatitudinis* previously theorised by Saint Augustine in the confessions (*Fecisti nos ad Te, Domine, et inquietum est cor nostrum donec requiescat in Te*).[33] Saint Augustine argued that man was a paradoxical being, insofar as man was the only being that craved absolute grace (*beatitudo*), and thus, it was because the yearning for the Absolute lay within human nature that only the Absolute could satisfy it. Therefore, man was constitutionally projected outwardly, propelled by the desire to reach a goal *naturalis quoad appetitionem, supernaturalis vero quoad asecutionem*,[34] to quote the scholastic formula. Hence, the importance of divine grace for human salvation according to Saint Agostine, as was apparent in his works arguing against the Pelagians.

Molina After Cajetan, one of the first authors who dealt specifically and systematically with the *status purae naturae* was the Jesuit Luis de Molina, author of the famous *Concordia liberi arbitrii* (1588), whose theories on the relationship between nature and grace were at the centre of the great *de auxiliis* debate that troubled early seventeenth century catholic theology. In the *Concordia* Molina states:

> Primus est status naturae humanae in puris naturalibus, sine peccato et sine gratia ac sine ullo alio dono supernaturali. Hunc statum nunquam homo habuit, neque unquam habebit:

(Footnote 31 continued)

property of the minor. Again, a child in guardianship may legally inherit property; but an heir is defined in law as the person who succeeds to the inheritance of the deceased, hence the child is the owner of the inheritance. Furthermore, we said earlier that the foundation of dominion is the fact that we are formed in the image of God (*imago Dei*); and the child is already formed in the image of God. The Apostle goes on to say, in the passage of Galatians quoted, 'the heir, as long as he is a child, differeth nothing from a slave, though he be lord of all' (Gal 4, 1)".

[32]de Vitoria 2010b (1538–1539), I, 20 (p. 248). "A person is master of his own actions insofar as he is able to make choices and another; hence, as Aquinas says in the same passage, we are not masters as regards our appetite for our own destiny, for example".

[33]"O Lord, You made us for You and our heart will be restless until it can rest in You".

[34]"…natural with regard to the appetite, but supernatural with regard to the thing which is to be achieved".

> Philosophi tamen naturales in eo crediderunt hominem fuisse conditum, neque aliud sine lumine divinae revelationis intelligere potuerunt [...] Secundus status est, in quo re ipsa primus parens ante peccatum fuit constitutus, qui innocentiae status appellatur.[35]

In Molina's *Concordia,* the idea of pure nature (*status purae naturae*) was introduced and it precedes the traditional Scholastic tripartite formula (*status naturae integrae, status naturae lapsae, status gratiae*). This hypothesis brings about the intrinsic conclusion that it is possible for humanity to be altogether encompassed in a worldly dimension (*in puris naturalibus*). A similar train of thought can be found with regard to the manner in which different kinds of law are listed in Molina's *De justitia et jure*: after divine law is mentioned, natural law follows suit pursuant to the natural end of moral and theoretical fulfilment within humanity, and the law governing the state of innocence, which involves a complex and dynamic interaction between nature and the supernatural, only comes in third, despite being the first to appear in human history, according to the biblical perspective.

Consequently, a parallel between natural law and Molina's status doctrine surfaces: just like pure nature, an abstract and hypothetical notion introduced in the *Concordia* inaugurates the enumeration of the various stages in the "history of salvation", thus introducing the idea of humanity as enclosed in space and time; the notion of *lex naturalis* contained in the *De justitia et jure* is at the forefront of the enumeration of the laws that are perceived as having guided mankind throughout history and through the various statuses, as if it were a structural and narrative necessity, therefore allowing for its theoretical distinctiveness.

The objection according to which natural law is derived from God as *naturae auctor*, as Molina expressly and thoroughly stated, was to no avail, since if it was to be believed that the supernatural was only extrinsically superimposed on nature, then it followed that any kind of subordination also had to be regarded as extrinsic.

Also Suárez in his *De divina gratia* treatise stated:

> Cajetanus et moderniores Theologi tertium considerarunt statum, quem pure naturalium appellarunt, qui licet de facto non fuerit, ut suppono [...] cogitari tamen potest, ut possibilis, et illius consideratio ad aliorum intelligentiam necessaria est, quia revera hic status est veluti aliorum fundamentum.[36]

A few observations ought to be made with regard to the passages cited above. First and foremost, the state of pure nature is imagined as the human condition devoid of sin and grace, that is to say what was added historically according to

[35]de Molina 1588, q. 14, a. 13, d. 3. "A first condition of the human nature consists of a natural state, without sin, without Grace, and without any other supernatural gift. Man, however, never had that condition, nor will he never have it. Naturalist philosophers, however, believed that man was placed in that condition, as they could not understand otherwise without the light of the divine revelation. [...] There is, however, a second condition, which consists in that our first progenitor was created before sin, and therefore called state of innocence".

[36]Suárez 1619, Proleg. IV, c. 1, n. 2. "Cajetan and the most modern theologians considered a third state, which they saw as purely natural, which in fact did not exist, although we can think of it [...] as being possible, and this consideration is crucial to comprehend the other states, as in fact this state underlies all the others, being their foundation".

Christian theology, whether in a negative or positive sense: on the one hand, sin is not innate, and it occurs after a certain period of time; on the other hand, grace, as its etymology suggests, is by nature a gift (the other gifts which are alluded to are the so-called preternatural gifts: exemption from pain, physical death, ignorance and so on). This status was clearly theorised by Molina and Suárez as being hypothetical; in fact, the very expression "*hunc statum nunquam homo habuit, neque unquam habebit*" (man has never been, nor will he ever be in, such a state) vaguely recalls Jean-Jaques Rousseau's famous words on the state of nature as a state that never existed and perhaps never would. As far as its hypothetical nature is concerned, the two Jesuit scholars vigorously asserted it, but in spite of this, about a century and a half later, Jansenius, the Bishop of Ypres, mounted a violent attack against both Pelagius and his followers and the molinist Jesuits in his work *Augustinus*, the former because of the assertion concerning the intrinsic goodness of human nature even after the original sin and the latter, whom Jansenius likened to the less famous heresy of the semi-Pelagians, because of the assertion concerning the (hypothetical) state of nature. Suárez, who fully agreed with Molina about the state of nature being hypothetical, was well aware of the novelty of the theory and that was why he mentioned *Cajetanus et moderniores theologi*[37] rather than the Fathers of the Church or the medieval scholastics. Nevertheless, the theoretical importance of this hypothesis is proven by its logical necessity with regard to the understanding of those who came thereafter.

Hobbes In the *Leviathan*, Hobbes stated:

> It may peradventure be thought, there was never such a time, nor condition of war as this; and I believe it was never generally so, over all the world: but there are many places, where they live so now. For the savage people in many places of America, except the government of small families. The concord whereof dependent on natural lust, haven no government at all; and live at this day in that brutish manner, as I said before.[38]

It is well-known that Hobbes theorised a status of perfect equality among all men, by which everyone had a right to everything (*jus in omnia*), and thus, everyone was at war against everybody else (*bellum omnium contra omnes*). This state of total belligerence made the state of nature unliveable, thus making the social contract and the creation of an absolute state a necessity. We could argue that Hobbes's state of nature is purely hypothetical because it is unliveable and thus cannot be posited, both psychologically and existentially, but Hobbes's observations are not clear-cut and retain a certain historical and theoretical ambiguity. For example, stating the impossibility of arguing the state of nature as a general principle does not exclude the possibility that it might exist in a more limited setting. A conformation of this view can be found elsewhere, even though the historical argument is moved away from England and other known countries, all the way to the fabled Americas, on the basis of more or less romanticised tales from travellers and literates. Therefore, the historical element of Hobbes's theory is set against a

[37]"Cajetan and the most modern theologians".

[38]Hobbes 1651, ch. XIII.

backdrop that is more fantastical than real, and the result is thus uncertain and has shaky foundations.

Locke In Locke's theory, the state of nature is a state of reasonableness, as it reflects the reasonable nature of the individuals that are a part of it and, more to the point, finds its intrinsic limit in the law of nature.

> To understand political power aright, and derive it from its original, we must consider what estate all men are naturally in, and that is, a state of perfect freedom to order their actions, and dispose of their possessions and persons as they think fit, within the bounds of the law of nature, without asking leave or depending upon the will of any other man.[39]

Whereas Hobbes only recognised the existence of *jus in omnia* in the state of nature, Locke acknowledged the existence of fundamental rights, also "primary", and other natural rights, also "secondary". The three primary rights are as follows: the right to life, the right to freedom, and the right to property (note the similarity to Vitoria in this last instance). As a matter of fact, if we were to give a literal interpretation of Locke's words, these fundamental rights would be bound up in the right to property. Locke states that by nature man is endowed with the right to property in respect of life, freedom and material possessions. Therein lies the difference between Locke and Hobbes: the acknowledgement of human reasonableness and inalienable rights under the term "property". The three fundamental rights are exercised within the state of nature, and the law of nature contains within itself the limit that Hobbes attributed to the establishment of civil laws, thus making Locke's state of nature historically feasible.

At this point, one could argue that Locke had the medieval, or even classical outlook in mind, and one could imagine a link between the Aristotelian and Lockean societies. However, two arguments can be raised to the contrary: (a) the first is that Aristotelian sociability comes before the individual, whereas Locke had a contractualist attitude and viewed the contract among individuals as the origin of social life, quite the opposite of Aristotle and (b) the second is that to Locke the limit was an isolating element that allowed for a more functional social life among human beings by reducing the chances of intersection; to medieval scholars, it was inherent to human nature, almost as if it were a transcendental condition for tight-knit sociability among men.

A few clarifications are in order: firstly, the state of nature does not represent a "golden age", a perfect state, or else men would not need to abandon it and stipulate a social contract. At this point, the secondary natural rights, i.e. the right to make one's own justice and the right to punish, become extremely significant. These represent the logical product of Locke's theorisation of the state of nature: this is essentially individualistic, made up of social atoms—i.e. individuals—each with their own primary natural rights, and all individuals are equal. It follows that, in the event that another individual violates an individual's rights, the latter, and only the latter, may punish the transgressor and restore balance. In the state of nature, there

[39]Locke 1690, Second Treatise, ch. II, § 4.

is no superior authority to defer to. It is the very dialectic between primary and secondary rights that propels mankind out of the state of nature.

There is a certain degree of uncertainty in Locke's state of nature, which justifies overcoming it. Locke's outlook on the state of nature is certainly more optimistic than Hobbes's: it is not a feral, belligerent state, but rather a state, the weakness, which is intrinsic in its optimistically conceived structure. It is a condition as fragile as complex machinery that runs the risk of being jammed by a grain of dust. It is a rational status susceptible of being rendered insufferable by a grain of dust, that is to say the possibility of someone not respecting another's rights. This is enough to put the state of nature in upheaval. The violation of a right may cause a chain reaction because, on the one hand, it is not a given that the empirically weaker individual will be able to obtain justice and, on the other hand, the punishment the victim inflicts may be fuelled by revenge, and thus be disproportionate to the offence. And then confusion, or even war, ensues. Therefore, while Locke's state of nature is not radically unbearable, it seems so weak, so fragile, that man feels the need to overcome it in order to stabilise, rather than radically change, the situation (as in Hobbes).

Interestingly enough, Locke stated:

> It is often asked as a mighty objection, where are, or ever were, there any men in such a state of Nature? To which it may suffice as an answer at present, that since all princes and rulers of "independent" governments all through the world are in a state of Nature, it is plain the world never was, nor never will be, without numbers of men in that state.[40]

By comparing Hobbes and Locke's theories, we can observe that both authors discussed the state of nature at great length, unlike Grotius. The difference between the two is that while Hobbes offered an ambiguous solution to say the least, Locke was seemingly straightforward, as he deemed the state of nature as existing synchronically only among sovereigns, and not as a past golden age, nor a state of total belligerence followed by social contract that established the civil state. Nevertheless, a precise analysis cannot ignore the statement that Hobbes made in the previously mentioned chapter XIII of the Leviathan:

> But though there had never been any time, wherein particular men were in a condition of war one against another, yet in all times, kings, and persons of sovereign authority, because of their independency, are in continual jealousies, and in the state and posture of gladiators; having their weapons pointing, and their eyes fixed on one another.[41]

There is another similarity between the two English philosophers. In the Second Treaty Locke stated:

> The promises and bargains for truck, etc., between the two men in the desert island, mentioned by Garcilaso de la Vega, in his history of Peru, or between a Swiss and an Indian, in the woods of America, are binding to them, though they are perfectly in a state of

[40] Locke 1690, Second Treatise, ch. II, § 14.

[41] Hobbes 1651, ch. XIII.

Nature in reference to one another for truth and keeping of faith belongs to men as men, and not as members of society.[42]

The stereotype of America as a pseudo-historical place (we could say "a non-place"), existing more as a fantasy than a reality, returns. They are flashes of a "hypothetical history", an oxymoron by which a situation that is defined as historical is set before a hypothetical backdrop.

Rousseau's "good savage" The starting point of Rousseau's philosophy is also represented by the state of nature: according to the philosopher, it is the only scenario from which it is possible to interpret history in action. The first ambiguity of Rousseau's theory lies in the state of nature: in his theorisation of the state of nature, there are indicators of the fact that Illuminism was fading. According to illuminist views, nature was an object that reason had to explain, whereas Rousseau saw nature as a reality to be comprehended and loved through sentiment before it could be dissected by reason. This re-evaluation of sentiment over reason, as well as the desire for a return to nature, clearly represented a preromantic motif, and it would be reprised in countless nuances. Rousseau's state of nature was apparently conceived as optimistic, but it was not inspired by the notion of man as a rational being as in Locke's theory, but rather by the circumstance that, initially, in the state of nature man lives isolated from others, and is thus insusceptible of giving or receiving offence. It is an ambiguous, purely negative kind of bounty, that of abstaining from wrongdoing, rather than the assertive, positive nature of actively pursuing good: thus the myth of the good savage emerges, i.e. the individual who lives isolated and happy in a state of isolation. The individualistic motif that had already appeared both in Hobbes and Locke's works went the furthest in Rousseau's theory. According to Rousseau, the state of nature was destined to unravel inasmuch as the state of isolation came to an end and social relationships came into being. Society came into being as the result of an unfair pact: man was good as long as he was alone; after he came into contact with other men, he became less good. It is one of the recurring themes in *Emile*'s pedagogy. At one point, the unravelling in question receives a sort of formal consecration: when men approach their kin, they move away from the state of nature, but they are definitively ripped away once property is introduced. As Rousseau described it, history began to worsen on the day a man planted a pole in the ground and identified something as his, and other men were so naïf as not to remove the pole or point out that there was no such thing as "mine" or "yours".

Rousseau was conscious of the fact that the state of nature had been dissolved but, at the same time, he felt that it had to be taken into account when interpreting history. Mindful of the well-known debate on the topic, one might question whether Rousseau's state of nature was conceived as a historical event or as a logical hypothesis, but the philosopher made it clear that it was essentially the latter: a state that has never existed, and perhaps never will, but without which history cannot be interpreted.

---

[42]Locke 1690, Second Treatise, ch. II, § 14.

6 Final Observations: Towards the Establishment of the Doctrine of Natural Law in the Eighteenth Century

The doctrine of natural law developed within late scholasticism raises important questions. One might ask whether this doctrine has managed to separate the natural from the supernatural, mankind from the God, and whether the autonomy recognised in favour of natural law resulted in a tendency towards absolute independence, despite the hefty limitations imposed upon it, which in turn was influenced by the secularisation brought about by Humanism and anticipated by Averroist movements. It is also a moot point as to whether this onset of dualism is merely hypothetical or whether the notion of pure nature, i.e. a status held together by commutative justice rather than charity and submission to the God, concedes too much to the pursuit of reason once it is employed to tackle practical legal and political issues.

Grotius shifted from a "sacred" notion of secularisation to a "profane" one, albeit gradually and moderately, in keeping with his peculiar temperament and works. At the beginning of the eighteenth century, he made a decisive contribution to the gradual detachment of the study of law from theology, a change that had been partially anticipated by the late scholasticism. The detachment in question was aided by the exacerbation of religious conflicts and by the rise of secular intellectual inclinations promoted by the humanist movement in the Renaissance, as well as by an accentuated naturalism and rationalism expressed through neo-stoicism and a revaluation of Aristotle's philosophy. Nevertheless, a bond still existed between Grotius's basic notions of metaphysics and natural law and the theological perspective.[43]

Pufendorf held that knowledge could take the form of natural law or theology. These two forms are distinguished by their originating source: the former stems from reason and the latter from revelation; the former perceives man as absolute, by taking into consideration his status in the natural world and the goals he pursues, whereas the latter speaks to the believer, guiding him to the realisation of a lifestyle that is meant to ensure his eternal salvation; the former regulates exterior conducts and the relationships that are formed between men, and the latter focuses on the dialogue between the individual and the individual's own conscience. Natural law is a human, worldly science, and in order to free it from the constraints of theology, Pufendorf (more than Hobbes and Locke) combined his ultimate beliefs with his methodology by resolving to promote natural law to the status of an autonomous scientific field exclusively dependent on human rationality, thus attempting to define natural *ratio*, material acts and sociability. The study of natural law was not meant to serve revealed truths, nor to contradict the dogma of revelation; it simply chose to disregard it. By refusing to allow the dogma of revelation to enter the

[43]See Todescan 2014b, 132 ff. and 319 ff.

narration of the founding arguments of natural law, and by solely giving importance to the light of reason (*ratio sibi relicta*), Pufendorf stressed the latter's crucial significance in building the system. Reason reveals the rules of natural law, and it identifies divine will as the source of obligation.

References

Auer A (1964) Säkularisierung. In: Lexikon für Theologie und Kirche, vol 9. Herder, Freiburg im Breisgau, pp 253–254

Cavalla F (2011) All'origine del diritto al tramonto della legge. Jovene, Napoli

Cavanna A (1982) Storia del diritto moderno in Europa. Le fonti e il pensiero giuridico. Giuffrè, Milano

de Lubac H (1978) Agostinismo e teologia moderna. Jaca Book, Milano

de Molina L (1588) Concordia liberi arbitrii cum gratiae donis. Riberius, Olyssipone

de Vitoria F (2010a) De legibus (1533–1534). In: Pagden A, Lawrance J (eds) Political writings (1991). Cambridge University Press, Cambridge, pp 153–204

de Vitoria F (2010b) De indis recenter inventis relectio prior (1538–1539). In: Pagden A, Lawrance J (eds) Political writings (1991). Cambridge University Press, Cambridge, pp 231–292

Fraile G (1964–1965) Hobbes y Rousseau con Vitoria al fondo. In: Anuario de la Asociación Francisco de Vitoria, vol 15. pp 45–62

Gentili A (1598) De iure belli. Excudebat Guilielmus Antonius, Hanoviae

Grossi P (1973) La proprietà nel sistema privatistico della Seconda Scolastica. In: Grossi P (ed) La Seconda Scolastica nella formazione del diritto privato moderno. Atti dell'Incontro di studio di Firenze (16–19 ottobre 1972). Giuffrè, Milano, pp 117–222

Grotius H (1925) The law of war and peace (De jure belli ac pacis, 1625) (Book I. trans: Kelsey FW, Introduction: Scott JB. Clarendon Press-Humphrey Milford, Oxford)

Hernández Martín R (1999) La lezione sugli Indios di Francisco de Vitoria. Jaca Book, Milano

Hobbes T (1651) Leviathan. Andrew Crooke, London

Larequi J (1929) Influencia suareciana en la filososofía de Grocio. Razón y Fe 87:226–242

Locke J (1690) Two treatises of government. Awnsham Churchill, London

Mongillo D (1970) L'elemento primario della legge naturale in S. Tommaso. In: Rossi L (ed) La legge naturale. Storicizzazione delle istanze della legge naturale. Dehoniane, Bologna, pp 103–123

Opocher E (1993) Lezioni di filosofia del diritto. Cedam, Padova

Pufendorf S (1727) Of the law of nature and nations, eight books (De iure naturae et gentium, libri octo, 1672) (trans: Kennett B). J. Walthoe et alii, London

Puig Peña F (1933, 1934) La influencia de Francisco de Vitoria en la obra de Hugo Grocio. Revista de Ciencias Jurídicas y Sociales 16:543–606; 17:12–113; 213–314

Suárez F (1612) Tractatus de legibus ac Deo legislatore. apud Didacum Gomez de Loureyro, Conimbricae

Suárez F (1619) De divina gratia. apud Didacum Gomez de Loureyro, Conimbricae

Thieme H (1973) Qu'est ce-que nous, les juristes, devons à la Seconde Scolastique espagnole? In: Grossi P (ed) La Seconda Scolastica nella formazione del diritto privato moderno. Atti dell'Incontro di studio di Firenze (16–19 ottobre 1972). Giuffré, Milano, pp 7–21

Todescan F (2001) Storicità e ipoteticità dello stato di natura nelle dottrine giusnaturalistiche del sec. XVII. In: Pedroso de Moraes Feltes H, Zilles U (eds) Filosofia: Diálogo de Horizontes. Festschrift em homenagem a Jayme Paviani. Educs-Edipucrs, Caxias do Sul-Porto Alegre, pp 139–148

Todescan F (2014a) Lex, natura, beatitudo. Il problema della legge nella Scolastica spagnola del sec. XVI. Cedam, Padova

Todescan F (2014b) Le radici teologiche del giusnaturalismo laico. Il problema della secolarizzazione nel pensiero giuridico del sec. XVII. Cedam, Padova

Todescan F (2014c) *Utrum omnis lex derivetur a lege aeterna*. Dogmatica giuridica e suggestioni teologiche nel 'sistema delle fonti' di Francisco de Vitoria. In: Beneyto JM, Vaca CR (eds) New perspectives on Francisco de Vitoria. Does international law lie at the hearth of the origin of the modern world? CEU Ediciones, Madrid, pp 41–123

Todescan F (2015) Le categorie giuridiche della dignità umana – La controversia sugli Indios nel pensiero della seconda scolastica. In: Kahlo M, Fiorillo V (eds) Wege zur Menschenwürde. Ein deutsch-italienischer Dialog in memoriam Mario A. Cattaneo. Mentis, Münster, pp 71–110

Truyol Serra A (1984) Francisco Vitoria y Hugo Grocio: Cofundadores del Derecho Internacional. La Ciencia Tomista 111:17–27

Vázquez G (1605) Commentaria ac disputationes in Primam Secundae Sancti Thomae. Compluti: ex officina Iusti Sanchez Crespo

Chapter 3
The Sovereignty of Law in the Works of Francisco de Vitoria

Simona Langella

Abstract Francisco de Vitoria's reflection on the role of the law is a key element of his work. The topic is the *leitmotif* of his oral and written legacy (See Langella in Teología y ley natural. Estudio sobre las lecciones de Francisco de Vitoria. BAC, Madrid, 99–152, 2011); with its various aspects, it was essential to the Master of Theology and Most Worthy Prime Professor at the University of Salamanca in solving a number of issues, ranging from the limits of civil and ecclesiastical powers to the question of Indians and their rights. This work aims to show that Vitoria, on the basis of his concept of the law, resolved a series of issues: not only those addressed by the *relectio De Indis*, to which he owes his fame, but also other serious matters, such as the limits of civil power—specifically of sovereignty, at a very delicate moment for nascent nation states—or of ecclesiastical power, with special regard to a spiritual reformation of the Church that the whole of Christianity perceived as necessary and indispensable.

1 Introduction

In 1526, Vitoria replaced Peter Lombard's *Liber Sententiarum* with Thomas Aquinas' *Summa Theologiae* as his course book.[1] He drew from this text the main theoretical fundamentals of his own reflections on pressing issues that mid-16th century European consciences were called to face for the first time. More precisely, the results of his reflections on the concept of law can be found in his commentary

[1]See Langella 2013, 25–69.

S. Langella (✉)
University of Genoa, Genoa, Italy
e-mail: langellauni@gmail.com

J.M. Beneyto and J. Corti Varela (eds.), *At the Origins of Modernity*,
Studies in the History of Law and Justice 10, DOI 10.1007/978-3-319-62998-8_3

to qq. 90–108 of Thomas Aquinas' *Summa Theologiae* I–II.[2] While discussing these questions, Thomas Aquinas investigates the topic of natural law in depth, which he interprets as the participation of the eternal law in men, that is to say the law or rule by which God created and governs the whole of creation. It was precisely Thomas Aquinas' assertion regarding the existence of a natural law that precedes any human law, valid for every human being, that would lead Vitoria to question its applicability to a series of issues that he himself tried to solve.

2 The Sovereignty of Natural Law: A Tool to Control Civil Power

In question 105 of the commentary to the I–II, dating back to 1533–1534,[3] while explaining the reason for the judicial precepts of Ancient Law, Vitoria defines the duties of the king in his relations with the political community.[4] In doing so, Vitoria clarifies that the king may indeed exert his power exclusively by means of laws. Consequently, not only is he required to enforce the law, but he must also do so to the highest degree.

Vitoria never doubted that the king should be subject to the law, even though during the course of his life and work, his position in this regard became more and

[2]In his commentary to I–II, qq. 90–108, dating back to the academic year 1533–1534, Vitoria initially defined the very essence of the *lex*, a definition that, as such, may be applied to any kind of law. Just like Saint Thomas Aquinas, despite understanding thoroughly the etymology of the word *lex* defined by Isidore of Seville in his *Etymologiae* (II, 10), Vitoria states that the law is the rule and measure of human acts, and that the word *ley* (law) comes from Latin *legare* (to bond), as it poses an obligation. Therefore, it belongs to reason, as it is the duty of the reason to issue commands. In other words, law in itself carries the obligation to act, as it is the rule and measure of human acts. See Vitoria 2010, 88 (q. 90, a. 1). See also Vitoria 1991, 155–157.

[3]See Vitoria 2010, 256–271 (q. 105, aa. 1–2). See also Vitoria 1991, pp. 197–204.

[4]During the academic year 1533–1534, Charles V visited the city of Salamanca and its University. Ramón Hernández Martín states that at the same time as the commentary to the *De legibus*, the Emperor attended a *lectio* given by Vitoria (precisely, on Friday 19th June 1534). See Hernández Martín 1995, 128–129. Indeed, Charles V spent a few days in Salamanca during that period, more precisely from 17th to 21st June 1534 (See De Foronda y Aguilera 1914, 389). According to Águeda M. Rodríguez Cruz, on the Friday following the eighth day of the festival of the *Corpus Domini* of 1534, Emperor Charles V listened to Francisco de Vitoria, sitting at one the desks, setting down one of the benches nearby. The scholar based herself on ms. 3825, *Carlos I de España y V de Alemania. Varias noticias y documentos para su historia*, f. 336v, preserved at the Biblioteca Nacional de Madrid (See Rodríguez Cruz 1990, 52). See also Heredia 1939, 119. Nevertheless, no record of this event can be found in the *Libros de Claustros* of 1534 (See Archivo de la Universidad de Salamanca, *Libros de Claustros*, libro XII, ff. 30–33), or in the side notes to Biblioteca Apostolica Vaticana, ms. Ott. lat. 1000, which includes the classes that Vitoria gave in 1533–1534.

more precise and articulated.[5] In his commentary to the *De legibus* and in his *relectio De potestate Papae et Concilii*, of 1528, Vitoria clarifies that there are two ways in which one can be subject to the law: the first is the *vis directiva*, to which everyone is subject; the second is the *vis coactiva*, to which not everyone is subject. The legislator is not obliged by coercive force, nor could he be punished by a superior for not complying with the law.[6] In actual fact, according to Vitoria, one cannot oblige oneself. Without a doubt, however, directive force obliges everyone.[7]

Although kings and rulers are the heads of state, they are a part of it as well, just as are their subjects, and hence they are also subject to the *lex*. Moreover, according to natural right, the roles as officers of the state must be proportionally distributed among all its members.[8] Also, based on natural right, the king must assume the responsibility of part of the duties of the state, as he receives part of the advantages.[9] Hence, provided that all other conditions are the same, in all matters related to the good of the state, the king must accept his portion of the responsibility, or he would act against the natural right itself.[10] Notwithstanding the above, Vitoria admits that he who creates the laws does not sin in the same way as the other

---

[5]With regard to the issue as to whether or not the king is subject to the law, it should be remarked that only starting from the commentary *De Legibus* (academic year 1533–1534) Vitoria adopts Saint Thomas' division between *vis directiva and vis coactiva*. As a matter of fact, in the *relectio De potestate civili* of 1528 Vitoria did not mention said distinction at all, although he already supported the theory according to which the legislator is also subject to the obligations set out by law. The arguments supporting this thesis were merely mentioned, and were basically limited to acknowledging that the obligatory character of the law is created by the king or the *res publica*. In the same way as the laws created by the *res publica* oblige all subjects, the laws created by the king also oblige the king himself. Vitoria also observed that the same occurs with the agreements, which are binding, although they are freely made: "*Quia in aristocratico principatu senatus consulta obligant ipsos senatores auctores illorum, et in populari regimine plebiscita obligant ipsum populum. Ergo similiter leges regiae obligant ipsum regem. Et licet sit voluntarium regi condere legem, tamen non est in voluntate sua non obligari aut obligari. Sicut in pactis; libere enim quisquis paciscitur, pactis tamen tenetur*". Vitoria 1960, 191. "There is confirmation of this in the practice of aristocratic principates, where the decrees of the senate are binding on the senators who pass them, and in popular governments, where the decrees of the plebs are binding on the whole populace. Hence the laws of kings are also binding on the king. The king is free to make laws as he chooses, but cannot choose whether to be bound by the law or not. It is similar to a treaty: anyone may choose whether or not to sign the treaty, but once made he is not free to choose whether he will be bound by its terms". Vitoria 1991, 40. These arguments are further developed and expanded in the *relectio* that Vitoria gave during spring 1534—*De potestate Papae et Concilii*-, precisely resorting to the distinction between *vis directiva* and *vis coactiva*, i.e. debating anew what he discussed during the classes he gave during that very same year.

[6]See Vitoria 2010, 150–154 (q. 96, a. 5) and Vitoria 1991, 180–182. See also Vitoria 1960, 455–456.

[7]See Torres 1931–1932, 141–143.

[8]See Vitoria 2010, 150–154 (q. 96, a. 5). See also Vitoria 1991, 180–182.

[9]See Vitoria 2010, 150–154 (q. 96, a. 5). See also Vitoria 1991, 180–182.

[10]See Vitoria 2010, 150–154 (q. 96, a. 5). See also Vitoria 1991, 180–182.

subjects if he does not respect them, owing to the fact that he compensates for his guilt by tolerating greater duties for the benefit of the community.[11]

However, the king is authorised to legislate only in his role as public representative, and laws must be made for the common or public good, not for the private good of the ruler or of some privileged individuals.[12] Here lies the difference between the king and the tyrant, between the just and the unjust law.[13] In this regard, Vitoria specifies that it is better to be subject to a just law issued by a tyrant, than to comply with no law at all,[14] because if a king without a rightful title (*si principes, qui non habent iustum titulum*) governed the kingdom, and the laws were not complied with, the *res publica* would fall into ruin.[15]

---

[11]See Vitoria 2010, 150–154 (q. 96, a. 5). See also Vitoria 1991, 180–182.

[12]"*Non licet principi condere legem quae non spectet ad bonum commune, alias tyranna est lex, non iusta, quia est persona publica quae ordinatur ad bonum commune et est minister reipublicae*". Vitoria 2010, 92 (q. 90, a. 2). "A prince may not invent a law which has no regard for the common good, since otherwise the law will be tyrannical, not just. The prince fulfils a public role which is itself ordained for the public good, and he is a servant of the commonwealth". Vitoria 1991, 157. Not only is he not entitled to create a law that is not aimed at the common good, but such an event could not take place as said law would not be a law: "*Bene licet principi bonum privatum suum respicere, sed non per legem. Secundo dico quod non solum non licet, sed nec potest fieri, quia talis lex non esset lex, et si constaret quod nullo modo respicit bonum commune, non esset ei parendum*". Vitoria 2010, 92 (q. 90, a. 2). "A prince may of course look out for his own private good, but not through the law. Second, I assert that a law cannot be against the common good, not only *de iure*, but also *de facto*, because in that case the law would be no law. If it were established that a law in no way concerned the common good, that law should not be obeyed". Vitoria 1991, 157.

[13]"*Hoc enim interest inter regem legitimum et tyrannum, quod tyrannus ordinat regimen ad proprium quaestum et commodum, rex autem ad bonum publicum ut tradit Aristoteles 4 Politicorum c. 10*". Vitoria 1960, 824. "This is the difference between a legitimate king and a tyrant: the tyrant orders the government for this own profit and convenience, whereas the king orders it for the common good, as Aristotle demonstrates (Politics 1295a 19–21)". Vitoria 1991, 303.

[14]Erasmus, in his *Institutio principis christiani*, also states that anarchy is far worse than tyranny: "*Anarchia quavis tyrannide perniciosor*". Erasmus 1703, 594 f.

[15]"*Certe videtur, quod leges, quae sunt convenientes rei publicae, obligent etiam si ferantur a tyranno, non quidem, quia a tyranno latae, sed ex consensu rei publicae, cum sanctius sit, ut serventur leges a tyranno latae, quam quod nullae serventur. Et profecto esset in apertam perniciem rei publicae, si principes, qui non habent iustum titulum, occuparent regnum, quod nulla essent iudicia nec aliquo modo possent malefactores puniri aut coerceri, cum non sit tyrannus iudex legitimus, si leges eius non obligant*". Vitoria 1960, 193. "It seems clear that laws which serve the commonwealth's purposes are binding, even when passed by a tyrant; not, to be sure, because they are passed by the tyrant, but because they have the commonwealth's consent, since utility and respect are better served by obedience to a tyrant's laws than by disobedience to all law. It would obviously be to the detriment of the commonwealth, were some prince with no just title to topple the government, that there should be no courts, no way to arraign criminals, no punishment for those who commit injustice. Yet this would be the inevitable result if the law of a tyrant emperor were not binding". Vitoria 1991, 42.

Nevertheless, civil laws are a reflection of the eternal and natural law[16] and therefore must be useful, feasible, honest, just and necessary.[17]

[16]As is the case for all other laws, the "natural law" also partakes in and is a reflection of the eternal law. In this regard, it must be stressed that despite the fact that all laws, in essence, participate in the eternal law, there is no doubt that the *lex naturalis* boasts a privileged relationship with it. See Vitoria 2010, 118 (q. 93, a. 3). See also Vitoria 1991, 168. Because of this, it has the nature of law to the highest degree. Finally, the natural law, although ignored, is in any case a real law and does not require to be promulgated in order to be obliging—see Francisco de Vitoria 2010, 98 (q. 90, a. 4). See also Vitoria 1991, 158–163—and, hence, it cannot be dispensed or revoked. The natural law is a reflection of the primordial needs of human nature, and therefore, it is just like nature itself: single, universal and immutable. See Lottin 1948, 97–100. All precepts contained therein are inscribed in a first, universal principle: *Bonum est amandum et malum fugiendum*. Moreover, as far as the first principles are concerned, the natural law is the same for everyone, both as regards its knowledge, and as regards the validity and truth of its principles. With regard to these, indeed, it is known by all men and is always true and just. In the same way as the first speculative principles are known by everyone, and are always valid, the same must be said for the first practical principles, due to their similarity with the speculative principles. However, as regards the conclusions that can be drawn from the first principles of the natural law, they are not always known by men, be it because of ignorance, or owing to the many circumstances that must be taken into account in order to know what is right and what is not. This means that the further the conclusions are from the first principles, the more mistaken the intellect can be about them. Indeed, drawing universal conclusions from some principles, to be applied to specific actions, requires the taking into account of several circumstances that may invalidate the correctness of the reasoning and is therefore the prerogative of the wise man. This leads to the acceptance of a progress in the knowledge of the natural law, in terms of clarification, that does not demonstrate an alteration in the *lex naturalis* but rather, a development in the knowledge that humans have of it. See García 1978, 124. Finally, as concerns the immutability of the natural law, it should be stated that it may change by "addition" only, this meaning that only circumstances may be added to it to improve it. On the contrary, it cannot be changed by "subtraction", this meaning that no principle can ever be abolished. Indeed, the first principles can never be altered by subtraction, although the secondary principles can vary. An instance of this can be seen in the conclusions drawn from the first principles. In actual fact, however, also concerning the secondary principles, the change does not properly concern the law; rather, the change takes place because of the variability of the matter to which it applies. The third property of the natural law implies that human or divine authorities cannot dispense with it. See Vitoria 2010, 194 (q. 100, a. 8).

[17]Through human reason, the eternal law reveals itself as natural and human law. It is the source and origin of all right laws, as they receive their mandatory force and normative character from the eternal law. The eternal law, the *ratio* governing the universe, governs all rational and irrational beings with its wisdom. However, if everything is subject to the eternal law by its own inclination, as far as knowledge is concerned, only the rational creatures are subject to it. See Vitoria 2010, 120 (q. 93, a. 6). See also Vitoria 1991, 168–169. Therefore, men are subject to the law in two different ways: by nature and because they are rational beings. This latter aspect is the basis of the *lex naturalis*. Strictly speaking, it not only belongs to reason, but it is naturally inscribed in the minds and hearts of men (the evidence of this existence was not only the authority of Saint Paul's, Rom 2:14, who spoke of a Law written on the hearts of men, but, more importantly, the promulgation of God's Decalogue, whose principles, according to Saint Thomas, *Summa Theologiae*, II–II, q. 122, a. 1, all belong to justice or to judicial precepts). Hence, not only does it conform to reason, but it is also intrinsically related to the same needs of human nature: reason, by examining the natural inclination of men, prescribes what men must or must not do to be fulfilled.

The power of the king is limited by a solid conception of law that, in Vitoria's political vision, has a hegemonic role.[18] In his theory, laws ensure the existence and unity of the political body. This makes the reason why the king is so greatly subject to the law apparent. On the other hand, it is the very same Aristotle in the III book of *Politics* who stated that, in the *polis*, the laws must be supreme, and that political power is merely in charge of their control.[19] Indeed, and without a doubt, according to Aristotle, it is truly preferable for the law to rule, rather than a citizen, because the law is impartial, as it is reason free from passion. That which is free from any element of affection is better than that which embodies it by nature; the law does not contain said characteristic, while every soul essentially does. Considering that passion belongs to those who have a soul, and that its effects corrupt even the best of men when they hold the power, it is best that the law be supreme in the *polis.*[20] Indeed, the justice of the laws guarantees equality; what is right, as it is equal, is also useful to the whole city.[21] In other words, law is order.[22] Without a doubt, the laws do not guarantee the unity of the state thanks to their contents only; they do so insofar as they are complied with and implemented, i.e. insofar as they "are supreme", maintaining order and consequently, the fulfilment of their purpose, i.e. the common good.[23]

[18]Natural law enunciates the intrinsic needs of the human being. Civil positive laws, or ecclesiastical laws, instead, indicate what is right, as it has been ordered or determined by the human will for the purpose of the good operation of the *res publica* or of the common good. Also in human positive laws, this is about an activity of reason (*ordinatio rationis*) that enunciates a norm or rule having a mandatory character. Civil law, in fact, is the result of human reason, just like natural law. The latter, however, is prior to positive law, and is the basis of the civil human law. Not only does this origin have an impact on the moral and juridical value of civil laws, but also on the very mandatory nature of their character; these, in actual fact, are not authentic laws if they are not derived from natural law. In the case of civil law, this is a determination or application of the common principles of natural law to specific actions. Therefore, by way of example, the right to property is derived from natural law, but the act of determining how to share the goods of the earth is not clear within this natural law; hence, with regard to the common good, human law will choose, among several determinations, the best one. See Francisco de Vitoria 1934, 74–75 (q. 62, a. 1).

[19]See Seel 1989, 70.

[20]See Aristotle, *Politics*, III, 10, 1281a 35–40. See also Aristotle, *Politics*, III, 11, 1282b 5–6.

[21]See Aristotle, *Politics*, III, 13, 1283b 40–45.

[22]See Aristotle, *Politics*, III, 16, 1287a 20–35.

[23]Vitoria also states that it is not only the intention of every legislator to make men good, but that it is the very quality of the law that makes subjects good. In doing so, however, he also highlights that the common good is made by private goods, and that it is impossible for somebody to behave with regard to the common good and, at the same time, to behave badly with regard to themselves. Hence, the aim of the prince is to make men good, and to induce them to virtue, as the common good is the aim of the legislator and the ultimate aim of the law. Thus, it is necessary that the law be especially aimed at the common good, which is happiness. This is the reason why Aristotle states that the right laws produce happiness. However, most of happiness is virtue, and one cannot be a good citizen simply by being wealthy, if one does not love virtue. In this way, the legislator intends to make men good. Without a doubt, this does not mean that, for Vitoria, the various authorities are no different: as a matter of fact, the civil princes wish to make men good within the limits of human happiness, while the ecclesiastic princes mean to lead them to eternal happiness.

It is the duty of the king to allow them to rule, by creating laws and enforcing them.[24]

It is for this reason that, among the virtues of those who rule, *iustitia* must prevail.[25] According to Vitoria, to preserve the public good, a special virtue is required, as it is difficult to behave properly with regard to compliance with the laws. "*Ad conservationem boni publici, speciali virtute est opus, quia est difficile bene se habere circa observationes legum*".[26] This special virtue—useful in time of both war and peace—is justice, the most perfect moral virtue.[27] The cornerstone of the government and the preservation of the kingdom, it is credited with the most perfect of acts, such as the power to prevent wars and riots, ensure equality and, most importantly, keep the peace through the laws.[28]

(Footnote 23 continued)

See Vitoria 2010, 114 (q. 92, a. 1). See also Vitoria 1991, 164–167. In this regard, in q. 10, a. 8, of II–II, he states: "*Disputando an lex civilis habeat solum reddere homines pacificos et ponere pacem inter cives, an etiam cum hoc debeat intendere homines esse bonos, determinavimus quod intentio principis condentis legem est et debet esse facere homines bonos*". Vitoria 1932, 192 (q. 10, a. 8).

[24]For the law to be applied, its promulgation is necessary. Positive human law does not oblige anyone if it is not promulgated, and has no strength or validity. Vitoria demonstrates this by asserting that issuing a law is ordering, but ordering is promulgating. If the prince issued a law that was obliging from the very moment of its creation to, for instance, sell the primogeniture, and somebody had sold it before, the contract would not be valid. On the contrary, the law would have been valid if it had been promulgated. The legislator is a public representative and cannot create a law without publicly promulgating it. For the human law to oblige, it is not sufficient that it is promulgated privately in a group, or among wise men. It needs to be solemnly promulgated. The prince only has the authority to create the law due to him being a public representative. Vitoria demonstrates this with an argument of reason: as a matter of fact, human laws must be aimed at easing the salvation of souls. If a private promulgation was sufficient, this would represent a great obstacle for men, as the obligations set forth could be ignored due to the ignorance of many. In any case, although a solemn promulgation is necessary for the human law to oblige, it is not necessary that it be promulgated before the whole community. See Vitoria 2010, 102–105 (q. 90, a. 4). See also Vitoria 1991, 158–163.

[25]As a matter of fact, comparing the classes that Vitoria dedicated to the explanation of prudence (See Vitoria 1932, 352–389, qq. 47–56) and those dedicated to justice, it is evident that Vitoria was more interested in this latter virtue (See Vitoria 1934–1935, vol. III, IV, and part of vol. V). About the application of the law and the "supra iustitiam" or "epiqueya" in Vitoria see Cruz 2009, 81.

[26]See Francisco de Vitoria 1934, 25 (q. 58, a. 6). As has already been stated, according to Aristotle, the laws must be supreme, provided that they were perfectly created. Of course, the one or more persons holding the power are supreme in all those cases where the laws cannot rule with precision because, as also stated by the Stagirite, it is not easy to give general rules that may apply to all cases (See Aristotle, *Politics*, III, 11, 1282b 5–10). Vitoria appears to be well aware of the difficulty pointed out by Aristotle while stating that the king, first of all, must acquire the virtue of justice as a *habitus*.

[27]"*Et sic patet iustitiam esse perfectiorem*". See Vitoria 1934, 27 (q. 58, a. 12).

[28]See Vitoria 1934, 27 (q. 58, a. 12).

3 Sovereignty of Natural Law: An Instrument for the Reformation of the Church

The work of Vitoria, however, does not end here. Indeed, between April and June 1534, with his *relectio De potestate Papae et Concilii*, Vitoria faced the thorny question of what measures would be efficient in establishing restrictive norms to fight cases of abuse of papal authority. He felt that the Church had to be reformed, but he never questioned the Pontiff's supreme authority and infallibility, even though some points of his doctrine, such as his strong resistance to the abuses of the Roman Curia, would impact on the attitude of the Spanish theologians during the Council of Trent.[29]

Vitoria declares a dual infallibility: the infallibility of the whole Church, gathered in a Council, and of the Pope. As regards faith and customs, the Council may not fail, and neither may the Pope.[30] For this reason, it is absolutely necessary that they agree on their decisions. Without a doubt, the final word on the causes does not belong to the Council, but to the Pope, in the same way that in temporal society the final word belongs to the king.[31]

The Pope, indeed, is entitled to dispense with[32] and repeal any statute and law of the Council, even if accompanied by an invalidating order (*decretum irritans*).[33] According to Vitoria, since the Pontiff is the supreme authority of the Church, he has full power to dispense with and repeal laws. If the Council could dispense in those cases where the Pope cannot, the Pontiff would no longer be the Vicar of Christ, vested with a supreme and universal authority, because the Council could

---

[29]See Urdánoz 1960, 412.

[30]See Vitoria 1960, 445.

[31]See Vitoria 1960, 484.

[32]Vitoria reflects also on the topic of the mutability of the human laws, especially by means of repeal and dispensation. He states that repealing a law means to annul it, while the dispensing with a law means the competent authority being exempt from the obligation to comply with a law because of reasonable cause: "*dispensare est tollere obligationem et relegare ius ad quod quis tenebatur*". Vitoria 2010, 164 (q. 97, a. 4). See also Vitoria 1991, 187. In other words, "dispensing" actually means to remove an obligation and to set aside the right to which someone was subject. The reason on which the law is based, however, remains invariable because, should it vary, the reason of the law would cease. Vitoria also states that in the case of the natural right or the divine right, a dispensation cannot be obtained if it is not based on a rational cause. With regard to the human right, however, the dispensation annuls the obligation of the positive law, while the obligation set out by the natural right remains: those who resort to a dispensation of this kind, therefore, avoid their part of the responsibility and offend those who do comply with the law. See Vitoria 2010, 166 (q. 97, a. 4). See also Vitoria 1991, 186–189. Moreover, one thing is the dispensation with the law, which still requires a part of the community to comply with it, and quite another is its repeal, which applies to the whole community. As a consequence, the legislator should pay more attention to dispensation, where a limited number of people are exempt from complying with the law, rather than on repeal where, since the law is no longer, no guilt is present. See Vitoria 2010, 160 (q. 97, a. 2). See also Vitoria 1991, 184–185.

[33]See Vitoria 1960, 451.

delegate these powers to another person, who would therefore have more power than the Pope himself.[34] It would be a great sacrilege to admit that a power could exist in the Church, greater than the one that Christ created for it, i.e. his own vicar. The Pope, indeed, did not receive his authority from the Council, but from Christ. For this reason, the Council cannot interfere with or limit the authority of the Pope, which directly comes from Christ.[35] If the faculty of dispensation with any ecclesiastical statutes is given to the Pope in his role of supreme shepherd, he preserves it even before a *decreto irritante.*[36]

However, in defending the supreme authority of the Pope, granted to him by divine law, Vitoria also condemns the abuses of the Curia of Rome in terms of dispensation with the law, thus introducing some Conciliarist aspects in the reformation of the Church.[37] In fact, Vitoria states that the Pope, in dispensing with laws and decrees, be these issued by a Council or by other Pontiffs, may fail, and commit a mortal sin.[38] This is not based on any kind of superiority of the Council as compared to the Vicar of Christ, but on the concept that it is not lawful to dispense with laws by choice, and without a reasonable cause, although said laws belong to human right.[39] The legislator, indeed, may not dispense with a law without a reasonable and just cause.[40] Right laws define what is useful and appropriate for the common good.[41] This purpose may not be achieved in specific cases, and these are the cases for which the dispensation is foreseen.[42] An irrational multiplication of these exceptions, without a just cause, would harm the common good.[43] The legislator would be acting wickedly, should he impose a law on some people, while at

---

[34]See Vitoria 1960, 447.

[35]See Vitoria 1960, 472.

[36]See Vitoria 1960, 451.

[37]See Urdánoz 1960, 420.

[38]See Vitoria 1960, 453.

[39]Of course, the immutability of the natural law implies that human or divine authorities cannot dispense with it. Vitoria points out that, as for human authority, it is clear that it is in charge of the custody and safeguarding of the natural and divine laws and, consequently, does not have the competence to modify them. See Vitoria 2010, 194 (q. 100, a. 8).

[40]See Vitoria 1960, 454.

[41]See Vitoria 1960, 454–455.

[42]Nevertheless, as has already been stated, for Vitoria natural law can neither be dispensed nor derogated. On the contrary, however, as far as human laws are concerned, Vitoria admits that they may be changed. See Vitoria 2010, 158 (q. 97, a. 1). See also Vitoria 1991, 183–184.

[43]Vitoria states that in the case of natural right or divine right, a dispensation cannot be obtained if it is not based on a rational cause. With regard to human right, however, the dispensation annuls the obligation of positive law, while the obligation set out by natural right remains: those who resort to a dispensation of this kind, therefore, avoid their part of the responsibility and offend those who do comply with the law. See Vitoria 2010, 166 (q. 97, a. 4). See also Vitoria 1991, 186–189.

the same time exonerating other people without a reason.[44] This principle also applies to the ecclesiastical laws, without which the Christian community may not be well governed and administered.[45] The supreme authority, the Pope, may not exempt himself without a reasonable cause from the rigour of his own mandatory laws, because the same prince, as stated by Saint Thomas, is subject to the law because of its directive force (*vis directiva*) and in the court of conscience (*in foro conscientiae*), although he is above it as regards changes to and reasonable dispensations from any law.[46]

Therefore, for some of the laws of the Church, it would be advisable that no dispensation is ever applied, namely those laws concerning the universal condition of the Church, the reformation of its customs and of any aspect that is necessary for its government.[47] Although they are not of divine right, they belong to the apostolic or primitive tradition of the Church, or are almost by way of necessity bound to its essential elements.[48] Hence, Vitoria states that with regard to very specific cases, where most of the difficulty resides, the Council may confirm its most important reformatory resolutions with a *decretum irritans.*[49]

Although Vitoria rejects the Conciliarist doctrine of the Paris Scholars, such as Gerson and Almain, and defends the authority of the Pope, at the same time he acts in support of the resistance to the very same Pope, in order to propose an effective remedy to the abuses of the Curia of Rome in terms of dispensations. In order to do so, he bases himself on Council resolutions sealed by invalidating order.[50] He thus asserts:

[44]One thing is the dispensation from the law, which still requires a part of the community to comply with it, and quite another is its repeal, which instead applies to the whole community. As a consequence, the legislator shall pay more attention in the case of dispensation, where a limited number of people do not comply with the law, rather than in the case of repeal where, since the law is no longer, no guilt is present: "*Quando autem omnes sunt exempti, nulli fit iniuria*". Vitoria 2010, 160 (q. 97, a. 2) and also Vitoria 1991, 185 ("but when all are exempted, no one is offended"). See also Vitoria 1960, 455.

[45]See Vitoria 1960, 454.

[46]See Thomas Aquinas, *Summa Theologiae*, I–II, q. 96, a. 5. See also Francisco de Vitoria 2010, 150–154 (q. 96, a. 5) and Vitoria 1991, 180–182. Vitoria clarified that there are two ways in which one can be subject to the law: the first way is the way of the *vis directiva*, to which everyone is subject; the second way is the way of the *vis coactiva*, to which not everyone is subject. The legislator is not obliged by the coercive force, nor could he be punished by a superior for not complying with the law. In fact, according to Vitoria, one cannot oblige oneself. However, as regards directive force, it obliges everyone. See also Vitoria 1960, 455–456.

[47]See Vitoria 1960, 456.

[48]See Vitoria 1960, 458. See also Urdánoz 1960, 421.

[49]Moreover, "*Facta tali declaratione et decreto concilii, si Summus Pontifex contrarium mandaret, possent vel episcopi, vel concilium provinciale etiam implorare principes ut quilibet eorum resisteret Summo Pontifici, impediendo mandata eius*". Vitoria 1960, 486.

[50]See Juan de Jesús María 1947, 118.

> Si per iniustas dispensationes vel per alia mandata insolentia procederent in perniciem Ecclesiae, posset convocari et congregari concilium, etiam contra eius voluntatem, ad resistendum Pontifici et obviandum eius insolentiae.[51]

While reading these daring statements of the very cautious Dominican Master, it is important to bear in mind that in his time, the topic of a call for a universal council was much debated and from it, a complete reformation of the Church was a much hoped for outcome. Most importantly, it must be highlighted that the subjection of the Pope to the Council declared by Vitoria is not the result of the jurisdictional authority of the Council over the Pope, but of the very nature of the circumstances. Indeed, the Pope would not be able to dispense with these laws, and the same can be stated as regards the Council.[52] Even though the jurisdictional powers of the Pope are fully above the Council, i.e. he is fully authorised to validly dispense with all decrees and statutes of the Council, and also repeal them, despite the invalidating order, in doing so he would sin: as regards moral obligations he is, in fact, subject to the resolutions of the Council, whenever it establishes laws that are aimed towards the good of the Church.[53] Similarly, he may not dispense with similar laws that were established by a predecessor of his. The superiority of the Council over the power of the Pope thus acknowledged by Vitoria is then reduced to a moral, not a legal obligation of the Pope with regard to a serious matter, i.e. to the very matter of the law.[54] However, having theologically and legally confirmed the papal authority, Vitoria does not renounce a strong criticism against those who do not want the Council to confirm some of its decisions with a *decretus irritans.*[55] Indeed, Vitoria states that:

> nos bene possemus philosophari et imaginari quod Summi Pontifices possent esse sapientissimi et sanctissimi viri, et quod nunquam dispensabunt sine legitima causa. Sed clamat experientia in contrarium[56]

---

[51]See Vitoria 1960, 488. It should be noted that, except for this proposition, Vitoria always refers to the legitimate Council, convened with the authority of the Pope.

[52]See Vitoria 1960, 460.

[53]This is how he completed his reasoning in proposition no. 14: "*Ergo si non obstante tali decreto concilii, adhuc Papa posset dispensare, in quo salvatur ista superioritas concilii supra Papam? Respondetur quod satis est* ad hoc *ut Papa teneretur, et male facit contraveniendo decreto concilii, vel sufficit iterum quod Papa non possit tollere talem legem nec irritare si concilium prohiberet, sed posset dispensare quia, manente tali lege, spectat ad eum omnis actus iurisdictionis in Ecclesia*". Vitoria 1960, 473.

[54]See Vitoria 1960, 482.

[55]Due to this strong criticism against the Roman Curia, Pope Sixtus V ordered this *relectio* to be included in the *Index Librorum Prohibitorum.* See Beltrán de Heredia 1939, 124.

[56]Vitoria 1960, 467. This is how he concluded this twelfth proposition: "distinguendo tempora, ut dicunt iuristae, et concordando iura. Tempore Conciliorum antiquorum erant Pontifices similes Patribus Conciliorum, quod ad retinendum et revocandum ab inmoderata et effusa licentia dispensandi non erat opus huiusmodi decreto. Immo si bene revolvantur iura et historiae apud antiquos patres non praesumebant Pontifices decreta Conciliorum ita faciliter et passim dispensare, sed tanquam oracula divina observabant. Nec solum non ita temere, sed fortasse nec semel dispensabant contra statuta Conciliorum, maxime circa leges graviores". Vitoria 1960, 471.

Having stated the need and lawfulness of not making obligatory those papal resolutions that are contrary to the laws that govern serious matters for the good of the Church,[57] Vitoria may consider how to go about resisting the destructive behaviour of the Roman Curia. Indeed, few ecclesiastical laws exist that are so serious that the Pope should never dispense with them. Even though for some of these laws, and under given circumstances, it would appear to be right and good to allow for a dispensation, it is without a doubt advisable not to do so, so as to avoid abuse of power.[58] The Dominican Master, however, specifies that once in a thousand years this may occur but that, in general, the law must not be left to human decisions.[59] On these laws, the Council, along with the Pope, may issue a *decretus irritans* to more specifically state those laws to which a dispensation should never be applied: "*Facta tali determinatione [sc. decreto irritante], nunquam liceret Papae dispensare in tali lege et peccaret mortaliter dispensando in tali lege ex quacumque causa*".[60]

Therefore, the invalidating order only implies a moral obligation[61] and does not entitle the Pope to dispense with a law; on the contrary, it makes it unlawful for him to do so.[62] In other words, Vitoria states that if it is not possible to exclude any exception and to make it impossible to dispense with human laws, the law should define the specific cases where the Pope is not entitled to lawfully dispense with laws.[63] Even though for him the unlawful dispensation is legally valid for all purposes, at the same time he asserts that resistance is lawful, justifying his own lack of obedience to these mandates.[64]

Vitoria then considers the conditions for a lawful disobedience from the requirements that, according to Saint Thomas, the law must comply with in order to create obligations for its subjects.[65] In the same way as an unjust law does not

---

[57]Vitoria bases himself on the authority of Thomas Cajetan in asserting that the Pope, in dispensing with laws and decrees of the Council or of another Pope, may fail and commit a mortal sin, as he is not entitled to dispense "*pro suo arbitrio et sine causa rationabili, etiam ubi nihil continent iuris divini*". Vitoria 1960, 453.

[58]See Vitoria 1960, 458.

[59]See Vitoria 1960, 460.

[60]Vitoria 1960, 461.

[61]However, in proposition 13, while recommending moderation, Vitoria points out that this order "*non deberet apponi in multis legibus, sed solum in paucis, hisque gravissimis et valde necessariis*". Vitoria 1960, 471.

[62]"*Tale decretum non facit* per se *quod Papa non possit dispensare, sed solum quod non liceat hoc*". Vitoria 1960, 472. This order does not breach his authority, which is overarching. Moreover, Vitoria states that for the Pope, this decree is a tool against the impertinence of princes and insolent men, and in this way scandal and gossip by many who speak negatively about the Roman Curia would be avoided. See Francisco de Vitoria 1960, 482–483.

[63]See Juan de Jesús María 1947, 131.

[64]"*Facta tali declaratione et decreto concilii sicut dictum est in decima conclusione, si Papa dispensaret subditi non tenerentur parere tali dispensationi*". Vitoria 1960, 481. Vitoria further specifies that "*licet non spectet at subditos hoc iudicare*". *Ibidem*. See also Vitoria 1960, 476–477.

[65]See Thomas Aquinas, *Summa Theologiae*, I–II, q. 96, a. 4.

oblige its subjects in *foro conscientiae*, a dispensation granted to somebody and harming somebody else would not oblige the subjects to acknowledge such dispensation[66]: "*Sed si ferret legem iniquam et iniustam et intolerabilem, vel alias valde gravem, subditi non tenerentur parere; ergo nec etiam si dispensatio sit huiusmodi*".[67] Hence, according to Vitoria, the subjects have the right to resist by not acknowledging the seriously unlawful dispensations issued against some ecclesiastical laws sealed with the *decretus irritans*, so as to show that said law, by reason of the very matter being debated, is by itself indispensable.

In this *lectio magistralis*, the Master's intention is to draft an action plan aimed at reforming the Church and, specifically, the Roman Curia. The key to this practical and speculative operation is applying to the dispensation the conditions of the just law established by Saint Thomas in *Summa Theologiae* I–II[68] and commented on by Vitoria.[69] In fact, Vitoria transfers these conditions to the dispensation so as to raise the dispensation to the level of a law.[70] In the same way as a law does not impose obligations if it does not comply with given requirements, the Pope's dispensations may not impose obligations on any subject if these do not meet specific requirements.[71]

4 The Sovereignty of Natural Law: An Instrument of Justice for Nations

The complex conceptual structure of the *relectio De Indis* (1539) can be schematically simplified by identifying a *pars destruens* and a *pars construens* which, respectively, analyse the illegitimate and legitimate titles for the *Conquista*.

In the first part, having rejected the medieval interpretation of the Pontiff as a *monarcha temporalis in toto orbe*, Vitoria defines two concepts, both proceeding from natural right, *dominium* and *ius gentium*.

As regards the concept of *dominium,*[72] it should be reminded that for a theologian, humans were the bearers of a "capacity to use things" not by human law,

---

[66]In the same way as the law must be created for the common good, the dispensation must also exist for the common good: "*Secundo probatur. Quia sicut leges debent fieri pro bono communi, (debet enim lex nullo privato commodo, sed pro utilitate omnium conscribi, c. Erit autem lex 4 d., ut ait Isidorus) ita etiam dispensatio, quae est quasi lex quaedam, debet habere rationem boni communis, alias erit dissipatio et non dispensation*". Vitoria 1960, 454–455.

[67]See Vitoria 1960, 478.

[68]See Thomas Aquinas, *Summa Theologiae*, I–II, q. 96, a. 4.

[69]See Vitoria 2010, 134–148 (q. 96, a. 4). See also Vitoria 1991, 173–179.

[70]According to Vitoria, "*dispensatio, quae est quasi lex quaedam, debet habere rationem boni communis, alias erit dissipatio et non dispensation*". Vitoria 1960, 454–455.

[71]See Urdánoz 1960, 138–139.

[72]See Langella 2014, 57–85.

but by natural law. In other words, Vitoria would propose *dominium* as an inalienable natural right.[73]

To the objection of the *opositores*, who saw in the natives' sins of anthropophagy or sodomy their inability to self-control and therefore, their incapacity with regard to *dominium*, Vitoria replied that guilt, madness or idiocy did not affect human dignity or human capacity to own: the natives' infidelity, and their state of sin, did not put into question their humanity, but only made it weaker.[74] Hence, Vitoria asserted that there was no cause that could legitimise the expropriation of the lands of the American Indians: the natural law and the faculty to possess or own things for their own use would apply to them, just as they applied to the rest of humanity.[75]

As regards the other fundamental concept debated in the *relectio* of 1539, it is noteworthy that it is not by chance that, in the *De Indis*, Vitoria stated that the *ius gentium* was derived from the natural law, clarifying all ambiguities of an interpretation that would see it on the cusp of the positive right. Indeed, for Vitoria, the *ius gentium* was of natural right, or derived from it: "*Vel est ius naturale vel derivatur ex iure naturali*".[76] However, in his commentary to the II–II, q. 57, a. 3, of 1535, Vitoria included the *ius gentium* in the positive right. After stating that "*quia omne aliud ius a iure naturali, est positivum. Dicitur enim positivum quia est ex aliquo beneplacito*",[77] he affirmed that "*ius gentium potius debet reponi sub iure positivo quam sub iure naturali*".[78] In doing so, Vitoria wanted to reject a conception of the natural right that was traditionally extended to irrational beings as well and, at the same time, to limit a conception of the *ius gentium* that included all precepts which, according to the Spanish theologian, belonged to natural right.[79] For Vitoria, the *ius naturale* was, on the one hand, closely linked to human reason and, on the other, to what was good in itself, regardless of anything else.[80]

In discussing this, it should be emphasised that for Luciano Pereña, it was impossible to state that Vitoria's position on the right of nations, defended during the lecture of 1535, changed in 1539 with the drafting of the *De Indis*. According to the scholar, Vitoria always supported the positive, constitutional and historical character of the *ius gentium*. In the *Relectio* of 1539, Vitoria wanted to demonstrate and affirm the rights of the Spanish with regard to foreign peoples.[81] As noted by

---

[73]See Vitoria 1960, 654. See also Vitoria 1991, 242.

[74]See Vitoria 1960, 655. See also Vitoria 1991, 243.

[75]See Vitoria 1934, 82 (q. 62, a. 1).

[76]Vitoria 1960, 706. See also Vitoria 1991, 278.

[77]Vitoria 1934, 7 (q. 57, a. 2).

[78]Vitoria 1934, 14 (q. 57, a. 2).

[79]See Vitoria 1934, 13–14 (q. 57, a. 2).

[80]"*Ius naturale est bonum de se sine ordine ad aliud*". Vitoria 1934, 14 (q. 57, a. 3).

[81]See Pereña Vicente 1952, 620.

Reginaldo Pizzoni, however, if the vision of the right of the nations was completely positive, the *relectio De Indis* and the *De iure belli* would have had no reason to exist. More specifically, the *De Indis* would have lost its character of a complaint against injustice perpetrated overseas, and this would have led to leaving the Indians at the mercy of the Spanish conquerors, abandoned to their greed.[82]

In the second part of the *De Indis*, after examining a series of titles that are generally acknowledged to be valid, and that are rejected by Vitoria, the Dominican Master detailed the possible legitimate and valid titles justifying the Spanish presence in America.

The first title proposed the topic of Spanish rights to cross the recently discovered lands, and to remain there without causing any harm to the Indians. The second title discussed afresh the question of the legitimacy of spreading the Christian faith. The third, fourth and fifth titles were related to the right of the converted Indians to be defended and required the *iustum belli* against those princes imposing idolatry. The sixth and seventh titles once again declared the rights of the natives that were fighting one another to resort, of their own free will, to the help of the Spanish administration. The last title finally referred to the utility, for the recently discovered peoples, of accepting the administration and government of the King and Queen of Spain, considering that they did not know science and mechanical arts, and had no advanced agriculture and craftsmanship.[83] As for the validity of this latter title, however, Vitoria had serious doubts.

In examining the legitimate titles, the new position of Vitoria is of a paramount importance, as it was based on a new vision: the natural society of all peoples.[84]

Both in the first part of the *De Indis*, where the Master lists and rejects the illegitimate titles for the *Conquista*, and in the second part of the *relectio*, where the legitimate titles are analysed, it is natural right, the source of all other human laws, that is to be the *fil rouge* of his reasoning. Rights are granted to both the Europeans and the Indians and along with them, also duties.

The illegitimate titles for the conquest are against natural right, as they deprive the Indians of their right to property, to self-government and freedom.[85] The Spanish, therefore, may not deprive them of their lands, as all peoples are entitled to own goods and to appoint rulers. It appears that the question is resolved in this way by Vitoria, in view of the natural right that originally provided the human kind with *dominium*.

[82]See Pizzorni 1988, 575.

[83]See Vitoria 1960, 704–726. See also Vitoria 1991, 277–292.

[84]See Urdánoz 1960, 598–600.

[85]See Vitoria 1960, 667. See also Vitoria 1991, 251.

In the same way, should the Indians deprive the Spanish of their natural right to cross their lands[86] and to trade with them[87]—a right derived from the original and universal availability of the common good and of the *cognatio*[88] of men, established among them by their own nature-, or hinder evangelisation,[89] persecute those who converted,[90] or even harm the innocent,[91] or, in brief, should they not live in compliance with the *ius gentium*, which is based on natural law, then they would be unfair and so should be punished.

These last considerations on Spanish rights were often misunderstood and interpreted as a means by which Vitoria could provide a legal basis to wars of colonisation.[92] In actual fact, the aim of Vitoria's reflection was to specifically, and not just formally, acknowledge the equality of the Indians, placing all subjects involved on the very same level, where duties and rights converge. Vitoria indeed recognises that the Indians are rational and free subjects. They are the bearers of rights and, as such, they are participants in natural justice, where duties and rights are intertwined by necessity and in a complementary fashion.

For Vitoria, in summary, natural law is the fabric on which the threads of universal justice can be woven, where conflicts and issues in relation to all topics, ranging from the merely political to the spiritual, are ordered according to a rational layout. In reality, his is a speculative analysis, notwithstanding the fact that it was born out of contingent historical events.

---

[86] "*Apud omnes enim nationes habetur inhumanum sine aliqua speciali causa hospites et peregrinos male accipere. E contrario autem humanum et officiosum habere bene erga hospites; quod non esset si peregrini male facerent, accedentes ad alienas nationes. Secundo, a principio orbis (cum omnia esset communia) licebat unicuique in quamcumque regionem vellet, intendere et peregrinari. Non autem videtur hoc demptum per rerum divisionem*". Vitoria 1960, 706. See also Vitoria 1991, 278.

[87] See Vitoria 1960, 708–709. See also Vitoria 1991, 279–280.

[88] "*Ut vim atque iniuriam propulsemus: nam iure hoc evenit, ut quod quisque ob tutelam corporis sui fecerit. Iure fecisse existimetur, et cum inter nos cognationem quandam natura constituit, consequens est hominem homini insidiari nefas ese*". *Digesta* I, 1, 3.

[89] See Vitoria 1960, 715–719. See also Vitoria 1991, 284–286.

[90] See Vitoria 1960, 719–720. See also Vitoria 1991, 286–287.

[91] See Vitoria 1960, 720–721. See also Vitoria 1991, 287–288. According to Vitoria, a serious breach of natural right is just cause for an intervention, known as intervention *humanitatis causa*. In this regard, in the commentary to the *De Legibus* of 1534, q. 105, a. 2, an affirmation is present, concerning respect for the life of innocents, that allowed Vitoria to perform a more in-depth analysis: "*Rex pro nulla causa et pro nulla utilitate reipublicae potest condere legem quod occidantur innocentes, etiam contra infedeles, quia est contra praeceptum iuris naturalis*". Vitoria 2010, 270 (q. 105, a. 2). See also Vitoria 1991, 204.

[92] See Todorov 1982, 191.

References

Cruz JC (2009) Fragilidad humana y ley natural. Cuestiones disputadas en el siglo de Oro. University of Navarra, Pamplona
Cruz R, María Agueda (1990) Historia de la Universidad de Salamanca. Fundación Ramón Areces, Congregación de Santo Domingo, Salamanca
de Foronda y Aguilera M (1914) Estancias y viajes del Emperador Carlos V, desde el día de su nacimiento hasta el de su muerte. Sucesores de Rivadeneyra, Madrid
de Heredia VB (1939) Francisco de Vitoria. Labor, Barcelona-Madrid-Buenos Aires-Rio de Janeiro
de Jesús María J (1947) ¿Francisco de Vitoria, conciliarista? Ephemerides carmeliticae 1:103–148
de Vitoria F (1932–1935) Comentarios a la Secunda secundae de Santo Tomás. In: de Heredia VB (ed) vol I–V. Biblioteca de Teólogos Españoles, Salamanca
de Vitoria F (1960) Obras de Francisco de Vitoria: Relecciones Teológicas. Critical edition of the Latin text. Spanish version, general introduction and introduction of the juridical-theological doctrine by Father Teófilo Urdánoz. Ed. Católica BAC, Madrid
de Vitoria F (1991) Political writings. In: Pagden A, Lawrance J. (eds) Cambridge University Press, Cambridge
de Vitoria F (2010) *De legibus*. Introduction by Langella S transcription and notes by García JB, Langella S translated into Spanish by García PC and translated into Italian by Langella S. Ediciones Universidad de Salamanca, Salamanca
Erasmus D (1703) Opera omnia. Lugduni Batavorum: Petrus Vander (reprint 1961–1962. Hildesheim: Georg Olms)
García JB (1978) El tratado 'De iustitia et iure' (1590) de Pedro de Aragón. Ediciones Universidad de Salamanca, Salamanca
Langella S (2011) Teología y ley natural. Estudio sobre las lecciones de Francisco de Vitoria. Madrid, BAC
Langella S (2013) La ciencia teológica de Francisco de Vitoria y la Summa theologiae de santo Tomás de Aquino en el siglo XVI a la luz de textos inéditos. SEE, Salamanca
Langella S (2014) Capax dei, capax dominii: la questio de indis en Francisco de Vitoria. In: JM Beneyto, Román Vaca C (eds) New perspectives on Francisco de Vitoria. Does international Law lie at the heart of the origin of the modern world? CEU Ediciones, Madrid, pp 57–85
Lottin O (1948) La loi en général, La définition thomiste et ses antécédents. In: Psychologie et morale au XIIe et XIIIe siècles. Problèmes de morale. Abbaye du Mont César-Duculot, Louvain, Gembloux, pp 97–100
Martín RH (1995) Francisco de Vitoria. Vida y pensamiento internacionalista. Madrid, BAC
Pizzorni R (1988) Lo *ius gentium* nel pensiero del Vitoria. In: I diritti dell'uomo e la pace nel pensiero di Francisco de Vitoria e Bartolomé de las Casas. Massimo, Milan, pp 569–583
Seel G (1989) La giustificazione del dominio nella *Politica* di Aristotele. In: Berti E, Valditara LMN (eds) Etica, Politica, Retorica. Studi su Aristotele e la sua presenza in età moderna. Japadre Editore, L'Aquila-Rome, pp 57–73
Todorov T (1982) La conquête de l'Amérique, La question de l'autre. Éditions du Seuil, Paris
Torres M (1931–1932) La sumisión del soberano a la ley en Vitoria, Vázquez de Menchaca y Suárez. Anuario de la Asociación Francisco de Vitoria 4:129–154
Urdánoz T (1960) Introducción. In: Obras de Francisco de Vitoria: Relecciones Teológicas, critical edition of the Latin text, Spanish version, general introduction and introduction of the juridical-theological doctrine by Father Teófilo Urdánoz. Ed. Católica BAC, Madrid
Vicente LP (1952) El concepto del derecho de gentes en Francisco de Vitoria. Revista española de Derecho internacional 5:603–628

Chapter 4
Vitoria, the Common Good and the Limits of Political Power

André Azevedo Alves

Abstract This chapter focuses on the relationship between Vitoria's notion of the common good (deeply embedded in the Thomist tradition but bringing with it some significant innovations) and his understanding of the limits of political power, both conceptually and in terms of its practical exercise. In order to shed light on that relationship, this chapter starts by laying out the fundamental aspects of Vitoria's traditional understanding of the common good in the context of a developing notion of individual rights that was to become central in modern political thought. The main theoretical implications of this understanding concerning limits on the extension and exercise of legitimate political power as understood by Vitoria are analysed and four prominent applications of Vitoria's conceptions about the limits of political power are discussed, namely concerning the controversial issue of legitimate resistance to abuses of political power, the role of *ius gentium* in establishing universal limits to the power of states in international affairs, the just war theory and the autonomy of Church and state. This chapter concludes with a brief reflection on the relevance of Vitoria's contributions in this specific area of political thought.

A.A. Alves (✉)
Catholic University of Portugal, Institute for Political Studies, Lisbon, Portugal
e-mail: azevedoalves@gmail.com

A.A. Alves
St Mary's University, Twickenham, London, UK

J.M. Beneyto and J. Corti Varela (eds.), *At the Origins of Modernity*,
Studies in the History of Law and Justice 10, DOI 10.1007/978-3-319-62998-8_4

1 Introduction[1]

Francisco de Vitoria is justly regarded as the founder of the School of Salamanca given the incredible scope of his contributions across a wide range of disciplines and his pivotal role in the development of late Iberian scholasticism.

What is in contemporary times described as "interdisciplinarity" was at the core of the vast contributions of the Salamanca School that brought together, analysed and integrated very diverse areas of human knowledge.[2] It should therefore come as no surprise that Vitoria's political contributions are deeply linked with sociological, anthropological and juridical insights. In addition, his reflections on the legitimacy of the conduct of states and individuals in the course of international affairs give him a strong claim to being one of the founding fathers of international law. The main features of his political contributions are set out clearly in three of his surviving *relectiones*: *De potestate civili* (on civil power), *De indis* (on the Indians) and *De iure belli* (on the law of war). Also of special interest are his commentaries to Aquinas' *Summa*, particularly on law and justice.

This chapter is specifically focused on the relationship between Vitoria's notion of the common good (deeply embedded in the Thomist tradition but bringing with it some relevant innovations in political theory) and his understanding of the limits of political power, both conceptually and in terms of its practical exercise. In order to shed light on this relationship, the following section lays out the fundamental aspects of Vitoria's traditional understanding of the common good in the context of a developing notion of individual rights that was to become central in modern political thought. The section after that deals with the main theoretical implications of this understanding concerning limits on the extension and exercise of legitimate political power as understood by Vitoria. The following four sections in this chapter analyse four specific and prominent applications of Vitoria's ideas about the limits of political power, namely concerning the controversial issue of legitimate resistance to abuses of political power, the role of *ius gentium* in establishing universal limits to the power of states in international affairs, the just war theory as a constraint on the action of states and the autonomy of Church and state. This chapter concludes with a brief reflection on the relevance of Vitoria's contributions in this specific domain of political thought.

---

[1]This chapter partially builds upon sections of the book *The Salamanca School* (co-authored with José Manuel Moreira, 1st ed. Continuum, 2010, paperback ed. Bloomsbury, 2013), and earlier versions were presented at the International Seminar "At the origins of modernity: Vitoria and the new world" (2–3—July 2015, Convento San Esteban, Salamanca) and at a CIEP Research workshop (23 September 2015, Catholic University of Portugal, Lisbon). The author would like to thank José Manuel Moreira, the participants in the sessions mentioned and two anonymous referees for their valuable comments on and constructive criticism of various versions of this paper. Responsibility for any and all errors and shortcomings remains solely with the author.

[2]Alves and Moreira 2013a.

2 The Common Good, "Objective Right" and Individual Rights

One of the key defining features of modern political thought was the development of a notion of individual rights that was seen as a departure from traditionally established conceptions of what can be described as an "objective right" (usually understood in the sense of justice and the common good).

The tension between the perceived demands of an "objective right" and a respect for individual (subjective) rights can be identified throughout Francisco de Vitoria's writings, and particularly when he deals with political issues. Depending on how one views Vitoria's political thought, he can be regarded either as one of the last traditional Thomists or as putting forward an account of personal autonomy and liberty that attempts to deal with the challenges of the modern period without jeopardizing traditional Thomist approaches to justice and the common good.

It is important at this point to recall that the precise origins of the theory of subjective rights is a controversial matter and this chapter certainly does not aim at solving that issue. An influential perspective, first laid out by Michel Villey in the 1940s, holds that the Roman jurists failed to contribute to the development of the concept of subjective right and points to the fourteenth-century nominalism of William of Ockham as the proper origin of natural rights theory.[3] Villey's main argument is that the Romans did not have the concept of subjective rights, thinking only in terms of objective right. The thesis—or at least its reach—is disputed by those who claim that the Roman jurist well aware of the *notion* of subjective rights even if they did not have an explicit *theory* of subjective rights. Regardless of the debate about the precise genealogy of subjective rights theory, it would appear that the pragmatic legal approach of the Romans limited their theoretical contributions to political thought in this regard. In terms of political theory, this means that it would indeed be only in the period of late scholasticism that the underpinnings of subjective rights theory start to be developed and it is in this concept that Vitoria's balance between the traditional concepts of objective right and the arising notions of (subjective) individual rights ought to be considered.

Vitoria, like later members of the Salamanca School, held what can be described as an organic view of political society, with the common good as its overriding goal. This view is, however, qualified by a general recognition that the binding character of natural law extends not only to individual subjects but also to positive law and to the rulers themselves. The result is a peculiar combination of a largely organic conception of the promotion of order and the common good with an emphasis on local and individual rights. The promotion of order is deemed a priority, but this common goal coexists with a wide range of individual, family and

[3]See Garnsey 2012, particularly Chap. 7 ("Property as a legal right"), for a developed summary of the debate between Villey and his critics and its implications.

local rights which limit both the power of temporal and spiritual rulers and which are seen as prevailing over unjust legislation.[4]

Although the notion of common good was essential for the definition of individual rights, it was mostly taken for granted and seldom subject to intense explicit scrutiny. While this may be regarded as odd by contemporary standards, one should note, as pointed out by Höpfl,[5] that the question "what is the common good?" was not usually a main topic of investigation in the Thomist tradition. The precise meaning and content of the concept was in practice the result of a mix of other related concepts and was also influenced by the specific circumstances of the social problems to which it was applied. More than a fully fledged and defined set of goals for social order, the notion of common good operated as an element of general guidance for reflections about political matters and political action.

Vitoria combines a strong adherence to the traditional Thomist conception of the objective right with a nuanced and in some ways innovative understanding of personal autonomy associated with a distinct sphere of individual freedom. As noted by Brett,[6] this is particularly clear in Vitoria's discussion of hunting and homicide. Thus, Vitoria explicitly objects to local lords enacting limitations on the people's liberty to hunt wild animals even if it is claimed that the limitations are in the interest of the subjects (for example, by helping them not to waste their time), because he regards the general preservation of liberty as taking precedence over the private good in a setting such as this.

The autonomous direction of each individual towards his conscientious perception of the good is seen by Vitoria as a liberty worth preserving even if from the perspective of an external political authority the real good is conceived differently and the person in question is judged to be in error.

In a similar vein, when discussing the act of killing in self-defence, Vitoria rejects the notion that only public or divine authority can justify killing and asserts a crucial role for private authority and private responsibility. In other words, Vitoria regards individual rights as indispensable components of a well-ordered society and therefore rejects limiting the notion of right to the obligation of acting in accordance with the law or the dictates of an external authority. Without neglecting the sense of objective right and political obligation, Vitoria's understanding of rights also includes the notion of a personal sphere of liberty that—while framed by natural law—relies primarily on the individual's authority and responsibility to use reason and freely decide his course of action in his particular circumstances.

In the same way that individual liberty is bound by natural law and must not lead to arbitrary acts, legitimate political power must not degenerate into absolutist or tyrannical forms. It is this dynamic and intertwined understanding of both the common good and individual rights that constitute the main limits on the extension and exercise of legitimate political power as understood by Vitoria.

---

[4]Hamilton 1963, 30.

[5]Höpfl 2004, 283.

[6]Brett 1997, 132–134.

3 The Commonwealth and the Limits of Political Power

Vitoria's conception of individual rights in the context of the common good led him to hold very strong views on the necessary limits of political power. In some ways, Vitoria may even be considered a constitutionalist (or at least pre-constitutionalist) author even though he did not elaborate his political arguments according to the (contemporary) technical definition of the term. The scholastic tradition which he furthered tended to either reject or strongly qualify the notion of a self-sustaining sovereignty of the ruler over and above the sovereignty of the people. In this tradition, the relationship between the citizens and the ruler is of a contractual or quasi-contractual nature, meaning that the exercise of political power is legitimate only if it respects the terms of the implied contract.

The medieval political maxim *Populus maior principe* meant that whatever the form of government, there remained an element of popular sovereignty that no ruler could dispose of at his own will. It is worth remembering here that in the context of the Thomist framework within which Vitoria operated, positive human laws are only held to be genuine laws to the extent they do not violate the general principles of natural law. As can be readily seen, there lies a first—and very significant—limitation on the exercise of political power: unjust pieces of legislation (i.e. those in opposition to natural law) are not to be considered law and do not in themselves command obedience (though depending on social circumstances and the consequences of disobedience, there may be other compelling reasons to obey them).

In his *relectio* on civil power (*De potestate civili*), Vitoria accepts that public power is from God in the sense that it is founded upon natural law but then adds that "the material cause on which this naturally and divinely appointed power rests is the commonwealth", which "takes upon itself the task of governing and administering itself and directing all its powers to the common good".[7]

The commonwealth delegates to political agents the authority to legislate, but for Vitoria,[8] it is clear who originally holds legislative power:

> (…) positive law derives from the commonwealth, and therefore the existence of the commonwealth itself and of its power to make laws must precede the existence of positive laws; consequently it may be deduced that this legislative power itself exists in the commonwealth by divine and natural law.

This process of delegation is of a secular nature and does not imply direct divine intervention in setting up governments. In fact, the idea that worldly governments are directly instituted by God was regarded not only as wrong, but as a dangerous heresy. But here Vitoria faces an apparent difficulty for he appears to wish to continue affirming that the power of legitimate kings proceeds from God while

[7] Vitoria 1991, 10–11.
[8] Vitoria 1991, 12.

simultaneously clearly pointing out that the original authority to legislate positive human law lies with the commonwealth, not the ruler.[9]

The solution to this paradox comes from the distinction between *potestas* (power) and *auctoritas* (authority). If power is understood as the royal capability to rule, then it may be said that, like other human capabilities, it is an innate endowment derived from God. However, if we think about authority (understood as executive "power"), then it lies originally with the commonwealth and is only exercised by the ruler upon delegation—even though it may be a non-explicit form of delegation.[10]

The distinction has important implications for the legitimate uses and boundaries ascribed to political power, which is no way unlimited. The ruler cannot in any way become the "owner" of the commonwealth: he merely receives (from the commonwealth) the authority to administrate collective affairs in accordance with the promotion of the common good. As summed up by Fernandéz-Santamaria[11]:

> The ruler, for example, may not alienate any portion of the national territory because the commonwealth is not his property. What has been transferred into royal hands, then, is not the state's potestas properly speaking, but its authority; the commonwealth does not invest the ruler with dominium over its parts but with the authority to act as its administrator. In other words, the prince is the nation's minister and caretaker; to rule means to fulfill the obligations implicit in the commonwealth's trust.

Although his capability to rule is derived from God, the political ruler is conceived by Vitoria[12] as an agent of the commonwealth entrusted with solving perceived problems of collective action.

The commonwealth as such cannot frame laws, propose policies, judge disputes, punish transgressors, or generally impose its laws on the individual, and so it must necessarily entrust all this business to a single man.

In the original condition or state of nature, however, there was no political power to be found and all men were free and equal. Man is a social animal that requires life in community both to better face the hazards of nature (because of his physical limitations) and to flourish fully, since justice and friendship can only be practised and experienced by living in society with other persons. However, political society does not derive directly from the social inclinations of man. Rather, the emergence of the state is explained by historical circumstances and not rooted directly in natural law.

Political power provides a solution to specific human needs—and to that extent it is not in contradiction with natural law—but the justification for the existence of the state must be sought in history and not directly in the general principles of natural law. From the perspective of natural law, both (hypothetical) pre-political and political societies are held by Vitoria to be in a somewhat similar position.

---

[9]Brett 1997, 136.

[10]Pagden and Lawrence 1991, xix–xx.

[11]Fernandéz-Santamaria 1977, 74.

[12]Vitoria 1991, 14.

Both are consonant with natural law but apply to different contexts and answer different needs. In prehistorical society, the state's coercive power was not necessary, but the conduct and requirements of actual historical man impose the establishment of political organization. This means that political power is affirmed as necessary in actual history but also that both the state and positive human law are only justified in so far as they contribute to the fulfilment of natural law.

In the process of arguing in favour of monarchy as the best form of government, Vitoria[13] provides another crucial insight about the relationship between liberty and political regimes. He starts by asserting that the claims of enjoying greater liberty by democratic "civil societies" are unfounded:

> Civil societies which have no sovereign and are ruled by a popular administration often boast of their liberty, accusing other civil societies of being the servile bondsmen of sovereigns. There are even some within this kingdom who subscribe to this view.
>
> Against this stupid and ignorant idea I offer my first corollary, which is that there is no less liberty under a monarchy than under an aristocracy or timocracy [rule of the multitude].

Vitoria[14] proceeds to justify his position on terms that show a sophisticated understanding of the distinction between the form of government, and the way political power is exercised:

> I demonstrate the major premise from what has been said already: under any type of government, each private individual is subject to the public power, which he is bound to obey, whether that power resides in one man or in a number of men or in the whole multitude. This power is the same, whether it be exercised by one man, or by the whole community or commonwealth, or by the nobles; there is clearly no greater liberty in being subject to three hundred senators than to one king. Indeed, men who are subject to the decree and government of the crowd have, by that token, all the more masters – unless anyone is so mad as to believe himself a slave when he obeys one wise king, and fancy himself free when he is subject to a barbarous mob.

This theoretical conception of the state is markedly distinct from absolutist and patriarchalist approaches but leaves two important questions insufficiently answered. The first is what the specific historical motivations may have been for men to give up their original condition of freedom. The second is about the conditions under which the establishment of political power may be regarded as legitimate. Vitoria did not provide full and complete answers to these questions, but the later Jesuit members of the Salamanca School would further develop ideas in this regard.[15]

It is nevertheless possible to state that even if tacit primordial consent was held to be sufficient, the widespread and consistent emphasis on the role of consent in the establishment of political power implicitly strengthened the notion that there were limits to government and to the exercise of political power, limits which also justified—at least in extreme circumstances and when no other workable options

[13] Vitoria 1991, 19.

[14] Vitoria 1991, 20.

[15] Skinner 1978, 158–166.

were available—the people legitimately resisting and even deposing and killing tyrannical political rulers.

4 Legitimate Resistance to Abuses of Political Power

The issues of legitimate resistance and tyrannicide were—understandably—two of the most controversial problems of the time; first, because they obviously risked jeopardizing the stability of existing political regimes and triggering the anger of rulers; and second because the discussion necessarily involved the problematic distinction between regicide (the unlawful killing of a legitimate monarch) and tyrannicide (the killing of a tyrant, an act which might be justified under some circumstances). The prevailing notion on this matter came to be that in extreme circumstances a ruler might be legitimately deposed.[16]

The common thread of the prevailing view was that rulers abusing their power in a tyrannical fashion could be deposed and even killed but only if the offences against the common good were sufficiently grave and if it was done through a valid judicial process. The judicial procedure, however, tended to be identified in strong terms as a requirement but was only vaguely defined, particularly in terms of defining who was supposed to have the final decision on the judgment in order for it to be considered valid. The requirement of grave violations against the common good essentially meant that given the risk of generating strife, disorder and civil war, the option of tyrannicide should by no means be taken lightly but only under fairly extreme circumstances.

Vitoria[17] evidences an affirmative but nevertheless reluctant attitude towards the possibility of legitimately deposing and even killing a tyrant. This is best exemplified when he states that although the commonwealth cannot reclaim its authority from a legitimate monarch if it has "transferred it unconditionally and in perpetuity to the king and its successors", it nevertheless retains by natural law a right to resist and if necessary depose a tyrannical ruler:

> (…) it remains true that if a king proves to be a tyrant in government the commonwealth can depose him, because even if the commonwealth has given away its authority it keeps its natural right to defend itself; if there is no other way, it may reject its king.

The imprecise definition of the conditions under which resistance would become legitimate and the process through which they could be determined obviously generated a practical tension between the general duty to obey legitimate authorities and the right to resist tyranny. Nevertheless, it is clear that also in this regard Vitoria's approach is consistent with his broader notions about the limits of political power.

[16] Gierke 1987, 45.

[17] Vitoria 1991, 200.

5 *Ius Gentium* and Limits to State Power in International Affairs

Francisco de Vitoria is generally and accurately regarded as having played a leading role in the foundation of modern international law. The application of the traditional Roman law concept of *ius gentium* was extended to a global setting, with universal application that was supposed to be independent of the will of particular rulers or legislators. The *ius gentium* as Vitoria conceived it was thus common to all mankind and could be recognized by reason even though it was not created through the deliberate will of any human legislator.

The *ius gentium*, with its universal applicability, assumed a crucial role in Vitoria's theory of international law and, indirectly, was also an important element for the limitation of the power of rulers and states. But since in this conception international law mostly assumes the form of unwritten law two additional questions arise: the first is about the binding force of the *ius gentium*; the second is about how to enforce it in practice.[18]

Vitoria[19] is clear in affirming the binding force of the *ius gentium*, and associating it with a notion of (presumably tacit) consent by all mankind:

> The whole world, which is in a sense a commonwealth, has the power to enact laws which are just and convenient to all men; and these make up the law of nations. From this it follows that those who break the law of nations, whether in peace or in war, are committing mortal crimes, at any rate in the case of graver transgressions such as violating the immunity of ambassadors. No kingdom may choose to ignore this law of nations, because it has the sanction of the whole world.

This meant that basic individual rights and fundamental principles of justice were not circumscribed to particular nations, empires or specific groups of people. This law of nations included basic rights to self-preservation, private property, diplomatic immunities and slavery as a form of safeguarding human lives in times of war. Vitoria—although not all members of the Salamanca School—went as far as considering the free movement of people and freedom of commerce as integrating the *ius gentium*, which led him to be fiercely critical of restrictions imposed in these areas.[20]

Vitoria's understanding that all peoples are in some way part of a global *societas naturalis* led him to uphold the existence of a universal *ius communicationis*. This meant individuals possessed universal rights of free movement in order to allow mutual communication and trade. The vigour of Vitoria's defence of *ius communicationis* as a binding restriction on the legitimate power of states and empires can be illustrated by the fact that Grotius to a large extent built his own defence of the positions of the Dutch Republic in its conflict with Portugal and Spain in Asia by

[18]Fernandéz-Santamaria 1977, 97–100.

[19]Vitoria 1991, 21.

[20]Alves and Moreira 2013b.

resorting to Vitoria's authority and to his reasoning in defence of free trade and open access to markets. As explained by Borschberg[21]:

> It should not escape attention that Mare Liberum specifically invoked the ius communicationis, or right of [free and unimpeded] communication, mentioned by Vitoria. (...) Vitoria's position was firmly anchored in a discourse that explored the right to evangelize and enter into contact with the indigenous peoples of the New World. Grotius' contribution (if this is even the appropriate expression) was to amplify the underlying intentions and programmes of Vitoria by heightening the emphasis on free trade and market access.

Denying or disregarding the *ius communicationis* was deemed by Vitoria a just cause for war which—irrespective of the appropriateness of later interpretations and extensions of the argument by Grotius and others—evidences the importance the founder of the Salamanca School attached to it as a safeguard of universal rights and as a limit to the actions of states in the domain of international relations.

6 Just War Theory as a Constraint on States

A particularly important application of *ius gentium* pertained to the regulation of military conflict. In line with the Thomist just war theory tradition, Vitoria stated that in order to be legitimate war must be declared for a valid motive and that it must also be waged justly to remain legitimate. Vitoria[22] summarizes his views on just war in his notable concluding statements to his lecture on the law of war (*De iure belli*):

> From all this we may deduce a few rules and canons of warfare:
>
> 1. First canon: since princes have the authority to wage war, they should strive above all to avoid all provocations and causes of war. (...) It is a mark of utter monstrousness to seek out and rejoice in causes which lead to nothing but death and persecution of our fellow-men, whom God created, for whom Christ suffered death. The prince should only accede to the necessity of war when he is dragged reluctantly but inevitably into it.
>
> 2. Second canon: once war has been declared for just causes, the prince should press his campaign not for the destruction of his opponents, but for the pursuit of the justice for which he fights and the defence of his homeland, so that by fighting he may eventually establish peace and security.
>
> 3. Third canon: once the war has been fought and victory won, he must use his victory with moderation and Christian humility. (...) He must give satisfaction to the injured, but as far as possible without causing the utter ruination of the guilty commonwealth.

It was recognized that the death of innocent people might be unavoidable, but it was only admissible if it came about as an accidental effect of an action essential to secure victory and every reasonable effort was made to avoid endangering the lives

---

[21]Borschberg 2011, 89.

[22]Vitoria 1991, 326–327.

of peaceful non-combatants. Thus, Vitoria[23] provides the example of the bombarding a "fortress of a city where one knows there are many innocent people, but where it is impossible to fire artillery and other projectiles or set fire to buildings" without harming the innocent and affirms that this is legitimate, provided the action is essential to pursue victory in a just war and that care is taken to minimize the evil effects of the war. Moderation and proportionality are also required in case of victory when it comes both to extracting reparations to imposing punishment.[24] Both should be reasonable and proportional to the wrongs inflicted by the guilty. Vitoria[25] goes as far as explicitly recognizing a right (and a duty) of individuals who firmly believe in conscience that a war is unjust to refuse to take part in it: "if the war seems patently unjust to the subject, he must not fight, even if he is ordered to do so by the prince".

For Vitoria, every reasonable effort should be made in order to avoid war, given the huge and terrible human costs it involved. Nevertheless, pacifism was regarded as an unrealistic and even irresponsible option. In some circumstances, there were just causes that made war legitimate. In those instances, war itself should be fought—as much as possible—within moral boundaries and humility, and moderation was recommended to victors, so that peace and security might be fostered in its aftermath.

7 Autonomy of Church and State

Building upon a Thomist framework, the independence and autonomy of secular power in its proper order (*in suo ordine*) was affirmed and positions arguing for the direct intervention of religious authorities in temporal matters were rejected. Vitoria[26] rejects the notion that the pope has temporal power and draws a clear distinction:

> Civil and temporal power is that which has a temporal end; spiritual power is that which has a spiritual end. I mean, then, that the pope has no power which is ordered to a temporal end, which is merely temporal power. (…) It is proved by argument that, as stated above, spiritual power is distinguished from temporal power by its purpose, because spiritual power aims at a spiritual end; but the supreme pontiff is nothing but the person or priest in whom the supreme power of the Church is vested; therefore he has no power which has a temporal purpose.

Unlike the clergy, secular authorities do not derive their temporal power from the pope nor do they answer to him on temporal matters. The pope possesses no

[23]Vitoria 1991, 315–316.

[24]Hamilton 1963, 150–152.

[25]Vitoria 1991, 307.

[26]Vitoria 1991, 88.

temporal powers through which he could alter civil laws, interfere in non-spiritual matters related to civil government or depose secular rulers.

While Vitoria[27] points out special instances where civil power may be subject to spiritual power—namely in situations where civil policy is "detrimental to the spiritual ministry"—he clear leans towards the autonomy of Church and state, a position that has two effects. Firstly, it limits the Church's scope for direct intervention in political affairs. Secondly—and most significantly from the perspective of limiting political power—it confines the actions of the state to a temporal sphere, subject to evaluation according to the pursuit of temporal ends, and bound by the notion of the common good and the rules derived from natural law.

8 Conclusion

In its heyday, the Salamanca School, of which Francisco de Vitoria is generally considered to be the founder, was probably the most influential force in shaping political ideas, at least in the West and in the regions of the world under its domain. Part of this influence was a result of the status of Portugal and Spain as prominent global powers in the sixteenth and early seventeenth centuries and so unsurprisingly the decline of the Iberian powers largely coincided with a decline in the influence of the School.[28] A conjunction of military, administrative and economic problems combined to produce this decline, but the influence of Vitoria's ideas proved more enduring than Iberian global dominance.

Among these ideas, Vitoria's conceptions about the limitation of political power in connection with the common good and his outspoken application of that doctrine to a number of salient issues are certainly among the most important for his and our own times. As shown in this chapter, Vitoria's ideas about the limits of political power are both traditional—to the extent they are broadly in line with the Thomist framework—and new—in the way that they anticipate and introduce some of foremost concerns of modern political thought in this area. Finally, Vitoria's contributions on the common good and the limits of political power are also relevant because of their universality and applicability in domestic and international affairs.

References

Alves AA, Moreira JM (2013a) The Salamanca School (1st ed. Continuum, 2010). Bloomsbury, New York

Alves AA, Moreira JM (2013b) Business ethics in the school of Salamanca. In: Luetge Christoph (ed) Handbook of the philosophical foundations of business ethics. Springer, Heidelberg, pp 207–225

---

[27] Vitoria 1991, 90–91.

[28] Pagden 2002, 82–87.

Borschberg P (2011) Hugo Grotius, the Portuguese and free trade in the East Indies. National University of Singapore Press, Singapore

Brett AS (1997) Liberty, right and nature: individual rights in later scholastic thought. Cambridge University Press, Cambridge

Fernandéz-Santamaria JA (1977) The state, war and peace: Spanish political thought in the renaissance 1516–1559. Cambridge University Press, Cambridge

Garnsey P (2012) Thinking about property: from antquity to the age of revolution. Cambridge University Press, Cambridge

Gierke O (1987) Political theories of the middle age (trans and with an introduction: Maitland FW first published in 1900). Cambridge University Press, Cambridge

Hamilton B (1963) Political thought in sixteenth-century Spain: a study of the political ideas of Vitoria, Soto, Suárez, and Molina. Oxford University Press, Oxford

Höpfl H (2004) Jesuit Political Thought: the society of Jesus and the State, Cambridge University Press, Cambridge, c. 1540–1630

Pagden A (2002) Peoples and Empires: Europeans and the rest of the world, from antiquity to the present. Phoenix Press, London

Pagden A, Lawrence J (1991) Introduction. In: Pagden A, Lawrence J (eds) Vitoria: political writings. Cambridge University Press, Cambridge, pp xiii–xxviii

Skinner Q (1978) The foundations of modern political thought—volume 2: the age of reformation. Cambridge University Press, Cambridge

Vitoria F de (1991) Vitoria: political writings. Pagden A, Lawrence J (eds) Cambridge University Press, Cambridge

Chapter 5
The Problem of Eurocentrism in the Thought of Francisco de Vitoria

Andrew Fitzmaurice

Abstract This paper focuses upon the reception of Vitoria's lectures 'On the American Indians', from the seventeenth century to the present. It argues that what Vitoria's text meant at various moments in time depended to a large degree upon which aspects of his discussion were emphasised. Those who have seen him as a defender of American peoples focused upon his discussion of occupation, while those who see him as an apologist for empire focus upon his analysis of the rights of communication. The paper concludes with an exploration of the current controversy over what purpose history, including the thought of Vitoria, serves for the present.

1 Introduction

In recent decades we have witnessed a debate over Vitoria in which he has been understood to be a critic of the Spanish conquests in America and an apologist for the same events. These almost diametrically opposed interpretations of Vitoria's thought were developing very soon after he delivered his lectures in Salamanca. To a large degree, the different ways of reading Vitoria have depended upon which aspects of his thought were emphasised. Those who have seen Vitoria as a defender of conquered peoples have tended to focus on his analysis of occupation and property. Those who have seen him as an apologist for empire focused either on his discussions of the natural right of communication or upon his discussion of what has been described more recently as cultural differences. In both cases, the understanding of Vitoria's work has often been driven more by debates about the present than about how Vitoria, himself, understood what he was doing.

In this paper I will examine three moments in the interpretation of Vitoria as a defender of the rights of the American Indians: namely, Grotius's discussion of Vitoria in *Mare liberum*; the discussion of the "Divines of Salamanca" by the Council of Virginia; and the reception of Vitoria in the work of nineteenth century

A. Fitzmaurice (✉)
The University of Sydney, Sydney, Australia
e-mail: andrew.fitzmaurice@sydney.edu.au

J.M. Beneyto and J. Corti Varela (eds.), *At the Origins of Modernity*,
Studies in the History of Law and Justice 10, DOI 10.1007/978-3-319-62998-8_5

and early twentieth century international lawyers. I will then turn to interpreters of Vitoria who focus upon the right of communication, from Samuel Pufendorf to postcolonial critics, and who accordingly view him as an apologist for empire. Finally, I will discuss recent debates over Vitoria and examine the charge of Eurocentrism in Vitoria's thought and in international law more generally.

2 Occupation

For Hugo Grotius, Vitoria was a critic of Spanish *dominium* and *imperium* in the Indies. Grotius was able to arrive at this conclusion because he focused upon Vitoria's analysis of the Roman law of occupation. Grotius attacked Portuguese and Spanish claims to *dominium* and *imperium* in the Indies, by devoting chapters in *Mare liberum* to the claims to title Vitoria had discussed in *On the American Indians*: first, the claim to dominion based upon discovery, then by the "Pope's gift", then "by title of war" or conquest, and finally by religion. In response to the claim to "title by invention", or discovery, Grotius followed Vitoria's reasoning that the "Indians" "have, and always had, their kings, their commonwealth, their laws, and their liberties": that is, lawful society was already constituted in a manner demonstrating that the "Indians" understood the operation of natural law.[1] He also extended Vitoria's analysis, and departed from it, arguing that discovery never provides title "for to find [i.e. possess] is not to see a thing with the eyes but to lay hold of it with the hands".[2] "Finding" is used here in the sense of the Roman Law of occupation, to take, and it is in this sense that finding could be possession. Grotius concluded:

> Vitoria therefore rightly saith that the Spaniards got no more authority over the Indians for this cause [i.e. Discovery] than the Indians had over the Spaniards if any of them had come formerly into Spain.[3]

Grotius wrote *Mare liberum* between 1604 and 1606 as chapter 12 of the larger work, *De Indis*, or *On the Law of Prize and Booty*, and he prepared it for publication in 1608. Meeting between 1606 and 1607, and so presumably without knowledge of Grotius work, the newly established Virginia Council of London discussed the work of the "Divines of Salamanca" on the justice of colonisation and arrived at a similar interpretation of the work of those Divines as had Grotius. The Council conducted a debate, recorded in its minutes, upon whether "some form of justification of our plantation might be conceived, and pass… into many hands". The conclusion of this careful debate was that the Council should avoid attempting to justify its colony. The first point noted was that Charles V's attempts at

[1] Grotius 2004, 13–15.
[2] Grotius 2004, 13.
[3] Grotius 2004, 15.

justification of the Spanish conquests had led him to submit the matter to "Casuists and Confessors" of Salamanca with the consequence that they had "declyn'd him from that severe and unjust course [of conquest]" and argued that there can be "gathered for him no title, of Dominion or property, but only a Magistracy, and Empire".[4] One of the more remarkable facts about this record is that it reveals the problematic nature of twenty first century historians' tendency to distinguish between "elite" discussions of legal and political ideas and, to use the common metaphor, discussions of law "on the ground". Clearly, the ideas of Vitoria and the "Divines of Salamanca" were employed by the agents of colonising projects in the seventeenth century as tools with which to address their own problems. The members of the Virginia Company, and the governing council itself, had found it necessary to read Vitoria and his followers and to discuss amongst themselves the implications of their writings for their enterprise. We learn from the minutes of their meeting that the members of the Virginia Council believed Vitoria had defended at least the dominium, if not the imperium, of the Americans.

The Council included its seven patent holders, amongst whom was Richard Hakluyt, the great English promoter of colonisation. Strikingly, Hakluyt translated Grotius' *Mare liberum* into English sometime between 1609 and 1616, thus making available to a wider audience, albeit through manuscript, the ideas that the Virginia Council had only so recently found difficult to refute. Indeed, Hakluyt's intended audience would almost certainly have included the members and promoters of the Virginia Company.[5] Given that the Virginia Company had changed its initial decision not to justify the colony, and was by 1609 engaged in an aggressive promotional campaign, we might conclude that, amongst other purposes, Hakluyt was making available the arguments with which the promoters had to engage in their pamphlets.

Vitoria's reputation as a defender of the rights of colonised peoples gained a great boost from late nineteenth jurists and this was largely because those jurists were deeply concerned by questions of occupation arising from the new wave of European empire in the 1870s and 80s. Henry Bonfils, professor of law at Toulouse, demanded: "Can territory occupied by barbarous and savage tribes be susceptible to acquisition by occupation?"[6] And he replied: "This was the doctrine generally adopted by the authors of the fifteenth, sixteenth and seventeenth centuries but rejected by Vitoria".[7] The French jurist Charles Salomon observed:

[4]"A justification for planting in Virginia" in Kingsbury 1906–1935, 1–3.

[5]David Armitage speculates on whether Hakluyt had members of the English East India Company, in their own rivalry with the Portuguese, as his intended audience, but he concludes that the occasion for the translation remains unknown. See Armitage, 'A note on the texts', in Grotius 2004, xxii. It is worth pointing out that the East India Company and the Virginia Company shared many senior members, including Thomas Smith and Robert Johnson. See Fitzmaurice 2007.

[6]Bonfils 1901, 305.

[7]Bonfils 1901, 305.

> If [the idea of natural slavery] is correct, the Spanish had the right to occupy that land, because all the territory discovered was res nullius, was unappropriated. Vitoria rejected without trouble this reasoning.[8]

The centrality of Vitoria to these arguments is typical amongst nineteenth century jurists. They resorted to Vitoria constantly in order to support sceptical views on colonisation as well as to make humanitarian arguments for colonisation. What they almost always shared, however, was a perception of Vitoria as a critic of empire. As such, Vitoria was perceived as a foundational figure in the tradition of imperial scepticism and he took a central position in histories of international law in that role. Ernest Nys, the Belgian historian of international law, did more than any other scholar to present this view of Vitoria, arguing that Vitoria's lectures "breathed with the love of humanity".[9] In 1917, Nys published Vitoria's works for the Carnegie foundation in the series of international law classics edited by James Brown Scott. Scott, an assistant to the Secretary of State, Elihu Root, was yet another champion of Vitoria as the defender of rights and would in 1934, himself, publish a work in which he argued for Vitoria, rather than Hugo Grotius, as the founder of international law.[10] According to Scott, Vitoria portrayed the Spanish conquests in the Americas as "despicable" acts.[11] Vitoria's condemnation, according to Scott, was based upon the questions of conquest and property. Thus, these late nineteenth and early twentieth century historians of international law argued that scepticism of empire and the birth of international law were born as one. In an almost mirror-like reversal, post-colonial historians have subsequently argued that international law and empire were inherently linked.

3 The Right of Communication

The understanding of Vitoria changes when we turn from questions of occupation to the natural right of communication. For Vitoria, the right of communication was a fundamental aspect of human sociability and was central to his understanding of natural law. It included, amongst its species, the rights of travel, commerce, and preaching. The portrayal of Vitoria as imperial sceptic, on the one hand, and imperial apologist, on the other, was most strikingly apparent in the contrasting views of Hugo Grotius and Samuel Pufendorf. While Grotius understood Vitoria to have condemned the Spanish conquests, Pufendorf pitted his own critique of conquest against what he perceived to be Vitoria's apology for empire. Grotius based his view upon Vitoria's discussion of occupation, while Pufendorf focused upon Vitoria's discussion of the right of communication. Pufendorf argued:

---

[8] Salomon 1887, 44.

[9] Nys 1894, 129. See also pp. 126–9 and Nys 1896, 126–7.

[10] Scott 1934.

[11] Scott 1934, 80.

> Franciscus a Victoria, Relectiones de Indis, Pt.V, § 3, does not win many to his position when he discusses the adequate grounds on which the Spaniards felt themselves entitled to subdue the Indians.[12]

He concluded:

> It is crude indeed to try to give others so indefinite a right to journey and live among us, with no thought of the number in which they come, their purpose in coming, as well as the question of whether… they propose to stay but a short time or settle among us permanently.[13]

While both Vitoria and Pufendorf ascribed to the notion of a universal natural law, for Pufendorf that law was based upon the universal rule of self-interest and self-preservation whereas for Vitoria it was based upon a universal human fellowship of which the right of "natural communication" was an important expression. The unsociable sociability of Pufendorf's natural law thus enabled him to put Vitoria's rights of communication into question.

Immanuel Kant took Vitoria's side of this debate, arguing in his *Third Definitive Article for Perpetual Peace*, in 1795, that "the right to visit" was a right "to present oneself for society" and that it therefore "belongs to all human beings". The earth's surface, he argued, "belongs to the human race in common". Kant therefore took the view that "universal hospitality" was a "cosmopolitan right". Such rights of visiting, for Kant as for Vitoria, included commerce with others. The consequence of the ever growing global ties would be to allow peoples to "enter peaceably into relations with one another" and to bring "the human race ever closer to a cosmopolitan constitution". Kant was aware, however, that Vitoria's arguments for communication had been abused and exploited as a justification for conquest, and in this respect he agreed with Pufendorf. On the exploits of European colonizers he declared "the injustice they show in *visiting* foreign lands and peoples (which with them is tantamount to *conquering* them) goes to horrifying lengths."[14] In the hundred years separating Pufendorf and Kant, and against a background of long and highly costly wars driven by European imperial rivalries, European philosophers and jurists had become increasingly skeptical of the legal arguments used to justify colonization and Kant's arguments in *Perpetual Peace* reflected those concerns.

4 The Contemporary Debate Over Vitoria

In the twentieth century, prior to decolonisation, Vitoria maintained the humanitarian reputation that had been established by the jurists of the *Institut de droit international*. As we have seen, James Brown Scott lauded Vitoria as both a humanitarian sceptic of empire and the founder of a "liberal" (to use his word)

---

[12]Pufendorf 1934, 364.

[13]Pufendorf 1934, 364–5.

[14]Kant 1996, 329.

international law. In his chapter on the "Liberalism of Vitoria", unfettered by fears of anachronism, Scott declared that "Vitoria was so liberal that even in our days his views seem ahead of the times" and a central aspect of that "liberalism" was his scepticism of empire.[15] This view of Vitoria as a critic of empire remained common in the twentieth century prior to decolonisation. It was also found, for example, in Lewis Hanke's highly influential 1949 work *The Spanish Struggle for Justice in the Conquest of America*. For Hanke, Vitoria was a defender of the "Indians". He was the first, argued Hanke, to put into question the Donation of Alexander of 1493, which had granted Spanish title to the western hemisphere.[16] Hanke conceded that Vitoria admitted the Spaniards' rights of communication, of travel and preaching, but he nevertheless viewed him as a critic of the conquests. He also pointed out that the impact of Vitoria's scepticism upon those conquests was indirect, through his influence upon his many pupils who could be found "throughout the Indies and in important positions in Spain".[17] For Hanke, as for Scott, Vitoria was a founder of international law as well as a humanitarian and, again, those two accomplishments were linked.[18] International law sought, it was argued, a global humanitarian regime.

By the early 1980s, however, the understanding of Vitoria as both a liberal humanitarian and a founder of international law was challenged by a number of historians, including Robert A. Williams and Anthony Pagden. Pagden's account of Vitoria presented a man who was deeply ambivalent about Spanish conquests and particularly about the right of occupation.[19] It was a contextual account of a thinker who found himself in a difficult political situation. Vitoria's arguments, if realised, would have left Charles V with "no property rights whatsoever" and only a "slender claim to jurisdiction".[20] He had come "perilously close" to arguing his emperor out of his American empire while at the same time being acutely conscious of the danger of his arguments. As a contextual account, Pagden's Vitoria could not be said to be characteristic of much of what has been written over the past thirty years. The tone might more truly be said to have been set by Robert A. Williams. In what might be described as one of the earlier post-colonial critiques of Vitoria, Williams took up the tradition that questioned Vitoria's account of the right of communication and commerce. Williams first developed his position in an article in 1983—shortly after the publication of Edward Said's *Orientalism*—and subsequently in his powerful and wide-reaching 1991 critique, *The American Indian in Western Legal Thought*.[21] Williams pointed out that the norms by which Vitoria questioned the justice of Spanish conquests were contained within the "Eurocentric discourse of

[15]Scott 1934, 275.

[16]Hanke 1949, 151.

[17]Hanke 1949, 152.

[18]Hanke 1949, 155.

[19]See, for example, Pagden 1986, 1991.

[20]Pagden 1991, xxvii–xxviii.

[21]Williams 1983.

reason embodied in the law of nations".[22] If the Indians refused missionaries or trade, both important forms of communication, then Vitoria's law of nations, according to Williams, would justify punishment and conquest. Thus Vitoria had provided a universalizing discourse based upon European norms that would justify the conquest of "normatively divergent peoples".[23] Moreover, Williams pointed out, Vitoria was prepared to countenance a further argument, the idea of guardianship, that would also justify Spanish *imperium* in the Americas—again, an argument that side-stepped the question of occupation. Whether or not Vitoria had agreed to the right of guardianship in the case of the Indies, he had, Williams argued, launched a further salient discourse in the armory of European legal justifications for the projection of sovereignty upon the non-European world. "Franciscus de Vitoria was", Williams concluded, "the first articulator of a European discourse of conquest founded on secularly rationalizable norms and values".[24] Williams articulated what has become a common criticism of Vitoria's thought: that is, Vitoria may not have drawn the conclusion himself that Spanish conquests were justified, but he provided the tools for subsequent European colonisers to justify their conquests. It is indeed true that Vitoria set the terms for the debate over the justice of European expansion for the following five hundred years.

For the past thirty years, historians and international lawyers have consistently portrayed Vitoria as an apologist for the expansion of European imperium. In order to do so, they have followed Williams' emphasis upon Vitoria's discussions of the right of communication and guardianship. Vitoria's account of occupation—an account that was believed to be so central to his thought from Grotius and the English colonisers of the seventeenth century through to the nineteenth century jurists of the *Institute de droit international*—has been brushed aside in these postcolonial analyses. According to James Anaya, writing in 1996, Vitoria produced a "precursor to trusteeship doctrine" and, "of more generally foreboding significance", he measured cultural expressions and social organisations by European standards. From this "Eurocentric bias", he "constructed a theory of just war to justify Spanish claims to Indian lands".[25] Similarly, for Antony Anghie, also writing in 1996 (and 2005), Vitoria's support for the rights of communication and commerce seemingly assume equality with Indians and reciprocity, and yet they endorse "endless Spanish incursions into Indian society".[26] The inevitable Indian violation of these norms justified a just war by the Spaniards and conquest. We thus see Pufendorf's critique repeated again through the focus upon Vitoria's discussion of the rights of communication. Ian Hunter has pointed out that these post-colonial critiques of Vitoria assume a 'global principle of justice' which, he argues, is itself a

[22]Williams 1990.

[23]Williams 1990, 106.

[24]Williams 1990, 106.

[25]Anaya 2004, 18.

[26]Anghie 2005, 20–21.

Eurocentric assumption.[27] At the same time, he observes, Vitoria's ius gentium was rooted in a particular and local context and it is therefore anachronistic to criticize him for failing to realize a 'transcendent global justice' which was not his concern.

This understanding of Vitoria has been multiplied numerous times in the scholarship on the history of international law, and European expansion, over the past twenty years. In what was until recently an almost separate intellectual space, some contextual work in the history of political thought provided a different view of Vitoria, for example in the work of Annabel Brett.[28] More recently, we have witnessed a reaction against the post-colonial critique of Vitoria in the work of the political philosopher Georg Cavallar and the historian of international law Pablo Zapatero who share, argues Hunter, a commitment to a global theory of justice with post-colonial critics and differ only upon whether figures such as Vitoria were true to it.[29] We now have a body of scholarship divided between the post-colonial critiques, which focus, on the one hand, on the discussions of the rights of communication and guardianship, and present Vitoria as an apologist for empire, and on the other hand, a group of scholars who regard Vitoria as more critical of the Spanish claims to dominium, and to some degree of imperium, and these scholars, like Grotius, place greater emphasis upon the first half of Vitoria's analysis which questions the right of occupation.

Martti Koskenniemi sought to move beyond this impasse in the scholarship in his 2011 article "Empire and international law: the real Spanish contribution".[30] The important issue, according to Koskenniemi, is not whether Vitoria supported the Spanish conquests or not. He notes that Vitoria clearly held good intentions regarding the peoples conquered by the Spanish. However Vitoria's contribution to the law of nations, argues Koskenniemi, was in his analysis of the concepts of *dominium*, *bellum iustum* and *ius gentium*.[31] Through Vitoria's work, these ideas were introduced to a context characterized by the emergence of states, the creation of a global economic system, and continuous warfare fought for the preservation and aggrandizement of those states.[32] Vitoria's achievement, therefore, was to create a theory of private property, embedded in his idea of *dominium*, that could be universalized through the *ius gentium*. Moreover, Vitoria's theory of property was one which abhorred a vacuum and so encouraged the exploitation of unrealized potential, the occupation of vacant territory or resources, wherever they could be found. His account of the natural right of communication supported the creation of an economic system of exchange across the globe. Europeans could then defend this universal understanding of property and commerce through the theory of just

---

[27]Hunter 2010, pp. 11–12.

[28]Brett 2011.

[29]Cavallar 2008, Zapatero 2009, Hunter 2010, p. 12.

[30]Koskenniemi 2011.

[31]Koskenniemi 2011, 11.

[32]Koskenniemi 2011, 12.

war. The combination of these elements, argues Koskenniemi, underpinned the ideological justification of European empire for the following five hundred years.

Clearly, Koskenniemi is sympathetic to the post-colonial reading of Vitoria but he does try to move beyond it. He combines within his analysis, and in contrast to many scholars, a discussion of both the question of occupation, the subject of the first half of Vitoria's *On the American Indians*, with a discussion of the rights of communication, which we find in the second half, and he does successfully put to one side the matter of whether Vitoria believed the conquests in the Americas to be just. It seems to me that Koskenniemi is right in much of what he says and that, in one sense, his argument is uncontroversial: namely, that Vitoria provided an important analysis of *dominium*, *ius gentium* and just war that proved to be central to the law of nations from his own day through to the present. He is clearly right, moreover, that this understanding was Eurocentric and served European interests and justified European domination of the non-European world.

At this point, however, Koskenniemi's argument tends to collapse back into the postcolonial critiques of Eurocentrism in international law.[33] Those critiques ignore or diminish the degree to which the ideas of *dominium*, *ius gentium* and just war were used to oppose European empires as well as to support them. The problem with postcolonial critique is that it appears to treat concepts as in some way the hostages of the contexts in which they are created, so that concepts used to justify a European order could not be used to critique that same order. We know, however, as historians, that these ideas—property, sovereignty, the law of nations, and just war—were all used by critics of European order and to oppose European empires.[34] They furnished such critiques not in order to support a global principle of justice, or universal history, but usually so as to defend local and particular interests, particularly motivated by concerns with the threat that empire could pose to metropolitan freedoms.[35] These critics were both Europeans and non-Europeans. Amongst Europeans, we can point to Vitoria himself, as well as his former student Domingo de Soto, as having used the idea of *dominium*, as well as the *ius gentium*, to defend the rights of the American "Indians". Grotius was certainly explicit about using commerce and just war to strengthen Holland and to resist Spain, but he also used the intellectual tools of property, just war and the law of nations to critique Spanish and Portuguese expansionism. Many nineteenth century European jurists also used the ideas of property and the law of nations to defend, as often as to deny, the rights of non-Europeans. When the late nineteenth and early twentieth century French jurist Gaston Jèze described a four hundred year old anti-imperial tradition, he began with Vitoria:

> As Vitoria already said in the sixteenth century, civilized powers have no more right to seize the territories of savages than savages have to occupy the European continent. The law of nations does not admit any distinction between the barbarians and the so-called

---

[33]See, for example, the recent debates in the reception of the *Oxford Handbook of the History of International Law*: Kirmse 2014; Samour 2014; Barreto 2015.

[34]See, for example, Pitts 2005; Muthu 2003; and Fitzmaurice 2014.

[35]Fitzmaurice 2014.

> civilized: men of all races, white or black, yellow or red, however unequal they are in fact have to be considered equal in the law.[36]

Jèze was not a mere theorist. He acted upon his own anti-imperial principles when he represented Hailé Sélassié, the Emperor of Ethiopia, in the League of Nations in order to challenge the Italian invasion of in the 1930s.[37] In this context, Vitoria's arguments concerning the Spanish conquests of the Americas had a new resonance.

Perhaps more importantly, and more troublingly for the claims of post-colonial and Third World Approaches to International Law (or TWAIL) scholars, is the fact that the tools of *dominium*, just war and the law of nations have been employed by non-European peoples for hundreds of years, not only in the post-colonial epoch, to push back against European empires. By way of illustration I will cite just two of countless examples of such usages. When France ceded claims to large territories in North American in the Treaty of Utrecht of 1713, the Wabanaki Confederacy of Native American peoples objected to the new English claims of title. The Wabanaki made a series of representations culminating in a letter they delivered to Georgetown in July 1721. This letter was written in Algonquian and translated by Jesuit missionaries into Latin, French and English and it was read aloud in all four languages to the English. The English version declared "my land don't belong to the, neither by right of Conquest, nor by Donation, nor by purchase".[38] Extraordinarily, these are three of the main bases for *dominium* examined by Vitoria in his *On the American Indians*. Here we find, therefore, the Wabanaki using the Europeans' own legal armoury in order to combat European claims to title. The letter goes on to examine each of the arguments of conquest, donation and purchase in detail, pointing out, for example, that in every instance that the English had fought the Wabanaki in wars they had failed to conquer them—"it's not thine by right of Conquest? When didst thou drive me from thence?"—while at the same time pointing to their own allodial title.[39]

Here then we find the supposedly European legal heritage, and many of the legal arguments employed by Vitoria, being employed by non-Europeans to oppose European empire. A more complex example, and one that underlines problems with the concept of Eurocentrism, comes from West Africa, and the port of Lagos, in the nineteenth century. Before colonisation, West Africa was a region in which communal property relations dominated land ownership. Prior, however, to the British annexation of Lagos in 1861, a market for private property in land began to develop in order to provide land to freed slaves from Brazil and Sierra Leone. After the creation of the Crown Colony, British administrators encouraged the development of private property, and yet the generation of repatriated slaves began to leave their private property to their descendants in communal ownership, thus resisting colonial

---

[36]Jèze 1896, 103.

[37]Milet 1996; Péan 1994, 45–61.

[38]Belmessous 2012, 116.

[39]Belmessous 2012, 116.

law.[40] In a further twist, later in the century, British administrators began to employ indirect rule over inland areas. For this they needed the support of chieftain families, yet the power of those families rested upon customary practices of communal ownership and was threatened with being undermined by private property. The administration therefore began to support customary forms of ownership, in opposition to private property, in order to maintain authority through the chieftains. Here we find not only that private property became a threat to empire, and that European law could be employed by indigenous groups to resist empire, but also that indigenous law could be appropriated to support the colonising power. Moreover, we find an entanglement of European and non-European understandings of property. Law, in this context, is fragmented, highly mobile and rapidly changing in local contexts, so that the notion of Eurocentrism has a very limited explanatory power.

When modern European empires declined in the twentieth century, the ideas of property, sovereignty, just war and the law of nations were translated to the new international order, along with much of the vocabulary of Western political thought and these concepts were extensively employed to further the process by which new states broke from European empires.[41] That transformation should give us further cause to be optimistic about the malleability of political ideas. It suggests that we are not prisoners of our intellectual landscape, that political concepts can be turned to different ends. Many contemporary scholars of the history of international law, including the scholarship of TWAIL (Third World Approaches to International Law), and historians and social scientists more generally, argue that the instruments of Western political and legal thought cannot easily transcend the historical circumstances of their emergence.[42] Given that those conditions include the use of those tools over centuries to justify European empire, expansion and hegemony, these scholars speculate on whether the ties are not merely accidental but causal. The conventions of political thought, I would argue, are just tools: the conditions of their production should not determine the ends to which they are put. They certainly should be capable of being transported into different historical circumstances albeit while changing their meaning at the same time. Such conventions are not, that is, trans-historical unit ideas of the kind that A.O. Lovejoy believed should be the subject of the history of ideas. What is true of material tools should be true of abstract tools. We do not regard with the same suspicion the ideological baggage of material tools transferred between cultures, whether that would be gunpowder, paper, or antibiotics. There is often a failure in what might be called the post-colonial scholarship on political thought to recognize that changes in the context of the terms of political discourse will lead to changes in the meaning of those terms.

---

[40]Mann 2012.

[41]I say "much of" because certain political vocabularies specific to empire, such as the vocabulary of occupation, including *territorium nullius*, were significantly diminished in the postcolonial political environment. See Fitzmaurice 2014.

[42]For international law, see, for example, Anghie 2005. For Western political thought, see, for example, Williams 1990; Mehta 1999; Tuck 1999; Tully 1995; Parekh 1995.

To understand what is meant by the utterance of political and legal terms in a particular case, we need to examine such terms in their contexts. Only from context can we understand what somebody is doing in appealing to a particular concept. In recent articles, the contextual approach to history of the so-called Cambridge school of the history of political thought has been criticized from a number of perspectives. Samuel Moyn, for example, has argued that, in the face of the global crisis in the humanities, history must be able to speak to the present. He therefore dismisses the concern with anachronism in the work of Quentin Skinner, the founder of the "Cambridge School", as "conventional antiquarianism" which cuts the present off from the past.[43] The historian of international law, Anne Orford, has criticized and defended anachronism.[44] Orford argues that "legal scholarship is necessarily anachronistic" because it is concerned with the operation of past concepts in the present.[45] The concern with anachronism in contextualist methodology, which is prominent in the "Cambridge School" methodology, is based upon a Wittgensteinian theory of the creation of meaning. Orford argues that international law, by contrast, must also be concerned with the "movement of meaning" over time. Expanding upon Orford's critique in a discussion of the uses of Vitoria in the present, Martti Koskenniemi has argued that 'Full-scale contextualism is a historicism insisting on the separation of chronologically distant moments from each other and the illegitimacy of producing judgements across contextual boundaries'.[46] He suggests that such rigor would 'exclude those [past] ideas as legitimate participants in today's debates'. Most disturbingly, he discovers a hidden agenda in such contextualism: 'open political engagement is avoided under the guise of a methodological point. The result is political through and through'.

It would be hard to argue with Koskenniemi, Moyn, or Orford, if the objective of the contextual approach to political thought, or to intellectual history more generally, was to insist that the arguments of historical figures in the past should remain imprisoned in time capsules never to see the light of the present, let alone the future. Such an approach to history would indeed deserve to be suspected of sinister motives. I am not aware, however, of any historians coming from the so-called 'Cambridge School' of intellectual history who would subscribe to such methodological notions. The approach of the Cambridge School methodology is avowedly political and it is concerned with the present as well as the past. It is driven, in part, by a political concern that the past should not be hitched to the political bandwagons of the present or that, at least, a history could be written that allows a skeptical eye to be cast over such attempts to hijack the past to political ends. In his early methodological writings, Quentin Skinner, for example, cited by both Orford

[43]Moyn 2015.

[44]Orford 2013. Orford is responding to critiques of anachronism in the history of international law, for example in Lesaffer 2007; Hunter 2012; and Cavallar 2008. These critiques draw upon the methodology outlined in Skinner 1969.

[45]Orford 2013.

[46]Koskenniemi 2014, 129.

and Koskenniemi, targeted the manner in which Whig history rather crudely flattened political thinkers of previous centuries into a triumphant liberal narrative intended to validate present political interests.[47] A further political purpose of the contextual approach to history, as stated by Skinner on many occasions, is to enrich our understanding of the vocabularies of political action available in the past *precisely* in order to enlighten our understanding of the array of political choices that can be made in the present and the future; to discover the different trajectories and previously overgrown paths that can be found.[48] This may not be a political mission for intellectual history that goes as far as Koskenniemi's suggestion that the 'validity of our histories' lies not in their correspondence with context but in 'how they contribute to emancipation today', but it is a mission nonetheless.[49]

Koskenniemi and Orford suggest, however, that it may be the followers of Cambridge contextualism who are most at fault, rather than the founders. The followers of Cambridge contextualism are most guilty of a political disengagement which apparently underlies a commitment to a current, neo-liberal, order.[50] Taking the first generation of the methodological followers of Skinner and Pocock, Anthony Pagden argues that we live in a world of porous boundaries, multi-culturalism, and pluralism which we cannot understand without reference to 'Europe's colonial past' while achieving such understanding makes us 'citizens of the world'.[51] Richard Tuck has shown how a history of relations between states that were based upon an analogy with aggressive rights bearing individuals offers insights into 'the very way in which we think about our moral behaviour'.[52] James Tully explicitly states that his work aims to encourage a 'critical attitude' to 'liberalism' and argues that 'historical studies of the formation of modern political thought' make possible a 'deeper understanding' of the 'problems raised by both liberals and their critics'.[53] Istvan Hont was skeptical of the idea that the history of political ideas might enrich the political languages of the present. The economic and political problems facing modern society, he argued, could not be solved by history. Nevertheless, while disavowing teleology he also denied the charge of antiquarianism, arguing that history 'helps us to ask better questions' and helps us engage with our 'political predicament'.[54]

The third generation of 'Cambridge School' scholars followed leads first explored by Pagden, Tully, and Tuck, down the newly discovered paths of the

[47]Skinner, 'History and ideology in the English revolution', in Skinner 2002, vol. 3, p. 238, an essay which opens: 'Ideological arguments are commonly sustained by an appeal to the past'. This essay was first published in 1965.

[48]See, for example, Quentin Skinner, *Liberty before Liberalism* (Cambridge, 1997).

[49]Koskenniemi 2014, 129.

[50]Koskenniemi 2014, 124.

[51]Pagden 1995, p. 1.

[52]Tuck 1999, p. 15.

[53]Tully 1993, p. 6.

[54]Hont 2005, p. 156.

intellectual history of empire and international intellectual history. There is no doubt that this generation of 'Cambridge'-inspired intellectual historians, along with their colleagues, have been motivated by the resurgence of 'empire' and Globalization following the Cold War to examine the pasts of empire. They have done so avowedly in order better to understand the present. According to David Armitage, the 'fundamental concern' for historians of international thought should be 'How did we—all of us in the world—come to imagine that we inhabit a world of states?'[55] Jennifer Pitts, an editor of *Ideas in Context*, argues that the 'recent sustained attention to questions of empire in political theory' arises partly from 'contemporary global structural inequalities'.[56] I have argued that 'if we really wanted to understand the historical and legal predicament of contemporary Indigenous peoples, we first needed to bring back into consciousness the multiple historical concepts' used to dispossess them.[57] Duncan Bell observes that the 'political context' for the 'scholarly reorientation' in the history of political thought to empire 'are clear': namely, contemporary conflicts, 'the spectre of neoliberal globalization' and 'burgeoning interest in questions of global poverty and inequality'.[58]

These 'Cambridge School' historians do not engage in an anachronism whereby they impose the present upon the past, but they do look to the past in order better to understand the genealogy of the languages of empire, among other political languages, which the present and the future inherit. There is no question, of course, that this is the context for our contemporary interest in Vitoria. Koskenniemi is right to point out that contextualists nevertheless impose their own frames upon the past. There are always questions we pursue, such as empire, and others we may ignore or diminish, such as, in the analysis of Vitoria, 'teaching young clerics about the management of the sacrament of penance', but the point of approaching the past in terms of its context is to minimize the distortions we create from our own perspective.[59] I am not aware of any Cambridge intellectual historian who has suggested that such distortions could be entirely overcome. In short, the contextual approach to history as an apolitical, or even antiquarian, vehicle of support for the status-quo of neo-liberalism, that has been the target of attacks in the recent historiography of international law, is something that simply does not exist. Historians of political thought would hardly seem to be likely candidates for an unthinking approach to their subject—politics. On the contrary, it is precisely because they are alert to the political and rhetorical uses of the past that they seek to deconstruct the political present through the use of the historical past. Such an approach may not encourage overt declarations of political ideology but it is nonetheless engaged with

---

[55]Armitage 2013, p. 13.

[56]Pitts 2010, 211.

[57]Andrew Fitzmaurice, 'Beyond "terra nullius"', at http://www.cambridgeblog.org/2014/11/beyond-terra-nullius/. See also Fitzmaurice 2014, p. 334.

[58]Bell 2016, p. 4.

[59]Koskenniemi 2014, 124.

the political process. It would appear that anxieties about the political disinclination of historians of political thought are a projection of anxieties and debates that lie more deeply in the discipline of international law itself.

In the case of the postcolonial understanding of political thought and international law, there is a failure to appreciate that meaning does change over time and this is precisely why the understanding of context is crucial. Meaning is created by the operation of terms within particular linguistic fields. If we ignore those linguistic contexts it becomes possible to ignore that meaning has changed. We need not therefore regard the intellectual heritage of Vitoria with quite such trepidation and suspicion. It is clear that he did indeed do much to bring *dominium*, the *ius gentium* and just war into modern political discourse but the meaning of those intellectual tools are not prisoner of the experience of European empires, any more than the political thought of West African peoples was incapable of being appropriated to support empire. At the same time, if we understand Vitoria, as much as we can, on his own terms and in his own time, we limit the distortion of the past in order to render service to the present. In so doing, we do not cut the past off from the present but, rather, establish an understanding of the foundations of modern political thought that provides accurate premises for the conduct of politics in the present and resists a political discourse that is indifferent to the verifiability of its claims. The indifference to the verifiability of political discourse seems to be a plague upon contemporary politics and one, I would argue, that is best combatted with a rigorous approach to context rather than the valorization of anachronism.

References

Anaya SJ (2004) Indigenous peoples in international law, 2nd edn. Oxford University Press, Oxford

Anghie A (2005) Imperialism, sovereignty and the making of international law. Cambridge University Press, Cambridge

Armitage D (2013) Foundations of modern international thought. Cambridge University Press, Cambridge

Barreto J-M (2015) Six books: international law, human rights and the politics of the turn to history. Crit Legal Thinking, March 27

Bell D (2016) Reordering the world: essays on liberalism and empire. Princeton University Press, Princeton

Belmessous S (2012) Wabanaki versus French and English claims in Northeastern North America. In: Belmessous S (ed) Native claims: indigenous law against empire 1500–1920. Oxford University Press, New York, p 116

Bonfils H (1901) Manuel de droit international public, 3rd edn, revised by Paul Fauchille. Arthur Rousseau, Paris

Brett A (2011) Changes of state: nature and the limits of the city in early modern natural law. Princeton University Press, Princeton

Cavallar G (2008) Vitoria, Grotius, Pufendorf, Wolff and Vattel: accomplices of European colonialism and exploitation or true cosmopolitans? J Hist Int Law 10(2):181–209

Fitzmaurice A (2007) The commercial ideology of colonization in Jacobean England: Robert Johnson, Giovanni Botero, and the pursuit of greatness. William Mary Q 64(4):791–820

Fitzmaurice A (2014) Sovereignty, property and empire, 1500–2000. Cambridge University Press, Cambridge
Grotius H (2004) The free sea, with William Welwod's critique and Grotius's reply, Armitage D (ed) (trans: Hakluyt R). Liberty Fund, Indianapolis
Hanke L (1949) The Spanish struggle for justice in the conquest of America. University of Pennsylvania Press, Philadelphia
Hont I (2005) Jealousy of trade: international competition and the nation-state in historical perspective. Harvard University Press, Cambridge
Hunter I (2010) Global justice and regional metaphysics: on the critical history of the law of nature and nations. In: Dorsett S, Hunter I (eds) Law and politics in British colonial thought: transpositions of Empire. Palgrave, New York
Hunter I (2012) The figure of man and the territorialisation of justice in englightenment natural law: Pufendorf and Vattel. Intellect Hist Rev 23:289–307
Jèze G (1896) Étude théorique et pratique sur l'occupation comme mode d'acquérir les territoires, en droit international. V. Giard et E. Brière, Paris
Kant I (1996) Toward perpetual peace. In: Gregor M (ed) Practical philosophy (trans: Gregor M). Cambridge University Press, Cambridge
Kingsbury SM (ed) (1906–1935) The records of the Virginia Company of London, vol 3, printed from Tanner Manuscripts, XCIII, folio 200. Bodleian Library, Oxford, pp 1–3
Kirmse SB (2014) Sleepy side alleys, dead ends and the perpetuation of Eurocentrism. Eur J Int Law 25(1):307–311
Koskenniemi M (2011) Empire and international law: the real Spanish contribution. Univ Toronto Law J 61(1):1–36
Koskenniemi M (2014) Vitoria and us: thoughts on critical histories of international law. Rechtsgeschichte – Legal History 22
Lesaffer R (2007) International law and its history: the story of an unrequited love. In: Craven M, Fitzmaurice M, Vogiatzi M (eds) Time, history and international law. Martinus Nijhoff, Leiden, pp 27–41
Mann K (2012) African and European initiatives in the transformation of land tenure in colonial Lagos (West Africa), 1840–1920. In: Belmessous S (ed) Native claims: indigenous law against empire 1500–1920. Oxford University Press, New York, pp 223–247
Mehta US (1999) Liberalism and empire. University of Chicago Press, Chicago
Milet M (1996) La Faculté de droit de Paris face à la vie politique, de l'Affaire Scelle à l'Affaire Jèze, 1925–1936. Éditions Montchrestien, Paris
Moyn S (2015) Bonfire of the humanities. The Nation, 9 Feb 2015, available at https://www.thenation.com/article/bonfire-humanities/
Muthu S (2003) Enlightenment against empire. Princeton University Press, Princeton
Nys E (1894) Les origines du droit international. Alfred Castaigne, Brussels
Nys E (1896) Etudes de droit international et de droit politique. Alfred Castaigne, Brussels
Orford A (2013) On international legal method. Lond Rev Int Law 1:170–177
Pagden A (1986) The fall of natural man, revised edn. Cambridge University Press, Cambridge
Pagden A (1991) "Introduction" to Francisco de Vitoria. In: Pagden A, Lawrence J (eds) Political writings. Cambridge: Cambridge University Press
Pagden A (1995) Lords of all the world: ideologies of empire in Spain, Britain and France c. 1500–1800. Yale University Press, New Haven
Parekh B (1995) Liberalism and colonialism: a Critique of Locke and Mill. In: Pieterse JN, Parekh B (eds) The decolonization of imagination: culture, knowledge and power. Atlantic Highlands, London, pp 81–98
Péan P (1994) Une jeunesse française. François Mitterrand, 1934–1947. Fayard, Paris
Pitts J (2005) A turn to empire. Princeton University Press, Princeton
Pitts J (2010) Political theory of empire and imperialism. Annu Rev Polit Sci 13, June
Pufendorf S (1934) De jure naturae et gentium libri octo, vol 2, translation of the edition of 1688 by C.H. Oldfather and W.A. Oldfather. Clarendon Press, Oxford
Salomon C (1887) L'occupation des territoires sans maître. A. Giard, Paris

Samour N (2014) Is there a role for Islamic international law in the history of international law. Eur J Int Law 25(1):313–319

Scott JB (1934) The spanish origin of international law: Francisco de Vitoria and his law of nations. Clarendon Press, Oxford

Skinner Q (1969) Meaning and understanding in the history of ideas. Hist Theory 8(1):3–53, reprinted in Skinner Q (2002) Visions of politics: vol 1 Regarding method. Cambridge University Press, Cambridge

Skinner Q (2002) History and ideology in the English revolution. In: Skinner Q (ed) Visions of politics: Hobbes and civil science, vol 3. Cambridge University Press, Cambridge

Tuck R (1999) The rights of war and peace: political thought and the international order from Grotius to Kant. Oxford University Press, Oxford

Tully J (1993) An approach to political philosophy: locke in contexts. Cambridge University Press, Cambridge

Tully J (1995) Strange multiplicity: constitutionalism in the age of diversity. Cambridge University Press, Cambridge

Williams R (1983) The Medieval and Renaissance origins of the status of the American Indian in western legal thought. South Calif Law Rev 57:1–99

Williams R (1990) The American Indian in Western legal thought. Oxford University Press, Oxford

Zapatero P (2009) Legal imagination in Vitoria: the power of ideas. J Hist Int Law 11:221–271

Chapter 6
On the Spanish Founding Father of Modern International Law: Camilo Barcia Trelles (1888–1977)

Yolanda Gamarra

Abstract This study intends to reconstruct the figure and intellectual work of Camilo Barcia Trelles (1888–1977) in order to better understand how the Spanish tradition of international law came to be recovered through the figure of Francisco de Vitoria (1483/92–1546) and what effects the recovery of his work had on the language of international law. This chapter, divided into three thematic pillars, attempts to discover the influence of Vitoria's thinking on Barcia's work and vice versa. Firstly, we consider why and with what purpose Barcia became interested in Vitoria's legacy; secondly, we focus on Barcia's works on Vitoria in the 1920s; and thirdly, we explore Barcia's legal cosmopolitan and liberal approach when recovering Vitoria's work and recognizing him as the founder of modern international law. This recognition was based on three axes: the configuration of a society of sovereign states, the identification of a set of individual rights of the states and the formulation of the principle of a "just war" as a sanction. We close with Barcia's contributions, through Vitoria's work, to the development of international law in Spain.

> On occasions, some peoples have the good fortune to have nobly human spirits that, when they overlay the influence of quantitative grandeur, come to embody the conscience of the world in their conscience, preaching objective justice and worshipping eternal truth (…) The teachers who moulded student consciences (…) were, first of all and above all, consciences in a perennial state of anxiety. They knew how to imprison what is eternal in human life: the cult of the truth. However, their work took on features of immortality.[1]

[1]Barcia Trelles 1928, 10.

Y. Gamarra (✉)
University of Zaragoza, Saragossa, Spain
e-mail: gamarra@unizar.es

J.M. Beneyto and J. Corti Varela (eds.), *At the Origins of Modernity*,
Studies in the History of Law and Justice 10, DOI 10.1007/978-3-319-62998-8_6

1 Introduction

This chapter explores how the Spanish tradition of international law began to be recovered by legal scholars through the figure of Vitoria in the final third of the nineteenth century and what effects that recovery had on the development of international law.[2] We focus on recovering the work of Camilo Barcia Trelles (1888–1977) as the first scholar of public and private international law to recognize Vitoria as the founding father of modern international law just when professional studies on the discipline began to emerge in the first decades of the twentieth century.

Spanish historiography of international law, with its own specific features, was the subject of the great debate regarding naturalism versus positivism and universalism versus particularism that flourished in European and American historiography in the nineteenth century, but was also the beneficiary of the revival of Vitoria's legacy.[3]

Since the final third of the nineteenth-century law historians, canon law scholars and philosophers of law have been dredging through the past, searching for some principles upon which Spanish national identity can be constructed. Spanish authors mined history looking for the roots of the Spanish state, and it was no coincidence that they focused on the Golden Age, the Age of Empire. Once the liberal jurists had been identified, they were used to justify the specific nature of the nation and place Spain among "civilized" nations. Then, in the first decades of the twentieth century, Barcia, a professional of international law and a disciple of Ernest Nys (1851–1920),[4] recovered and internationally disseminated Vitoria's legacy.

Spanish authors from the end of the nineteenth century and beginning of the twentieth century saw their own humanitarian feelings, legalism and sense of civilizing behaviour reflected in the part of the Spanish renaissance that revived and modified the ideas of Thomas Aquinas (1225–1274), and formulated a legal answer to the challenges caused by the conquest in the Americas and the clash of religions. Decades later, under Franco's regime, Spanish legal internationalists reclaimed the legacy of the liberal imperialists from the nineteenth century by identifying them with orthodox Catholic thought.[5]

In recent times, Spanish international legal doctrine has focused its historiographic interest to the examination of the idea of justice,[6] war and humanitarian

---

[2]On a global view of the history of historiography see Kénovian and Rygiel 2015, 9–24.

[3]Gamarra and de la Rasilla 2012, 21 *et seq*. See also Fernández Sánchez 2013

[4]On Ernest Nys as the first professional historian of international law see Koskenniemi 2012a, 943 *et seq*.

[5]Koskenniemi 2011a, 5.

[6]Pereña 1992.

law[7] and, human rights.[8] Nevertheless, a group of scholars of the work of Vitoria who defend his legacy under a liberal approach is emerging.[9]

In the twenty-first century, the re-reading of the works by the authors from the School of Salamanca is due, on the one hand, to the painstaking work of internationalists who subscribe to the Critical Legal Studies School (post-colonial theory)[10] and, on the other, to works on international constitutionalism.[11] The two currents of thought provide opposing visions of Vitoria's legacy.[12]

On the one hand, the interest in Vitoria's work has been influenced by the post-colonial scholarship in international law.[13] Legal scholars have returned to the work of the classical Spanish writers of the School of Salamanca,[14] addressing the colonial origins of international law[15] and making analogies with the political organization of the Middle Ages.[16] The new generation of critical authors has reconstructed a historical process of "rise, fall and rise" of the "standard of civilization", connecting its revival with the current existence of a (neo)colonial paradigm in international law in an era of globalization and global governance.[17] Most of them consider that the various actors of international society are using international law to impose a (neo)liberal globalized civilization on the world.[18] In particular, the Third World Approaches to International Law (TWAIL) current of thought[19] attempts to trace a line of continuity between different periods of historic imperialism, and especially between those of the sixteenth century and the end of the nineteenth century with the contemporary structures of global governance as exemplified in the globalized post-Cold War scenario.[20]

On the other hand, interest in Vitoria's legacy has been encouraged by international constitutionalism and an innovative cosmopolitan vocabulary.[21] The processes include the rise of European constitutionalism and its model of constitutional pluralism or "multilevel constitutionalism",[22] that recognizes analogies in other regional integration processes. We can also add the revitalization of the domestic

---

[7]Pastor Ridruejo 2012, 79 *et seq.*

[8]See Carrillo Salcedo 1993, 49 *et seq.*

[9]See Castilla Urbano 1992, or Zapatero 2009, 221–271.

[10]See Craven 2016, 21 *et seq.*

[11]See Schwöbel 2011, 78 *et seq.*

[12]Gamarra and de la Rasilla 2012, 21–24.

[13]See Prashad 2008.

[14]For example, Haggenmacher 1988, 29.

[15]See Anghie 2005, 13 *et seq.*; and Koskenniemi 2011a, 3.

[16]See Canning 1987. See also the classical work of von Gierke 1900.

[17]Among others, see Fidler 2001, 140 *et seq.*

[18]Schröder 2002 and Braithwaite 2008.

[19]Chimni 2006, 3–27.

[20]Gamarra and de la Rasilla 2012, 22.

[21]Niemela 2008, 306 and Bhandari 2016.

[22]Petersmann 2012.

constitutional model after the end of the Cold War and the development of a growing interest in comparative international law.[23]

This chapter is constructed around three thematic pillars, in order to discover the influence of Vitoria's thinking on Barcia's work and vice versa, i.e. the influence of Barcia on the recovery of Vitoria's work. Firstly, we begin with why and for what purpose Barcia studied Vitoria's work, and the legacy of the authors from the nineteenth century. Secondly, we establish a parallelism between the study of Vitoria's work and the professionalization of international law studies. Thirdly, we focus on how Vitoria's work influenced Barcia's international legal thinking and how it was disseminated internationally in the period between the World Wars, especially using the League of Nations for comparative purposes. Based on Vitoria's legacy, this chapter deals with the problems related to the configuration of a society of sovereign states, the creation of a set of individual rights of the states and the formulation of the principle of a "just war" as a sanction. It closes with some reflections about the influence of Barcia's studies on the development of international law in Spain.

2 Nationalism and Orthodox Catholicism in the nineteenth Century

In the final decades of the nineteenth century, a debate arose about the powers of Spain and its abilities to project them internationally. The design of Spanish international policy was dependent upon the preparation of its own national identity—something that, at the beginning of the twentieth century, ended up being called "the idea of Spain".[24]

The first chairs in public and private international law were established in the 1880s, through the proclamation of the Gamazo Act (1883), in the schools of law of Spanish universities: in addition to The Central University (of Madrid), Barcelona, Granada, Oviedo, Santiago de Compostela, Seville, Valencia, Valladolid and Zaragoza.[25] The first professors of international law included the Roman law scholar Juan de Dios Trías y Giró (1859–1914) in Barcelona, the canon law scholar Rafael Conde y Luque (1835–1922) in Madrid and the civil and canon law scholar Nicolás López R. Gómez in Valladolid. In the remaining universities, chairs were filled through state examinations, these being passed by, among others, the professors Manuel Torres Campos (1850–1918) (Granada), Luís Gestoso y Acosta

[23]Koskenniemi 2011b, 1 *et seq.*

[24]See Pasamar Alzuria 1993, 183 *et seq.*

[25]See Gamarra 2011/2012, 3 *et seq.*

(1855–1931) (Valencia), Joaquín Fernández Prida (1863–1942) (Valladolid/ Madrid), Aniceto Sela y Sampil (1863–1935) (Oviedo), Salvador Cabeza y de León (1864–1934) (Santiago de Compostela) and Adolfo Morís Fernández-Vallín (1860–1952) (Seville).

The works produced by the 1880s Spanish generation of international lawyers were characterized by a fusion of currents of thought with a socio-historical approach, positive law and an iusnaturalist perspective. The contributions of the first generation of professors to the field of international law and international politics were scarce. In the final decades of the nineteenth-century textbooks of international law or treaties were edited and works of the most prominent European internationalists were translated such as Friederic von Martens or Pasquale Fiore textbooks.[26] We can perhaps make two exceptions to the above statement; the first is the work carried out by Sela through his lectures and the second is the monographs and academic speeches by Ramón Dalmau, the Marquis of Olivart (1861–1928).[27] In 1886, Dalmau translated into Spanish the *Relectiones De Indis* for the first time.

In this context, various currents of thought attempted to use the work of the Spanish classics in pursuit of that national identity, which—together with the work of the Dominican order by religious authors such as Getino, Beltrán de Heredia, Urdánoz, Hernández-Martín—[28] facilitated the recovery of Vitoria's legacy.

Eduardo de Hinojosa y Naveros (1852–1919) was considered as the father of modern Spanish legal historiography.[29] Hinojosa wrote *La influencia que tuvieron en el Derecho público de su patria, y singularmente en el Derecho penal, los filósofos y teólogos españoles anteriores a nuestro siglo* (1890), recovering the scholasticism of the sixteenth century.[30] Hinojosa's inaugural speech on joining the Royal Academy of History (1889) on the subject of the Dominican friar Francisco de Vitoria, *Francisco de Vitoria y sus escritos jurídicos* (1889)[31] is particularly interesting. He argued that Vitoria was the first writer to clearly and scientifically

[26]Fiore 1894–1895 and von Martens 1882–1883.

[27]See Blanc Altemir 1999.

[28]Other authors who explored the Vitori's legacy was Álvarez de los Corrales, Bravo Murillo, Pérez de Gomar, López Sánchez, Calvo, Fabié, Marqués de Villaurrutia, Ceferino González, Conde y Luque, Hinojosa, Menéndez y Pelayo, Fernández Prida, Abad y Cavia. See Alonso Getino 1946.

[29]Perez de Guzman y Gallo, 531–534. See, also, Peiró Martín and Pasamar Alzuria 2002, 326 and 327, and Peiró Martín 2013, 63, 95 and 292.

[30]In this work, Hinojosa proposed two features that would have an influence on later generations. The first is a desire to emphasize the renewal of renaissance methodology started by Vitoria and the continuity of the neo-Thomist genealogy of traditionalist Catholic thought in Spain. The second feature states that Hinojosa was aware of the parallels between "the issue of the authority of the Spanish monarchs to conquer the New World" and the concerns of immediate interest for international lawyers at the peak of imperialism, an issue that "has also preoccupied the authors of international law during our day, without yet having found a consistent and definitive solution", see Hinojosa y Naveros 1890, 186. This paper received an award from the Academia de Ciencias Morales y Políticas in 1889. See García Gallo 1948

[31]Hinojosa y Naveros 1889, 38.

formulate the principles of justice on which international relations were based in time of war. The speech was responded to by Marcelino Menéndez y Pelayo (1856–1912), the greatest exponent of the nationalist and Catholic School in Spanish historiography. He recognized that Vitoria was the father of the science of international law.[32]

The legacy of these authors of the nineteenth century was brought together in the second attempt to recover the work of Vitoria in the 1920s. Barcia was the leading specialist on the "Spanish School" of international law in the Spanish language and on the role of Vitoria in laying the foundations of the modern historiography of international law. Let us focus again on the initial years of Barcia's education in order to better understand why he was interested in Vitoria's work and how he conveyed his knowledge in international law.

Barcia studied his degree in law at the University of Oviedo, and was awarded the Extraordinary Degree Award (1909). At the beginning of the twentieth century, the University of Oviedo, and particularly its School of Law, represented one of the liveliest bodies supporting the reconstruction that concerned the educated Spain after the "disaster" of 1898.

After its creation in 1876, the elite of the Free Educational Institute (ILE) (the so-called institutionists) embodied the conscience of Spanish liberalism. They would be followed by a large part of the bourgeois population.[33] It was necessary, in the eyes of the institutionists, to create a different structure from the state that would put an end to despotism and replace its moral corruption with honesty and respect for the law.

Barcia lived his life as a student at the University of Oviedo against this background and there he met Aniceto Sela Sampil, one of his legal internationalist lecturers who nurtured his vocation in this direction.[34] Sela influenced him with his idea of peace based on justice, precisely when the second Hague Peace Conference was being held (1907).[35] He also influenced him in a methodological concern that was positioned within the positivism current by reflecting, in the study of the international legal system and in its teaching, the influence of the practice of states in their reciprocal relations. Barcia paid attention to both "realities" and the state of "theory".[36] This led to an examination of international relations defined by the "policy of force" and also by the first signs of cooperation between states in support of common interests and, later, signs of integration into higher organizational hierarchies (the League of Nations).

In 1909, Barcia moved to Madrid to study his doctorate. Then, he met another Asturian, Joaquín Fernández Prida from the same generation as Sela, and Rafael Altamira y Crevea (1866–1951), a legal historian and a judge at the Permanent

[32]Menéndez y Pelayo 1890, 91. See also Menéndez y Pelayo 1911.

[33]Tuñón de Lara 1982.

[34]See de Fernández Rozas and Andrés Sáenz de Santa María 2010, 539 *et seq.*

[35]González Campos et al. 1964, 561–583.

[36]See the books written on international politics in the 1920s, Barcia Trelles 1924, 1925.

Court of International Justice.[37] Barcia was a keen student of Fernández Prida's lectures on the history of international law and he learned from him "good speech, precision, the accuracy of a well-used word to thought".[38] Under his guidance, he attained his doctorate with distinction from the Central University (1915) with his thesis entitled *The Annexation of Bosnia-Herzegovina into Austria-Hungary*.[39]

In his youth, another strong influence on Barcia was Rafael María de Labra (1840–1918), whom he met through a family connection. Labra, one of the founders of the ILE, had been an advocate of international law, a defender of freedom and equality and, above all, of the abolition of slavery in the former Spanish colonies. Barcia frequented the Athenaeum of Madrid, a cultural institution of the first order led by Labra. There is evidence from this period of his participation in several newspapers in Madrid, particularly in *La Libertad*, where he commented on the incidents that led to the end of the Great War of 1914, the foreign policy followed by the great powers, Spanish foreign policy and even on the nature of the League of Nations.[40]

Barcia's seeking of broader horizons in order to attain a strong education was met through several grants given by the Spanish Board for Advanced Studies and Scientific Research in the first decade of the twentieth century.[41] The aid allowed Barcia to broaden his studies of international law in Brussels in 1912, with Ernesto Nys; and later, in Berlin, between 1913 and 1914, with von Triepel, von Liszt Kaufmann and von Martitz; and in 1916 in Berne, with Max Huber.

Of all of these authors, Nys' influence was especially strong. Between 1880 and 1890, the Belgian law historian was the first expert to call attention to the tradition of late Spanish scholastic thought, particularly the University of Salamanca, which had proved to be critical in terms of the methods of the Spanish *conquest* and had promoted domestic and universal laws to control and direct its course.[42] Nys studied how Dominican theologians such as Vitoria (1483–1546) sided with Bartolomé de las Casas (1484–1566), the best-known defender of the native Indians, insisting on their humanity and on their property and jurisdiction rights.

The knowledge acquired by Barcia with Nys about Vitoria's work, along with the legacy of Spanish authors from the nineteenth century encouraged him to study the theologians and jurists from the sixteenth century. Barcia decided to study Vitoria's work because he was the figure who stood out among Spanish internationalists in the sixteenth and seventeenth centuries, and because he was the first to offer innovative principles to specifically international problems. According to Barcia, in addition to the opinion of thinkers, there was another problem,

---

[37]Gamarra 2012b, 1–49.

[38]Miaja de la Muela, 1958, p. 19.

[39]Barcia Trelles 1915 (available at the University Complutense of Madrid).

[40]See *Expediente de catedrático*, 7481-11, Archivo General de la Administración. Alcalá de Henares.

[41]Espaliú 2012, 163 *et seq.*

[42]Nys 1889, 532, 1890, 1914.

which consisted in legally determining what the consequences of the discovery of territories were for the purposes of extending political sovereignty of those who added unknown lands to civilization.[43] For Barcia, Vitoria was a creator, a moulder of consciences.[44]

3 The Nation State, the Rule of Law and Freedom in the twentieth Century

Spanish students with grants of 1914 returned to Spain with something more than new knowledge or the learning or improvement of certain techniques. They were bearers of a new vision of Spain itself. The generation of grant-receiving students of 1914, in an attempt to justify the Spanish nation, looked to the past and found that Vitoria had broken with medieval tradition and had given rise to a style of coexistence that was characteristically Spanish.

In the 1920s, a process of renewal began in the chairs of public and private international law, thereby contributing to the professionalization of the discipline. New professors with new ideas and new methodologies were incorporated into the chairs of international law: José de Yanguas Messia (1890–1974) at the University of Madrid (1920), or José María de Orué y Arregui (1894–1953) at the University of Valencia (1925), or Luis Gestoso Tudela (1886–1957) at the University of Murcia (1921), or José María Trías de Bes y Giró (1890–1965) at the University of Barcelona (1916).[45] In 1919, Barcia passed the state examinations and gained the chair of public and private international law at the University of Murcia, and in 1920, he moved to the University of Valladolid where he remained until 1939.[46]

Barcia, along with José de Yanguas Messía and José María Trías de Bes, cooperated closely.[47] The three of them published works on the Spanish classics from the sixteenth and seventeenth centuries, as did other Spanish internationalists in the period around the World Wars. Later, a new generation of legal internationalist carried on with the study of the Spanish classics from a different political approach: Franco's dictatorship. Luís García Arias (1921–1973),[48] Alejandro

[43]Barcia Trelles 1928, 11.

[44]Barcia Trelles 1928, 14.

[45]See *Diccionario de Catedráticos españoles de Derecho (1847–1943)*, available in http://portal.uc3m.es/portal/page/portal/instituto_figuerola/programas/phu/diccionariodecatedraticos/lcatedraticos.

[46]*Expendiente de catedrático* of D. Camilo Barcia Trelles, nº 7481-11, Archivo General de la Administración.

[47]See Barcia Trelles 1974, 20.

[48]García Arias 1947, 151–169.

Herrero Rubio (1907–2004),[49] Adolfo Miaja de la Muela (1908–1981)[50] or José Gascón y Marín (1875–1962)[51] studied Spanish classic scholars under a National Catholicism approach.

During the years at the ILE, Barcia started a friendship with Fernando de los Rios (1879–1949), who was a socialist politician and professor of political law.[52] Between Barcia and De los Rios there was a scientific osmosis based on friendship and intellectual purposes.[53] Both were strongly influenced by authors such as Hermann Cohen (1842–1918), a German Jewish philosopher, one of the founders of the Malbourg School of Neo-Kantianism. During his stay in Germany, De los Ríos contacted with the neo-Kantian socialism.

Both of them analysed the origins of the modern nation state and the quirky position of Spain within the Renaissance currents. They rediscovered Spain through the study of the theologians and jurists of the sixteenth century: Vitoria, Domingo de Soto, Francisco Vázquez de Menchaca, Francisco Suárez, among others.[54]

De los Ríos studied the relationship between power and people, that is, coexistence of the state and the individual, i.e. the conflict between authority and freedom. De los Rios defended that with the use of socialism, the dignifying of existence and the organization of a truly international society could be achieved. Barcia, on the other hand, moved away from socialist approaches to liberal ones.

In the 1920s, there was a new opportunity to recover Spanish classics from the sixteenth century. Primo de Rivera's dictatorship had reached a certain national consensus, above all regarding the pacification of Morocco. At that time, a group of internationalists and professors in law decided to join forces around the name of Vitoria to remember and update his doctrine (and that of the other classics) and create a network of contacts that would allow Spain to expand, through *cultural diplomacy*, its weak international presence.

Talking about Vitoria meant referring to the University of Salamanca, which was the university chosen to develop the project on the internationalization of the Spanish classics of the Golden Age. In 1926, on the celebration of the 4th centenary of the appointment of Vitoria to the chair of *Prime Theology* at Salamanca, they decided to form an association, a chair and an institute of international law bearing his name. They did this at the university conference in honour of Vitoria, which was attended by the Minister for Public Instruction, Eduardo Calleja (1875–1950), and the Minister of State, José de Yanguas Messia, as well as the ambassadors from Uruguay, Holland, and several professors in international law.

---

[49]Herrero Rubio 1947 (prologue of Camilo Barcia Trelles), 1952, 309–450, 1953, 1959 (2nd ed.).

[50]Miaja de la Muela 1934, 1945, 131 *et seq.*, 1949.

[51]Gascón y Marín 1946, 191–123.

[52]Villar 2012, 553 *et seq.*

[53]In 1920, Barcia was the Socialist Party candidate in the general elections to the Parliament from Alicante.

[54]de los Ríos 2007, 37 *et seq.*

Barcia was commissioned by the University of Valladolid to give two conferences before an "academic embassy" composed of Dutch jurists (Treub and Van der Mandere) in order to honour Vitoria in the University of Salamanca. As a result of these conferences, the Hague Academy of International Law, in particular James Brown Scott (1866–1943) and Antonio Sánchez de Bustamente (1865–1951), invited Barcia in the summer of 1927 to give a course of ten lessons about Spanish jurists and theologians of the sixteenth century. That year, the team of professors was composed of Baker, Lebée, de Boeck and van Eysinga and also, Kraus, Niboyet, Streir, Seligman and other younger professors such as Alfred Verdross and Henri Rolin.[55]

Barcia discovers Vitoria, and Vitoria reveals Barcia.[56] If Barcia was responsible for the revelation that Vitoria was the real creator of the science of international law, in turn it was because of Vitoria that Barcia's name became familiar to those who worked on international legal questions. However, there were those who attributed a certain "southern enthusiasm" to his exaltation of Father Francisco.[57]

The initiative to create an association coinciding with the launch of the Ibero-American Exposition in Seville was another manifestation of the desire of the Directory (Primo de Rivera's dictatorship) to increase cultural ties between Spain and Latin American countries. This was included in the statements made by the Uruguayan Ambassador, Benjamín Fernández Medina (1873–1960), and the Spanish Minister of State, Yanguas Messía. While for the former the creation of the association was an instrument to be used to "cooperate cordially once again in the exchange of relationships between Europe and America", for the latter it was an opportunity to create a new Spanish foreign policy towards America.[58]

On 14 July 1926, the Spanish association was established in Madrid, bearing the name of the professor from Salamanca Francisco de Vitoria, considered to be the most representative figure from Hispanic legal tradition, at the initiative of José de Yanguas Messia, Fernández Medina and Eduardo Callejo, with its founding members being Fr. Luis G. Alonso de Getino (1877–1946); Rafael Altamira, Camilo Barcia, Joaquín Fernández Prida, Manuel González Hontoria (1878–1954); Ramón Dalmau, Marqués de Olivart, Sánchez de Bustamente, Félix Gordón Ordás (1885–1973); and Salvador de Madariaga (1886–1978). The mere mention of these names gives an idea of the plurality of the ideological opinions and agreement as to the importance and work of Vitoria.

The objectives of the Spanish association "Francisco de Vitoria" were summarized in its articles of incorporation, with the first being to:

> state the existence of a Spanish legal school of international law, from a tradition that has caused our writers to declare that the Spanish were not only the precursors of Grotius, but were also the first to disseminate and support doctrines which Grotius undoubtedly

---

[55]See Barcia Trelles 1927b, 652 and 653.

[56]Miaja de la Muela 1958, 27.

[57]Octavio 1930, 219.

[58]See Rodríguez-San Pedro Bezares and Polo Rodríguez 2008, 152 *et seq.*

> developed more broadly and methodically, but that are and should be considered to be the strongest and most important source of inspiration for this branch of law.[59]

The second of the objectives of the association was, precisely, to collect and publish all of the legal, theological, philosophical and political treatises by Spanish, Portuguese and American authors that had contributed to "the formation of international law or had defended principles of justice for relationships between peoples",[60] thereby cementing the prestige of the Hispanic world and:

> honoring the great thinkers and exemplary men of our race for their ideas and character; (and) demonstrating our legal, political and educational tradition, which is inferior to none and in many ways superior to almost all.[61]

One of the most immediate results of the activities of the association was the creation at the University of Salamanca of the *Francisco de Vitoria* Chair, which was held by famous Spanish and foreign jurists, with the first two academic years being dedicated to an analytical explanation of Vitoria's *Relections* about Indian natives and war.

Another of the activities consisted in the beginning of the arduous work of editing, translating and publishing of the works by the authors of the Spanish School, and in particular of the *Theological Relections* by Vitoria based on the published editions—the first appeared in Lyon in 1557 in Latin, followed in the same century by others in Ingolstadt, Salamanca, Antwerp and Venice, with the series continuing in the seventeenth and eighteenth centuries, and by the best manuscripts preserved in Madrid, Lisbon, Palencia, Vienna, Granada and Valencia.

In the twentieth century, the first editions of Vitoria's work appeared in Spanish, French and English. The latter edition, of 1917, by the Carnegie Institution, contained the *Relections De Indis* and *De iure belli*. In 1932, the version by professor James Brown Scott (1866–1943), assistant to the Secretary of State, Elihu Root, was published in Washington as an appendix to his work *The Spanish Origin of International Law. Francisco de Vitoria and his Law of Nations*.[62] His work was recognized in 1933 when he was awarded an honorary degree by the University of Salamanca, and the University of Valladolid dedicated a chair to him, the "James Brown Scott" Chair.

In 1932, on the occasion of the commemoration of the 4th centenary of the *Relections*, it was Brown Scott who proposed that international recognition should be given to the professors of the Spanish School. He also promoted the creation of the Vitoria-Suárez International Association, whose articles of incorporation were approved at the meeting of the Institute of International Law (IDI) held in Oslo (1932). The work of the Vitoria-Suárez International Association, created at the suggestion of Brown Scott and chaired by Nicolas Politis, with Spanish jurists such

[59] Articles of the Francisco de Vitoria Association, Archive of University Carlos III of Madrid.

[60] Yanguas Messia 1933, 6 and 7.

[61] Yanguas Messia 1933, 7.

[62] Brown Scott 1934.

as Barcia, Fernández Prida, Sela Sampil, Trías de Bes, and Yanguas Messía as founder members, as well as recognizing Vitoria, also included the initiating of a plan to publish works that included an analysis of the doctrines of Augustin de Hippo on the rights of man and another of Thomas Aquinas in order to define the ideological origins of Vitoria's theory of international law.

The mere mention of these names explains the interest in Catholic circles, which were always on alert whenever there was an attempt to recognize Hispanic thought internationally. These sectors underlined the legacy of orthodox thought in international legal tradition by stressing Spanish historical continuity and by not condemning monarchic institutions, under the seal of which Spanish dealings in America and the world in the sixteenth and seventeenth centuries were carried out. The reappraisal of the figure of Vitoria would appear as a clear example of this spirit of fusion and harmony that Spanish jurists wanted so much, both for Europe and for Spain.

In the 1920s and 1930s (the Genevan period), Spanish theologians and jurists from the sixteenth century were identified as precursors of the new profession by the North American internationalist Brown Scott, a strong supporter of arbitration and of the League of Nations.[63] Brown Scott was an expert on the theses presented by Barcia in his course at the Hague Academy of International Law.[64] Brown Scott admired the humanitarian aspect in the works of these Spaniards and especially their tendency to debate the Spanish empire in terms of natural law and the law of peoples (*ius gentium*). Scott paid particular attention to the two lessons that were published (*relectiones theologicae*) that had been given by Vitoria in 1538 and 1539 in Salamanca, in which he defended the rights of native Indians and also established rules for Spanish trade and the religious conversion of recently conquered territories.[65] According to Brown Scott, this was a perfect example of a propagandist who, for reasons of conscience and for the benefit of humankind, rebelled against the excesses committed by his own nation.[66] In more than one occasion, Brown Scott repeated:

> I, James Brown Scott, citizen of the United States and a protestant, proclaim that Francisco de Vitoria, the Spanish Catholic friar, was the founder of international law.[67]

At the same time, the understanding between Barcia and Salvador de Madariaga led the former to be influenced by the latter in his thinking. Madariaga frequently mentioned Vitoria when explaining the reasons for the presence of Spain in the League of Nations,[68] and even to define the (future) programme of republican

[63]On the figure of J. Brown Scott, see Coudert 1943, 559–561; Finch 1944, 183–217.

[64]At the same time, the American Chair of the University of Valladolid published the book of Brown Scott 1928.

[65]See Koskenniemi 2012b, p. 41.

[66]Brown Scott 1934. See a debate on this in Rossi 1998.

[67]See Miaja de la Muela 1958, 30.

[68]Egido León 1986, 106–113.

foreign policy (1931–1936).[69] Barcia established a parallel between Vitoria's principal ideas and the principles included in the League of Nations Pact: universality, objective justice, peace, sovereign equality and "just war". These principles were invoked by Barcia when he argued that Vitoria was the founding father of modern international law.

4 An Objective International Law

Barcia was the first Spanish internationalist to give more than one course at the Hague Academy of International Law. In 1927, the first of the three he gave was called "Francisco de Vitoria et l'École moderne du Droit International".[70] This was followed by "Francisco Suárez (1548–1617): les théologiens espagnols du XVIe siècle et l'école moderne du droit international",[71] and "Fernando Vázquez de Menchaca. L'école espagnole du Droit international du XVIe siècle".[72]

Barcia recognized that the conditions were right for Vitoria to leave his immortal teachings to posterity. First, there was the approach to new problems arising from new realities (the discovery and conquest of America). Second, there was the existence of an objective, cultured movement that was ready to deal with these questions (Vitoria's actions in the university).[73] Barcia considered Vitoria to be the founding father of international law because he was the first to recognize the existence of an international society of nation states subject to an objective international law.

Barcia began his first course on Vitoria by following the *De Indis* system. After offering a brief description of Vitoria, he put forward the arguments that Spain used at the beginning to try to legitimize the conquest of the New World, which were, above all, of a religious nature.[74] The legal foundation of the initial occupation of the Antilles by the Crown of Castile was based on papal bulls issued by Alexander VI in 1493.[75] The bulls played an essential role at that time in view of the fact that the donation (made by the Pope) was linked to universal ambitions (*dominium universale*).[76] This was met by criticisms from the French, English and the Spanish themselves.

[69]Gamarra 2012a, 185 *et seq.*

[70]Barcia Trelles 1927a, 113–336.

[71]Barcia Trelles 1933, 389–549.

[72]Barcia Trelles 1939, 433–530.

[73]Barcia Trelles 1928, 23.

[74]Barcia Trelles 1927a, 114 and 115.

[75]Barcia Trelles 1927a, 149 *et seq.*

[76]*Dominium* described the relationship that held together the three parts of the triad into which the Roman jurist Gaius had divided the natural world: persons, things and actions. For naturalist, *dominium* is conferred by the God's law, and for Lutheran, *dominium* is conferred by God's grace. Melchor Cano points out *dominium iurisdictionis* derives from the will of the community and *dominium rerum* from natural law. See Pagden 1987, 79 *et seq.*

In Spain, as Barcia stated, the Maestro of Salamanca and its school repudiated the authority of the bulls, using exactly the same arguments as had been used by the French and the English. Why was the Spanish monarch (Charles V) setting himself up as heir (master) of half the world? They acknowledged the Pope's status as spiritual director of all Christians, but they did not accept that he could exercise *dominium* over the secular world, or have the slightest degree of authority over non-Christians.

In his *Theological Relectiones*, given in Salamanca in the 1520s and 1530s, Vitoria asked himself with what right (*ius*) the barbarians had been subjected to Spanish rule.[77] As Barcia wrote, Vitoria rejected all the forms of legitimization of the conquest initially claimed by the Spanish: the *ius inventionis*, in the realm of Private Law, invoked by Christopher Columbus; the idea of a universal sovereignty of the Empire or the Church; and the idea that the Indians were heathen sinners. Vitoria also rejected voluntary submission, whose spontaneity was legitimately questionable, and the idea of a special concession from God to the Spanish, about which Vitoria was fairly ironic because it seemed to him to be highly improbable and because it flew in the face of Common Law as well as of the Holy Scriptures.[78]

Facing the non-legitimacy of these rights, Barcia argues that Vitoria offered what he considered were the only legitimate justifications for the conquest and the origins of the modern international law. There were basically three ideas in his main argument: firstly, the establishing of world order as a natural society of sovereign states; secondly, the theoretical formulation of a set of natural rights for peoples and states; thirdly, the reformulation of the Christian doctrine of "just war", which he defined as a legal sanction for wrongdoings suffered.

The first and most important of these theories was the representation of the world order as a *comunitas orbis*, in other words, a society of *respublicae* or sovereign states, equally free and independent, subject externally to the same international law and internally to the constitutional laws that they had set for themselves.[79] The old universalistic idea of the mediaeval *comunitas*, under the universal domain of the Emperor and the Pope, was rejected and replaced by the idea of an international society of nation states, conceived as legal entities independent of each other but subjected to an objective international law.

It was in this "outstanding" idea of the *communitas orbis* as a natural society of free and independent states that Vitoria saw the foundation of the second basic idea of his construct: the idea of external state sovereignty. This idea was identified with a set of natural human rights providing, firstly, a new legitimization of the conquest and secondly, the ideological framework, Eurocentric in nature, of international law, its usage for colonialism and even its warlike tendencies.[80]

---

[77]In 1539, Francisco de Vitoria proclaimed his *Relectio* on the American Indians, *De Indis*, in which he questioned the legitimacy of the Spanish conquest of America.

[78]Barcia Trelles 1927a, 160 *et seq.*

[79]See Truyol y Serra 1993, 24. See also Fernández Sánchez 2015, 113

[80]See on the Eurocentric international law approaches the ideas of Koskenniemi 2011c, 152 *et seq.*

As Barcia wrote, the first natural right formulated by Vitoria was the *ius communicationis*, derived from the idea of the "natural society" of nations.[81] The second right was the *ius commercii* which was the legal recognition of a great unified world market.[82] The third right was the *ius occupationis* of uncultivated lands and anything not gathered by the Indians, including gold and silver.[83] The fourth was the *ius migrandi*, the right to go to the New World and obtain citizenship there.[84]

To these human rights, Vitoria added another four divine rights (that were just as asymmetric and even more liberal): i) the *ius praedicandi et annunciandi Evangelium*; ii) the duty of the Indians not to obstruct the exercise of this right;[85] iii) the duty-right of the *correctio fraterna* of the barbarians, iv) and the duty-right to protect the converts against their lords (who in turn would be replaced by Christian sovereigns in the event that the majority of the subjects had converted).[86] Indeed, one of the arguments invoked in authorizing the monarchy of Castile to claim sovereignty and property rights in America was the voluntary transfer of the American Indians' (natural) legislative authority to the Empire.[87] And then, of course, there was the right of the Spanish, in the event that the Indians refused to be swayed by their reasons, to defend their rights and safety, even by resorting to war as an extreme measure.

As far as Vitoria and his successors were concerned, one of the legitimizing arguments for the conquest of America was the fact that the natives had offered resistance to the allegedly legitimate right of the Spanish to "travel" to their lands, thereby violating their "right of society" and "natural communication" (*ius communicationis*), and therefore, they were liable to punishment through the conquest.[88]

The idea of the international community as a natural society of sovereign states put forward by Vitoria enabled him to lay the foundation for his third basic idea as Barcia puts out: a new doctrine of the legitimization of "just war" (and through this, conquest), defined as redress for *iniuriae* and thus as an instrument for enforcing law.[89] From this came a simple legal formulation of war as a sanction aimed at ensuring the

---

[81]Barcia Trelles 1927a, 195 *et seq.*

[82]Barcia Trelles 1927a, 206 *et seq.*

[83]Barcia Trelles 1927a, b, 219 *et seq.*

[84]Barcia Trelles 1927a, b, 215–218.

[85]For the Christian use of the conquest as the material and spiritual appropriation of the New World, through the demonization of the native religions, forced conversion and the claim that the Indians were inferior, destined to obey and serve, see Zavala 1971 and also Todorov 1987.

[86]Barcia Trelles 1927a, b, 195 *et seq.*

[87]Bartolomé de las Casas himself, the most fervent defender of the rights of the American Indians, maintained that "the only right Your Majesty holds is as follows: that all or most of the Indians freely wish to be your vassals and look on it as an honour". Francisco de Vitoria had defended the same idea in *De Indis*. See Hanke 2002

[88]Pagden 1987, 85.

[89]Barcia Trelles 1927a, 242 *et seq.* War occupies a central position in Vitoria's construct, see Verhoeven 1988, 112 *et seq.*

effectiveness of international law that was to last until Kelsen. War was lawful and necessary, Vitoria maintained, precisely because states were subject to human rights, and in the absence of a higher court, these could only be defended through war.[90]

5 At the End of the Day ...

Our intention through the reconstruction of Barcia's work on Vitoria's thoughts has been to explain the nature of the predominant legal internationalist thought in Spain, which can be identified with the discourse of objective positivism in support of the establishment of an international community designed by internationalists in the interwar period. That objectivism, with sociological roots, which is retraceable, to different degrees, to G. Scelle, through the influence of L. Duguit, and to the American legal realism of interwar period (Pound, Holmes) found in the Spanish doctrine, was influenced by natural law, fertile ground for its development by the contemporary international legal scholars.[91]

Barcia was characterized by his liberal thinking, Christian foundations and celtic lineage (which helped him not to reach hasty or unilateral conclusions).[92] His friend José de Yanguas Messía summarized Barcia's qualities as "objectivity, clarity, order, a balance of the real and the ideal in his understanding of international life, a broad vision and calm judgement".[93] He was remembered in the history of the discipline as a fine analyst of international reality who was more interested in explaining behaviour than in sterile technical or legal discussions and, above all, as a defender of the Spanish origin of modern international law, something that he had been proud of having defended when no one else was doing so in the midst of an "almost absolute solitude".[94]

Barcia was in Valladolid at the time of the military uprising of the 18 June 1936. He was accused of being a "Mason and leftist" (his brother Augusto was a minister of the Second Republic) and was removed from office in April of 1937. In 1937 and 1938, he worked for free for the press and publicity service of *Falange* on international issues.

In 1939, Barcia was "transferred" to the University of Santiago de Compostela from the University of Valladolid.[95] This was because of the Francoist university

---

[90]This interpretation of Vitoria's writings was suggested by James Brown Scott: as far as Vitoria was concerned, war was "a legal action brought by force in the absence of a higher Court", Brown Scott 1928, 107. Also, Barcia Trelles 1927a, b, 277, 330 *et seq.*

[91]Gamarra and de la Rasilla 2012, 21 *et seq.*

[92]Miaja de la Muela 1958, 16.

[93]Yanguas Messía 1958, 13.

[94]Forcada 2012, 274 *et seq.*

[95]See *Boletin Oficial del Estado* (Official Spanish Journal), 18 August 1939.

purge, and soon after his arrival he was to suffer the effects of a second purge.[96] During the Francoist dictatorship, there were those who accused Barcia of being a Mason, although one of his friends denied this, linking him to the Rotarians.[97] This accusation was spread after the Francoist uprising and purges because he had spoken about the League of Nations and had agreed with the Republican movement. It was his friend Yanguas Messía who helped Barcia in successive purges by establishing a real network of self-protection. His disciples Luís García Arias, Alejandro Herrero Rubio and Adolfo Miaja de la Muela carried on his work studying Spanish classics from a National Catholicism approach.[98] This approach was not very different from that defended by the liberal Catholics in the nineteenth century and beginning of the twentieth century.

Barcia's close contact with Vitoria's work gave him a "strong iusnaturalist foundation"[99] and liberal approach to international law that can be seen in his idea that "law is a technical, instrumental medium and not an end in itself, at the service of fundamental human values".[100] His technical analyses were accompanied by a complementary evaluative analysis based on the doctrines of Spanish theologians from the sixteenth century, particularly the teachings of Vitoria.[101]

At the end of the day, Vitoria's model and Barcia's thinking too, precisely because they are so distinctive, still guide international legal thought and still nourish two opposing but synchronous ideas: firstly, the legal utopia (and regulatory doctrine) of worldwide coexistence based on law, and secondly, the previously Christianocentric and later Eurocentric doctrine of the legitimization of the colonization and exploitation of the rest of the world by European states. Colonization was in the name of "values" that were constantly in flux depending on the period, but declared to be universal at all times: first, the mission of "evangelization", then of "civilization", and finally the present-day "globalization" of so-called Western values (democracy, the rule of law and human rights).

References

Alonso Getino L et al (1946) Fray Francisco de Vitoria, fundador del Derecho internacional moderno. (Conferencias pronunciadas en la inauguración de su Monumento Nacional en la ciudad de Vitoria). Ediciones Cultura Hispánica, Madrid

Anghie A (2005) Imperialism, sovereignty and the making of international law. Cambridge University Press, Oxford

[96]Claret Miranda 2006, 184. See, also, 123, 129 and 134.

[97]Peláez 2005, 134 and 135.

[98]Gamarra 2016.

[99]Pérez González 1988.

[100]Miaja de la Muela 1958, 64.

[101]Barcia Trelles 1928, 215 and 216.

Barcia Trelles C (1915) La anexión de Bosnia-Herzegovina a Austria Hungría. Thesis unpublished, University Central of Madrid, Faculty of Law

Barcia Trelles C (1924) La política exterior norteamericana de la posguerra. Universidad de Valladolid, Valladolid

Barcia Trelles C (1925) El imperialismo del petroleo y la paz mundial. Universidad de Valladolid, Valladolid

Barcia Trelles C (1927a) F. de Vitoria et l'École moderne du Droit International. Recueil des cours - Académie de droit international II:113–336

Barcia Trelles C (1927b) La Academia de Derecho internacional de la Haya. Impresiones de un testigo. Revista Universidad (Revista de Cultura y Vida Universitaria), 652–653

Barcia Trelles C (1928) Francisco de Vitoria fundador del derecho internacional moderno. Universidad de Valladolid, Valladolid

Barcia Trelles C (1933) Francisco Suárez (1548–1617): les théologiens espagnols du XVIe siècle et l'école moderne du droit international. Recueil des cours - Académie de droit international I:389–549

Barcia Trelles C (1939) Fernando Vázquez de Menchaca. L'école espagnole du Droit international du XVIe siècle. Recueil des cours - Académie de droit international I:433–530

Barcia Trelles C (1974) Mi amigo Pepe Yanguas. Revista Española de Derecho internacional, Homenaje al Profesor don José de Yanguas Messía XXV:1–19

Bhandari S (2016) Global constitutionalism and the path of international law. Transformation of law and state in the globalized world. Brill/Nijhoff, The Hague

Blanc Altemir A (1999) El Marqués de Olivart y el derecho internacional (1861–1928): sociedad internacional y aportación científica. Universidad de Lérida, Lérida

Braithwaite J (2008) Regulatory capitalism: how it works, ideas for making it work better. Edward Elgar, Cheltenham

Brown Scott J (1928) El origen español del Derecho internacional moderno. Preliminary study writen by Camilo barcia, Universidad de Valladolid, Valladolid

Brown Scott J (1934) The Spanish origin of international law: Francisco de Vitoria and his law of nations. Clarendon Press, Oxford

Canning J (1987) The political thought of Baldus de Ubaldis. Cambridge Studies in Medieval Life and Thought, Cambridge

Carrillo Salcedo JA (1993) Aportación de Francisco de Vitoria a los fundamentos filosóficos de los derechos humanos. In: Mangas Martín A (ed) La Escuela de Salamanca y el Derecho internacional en América. Del pasado al futuro. Asociación Española de Profesores de Derecho internacional y Relaciones internacionales, Salamanca, pp 49–54

Castilla Urbano F (1992) El pensamiento de Francisco de Vitoria: filosofía política e indio americano. Antropos, Barcelona

Chimni BS (2006) Third world approaches to international law: a manifesto. Int Commun Law Rev 8:3–27

Claret Miranda J (2006) El atroz desmoche. La destrucción de la Universidad española por el franquismo, 1936–1945. Crítica, Barcelona

Coudert FR (1943) An appreciation of James Brown Scott. Am J Int Law 37:559–561

Craven M (2016) Theorizing the turn of history in international law. In: Orford A, Hoffmann F, Clark M (eds) The Oxford handbook of the theory of international law. Oxford University Press, Oxford, pp 21–37

De los Ríos F (2007) Religión y Estado en la España del Siglo XVI. Edition of Antonio García Pérez. Prologue by Ángel del Río. Centro de Estudios Andaluces, Seville

Egido León Á (1986) Madariaga reivindicador de la figura de Vitoria como fundador del derecho internacional. In: Salvador de Madariaga, 1886–1986. Libro-Homenaje con motivo de su centenario. Ayuntamiento de La Coruña, La Coruña, pp 106–113

Espaliú C (2012) La Junta para Ampliación de Estudios e Investigaciones Científicas y el Derecho internacional. In: Gamarra Y, Rasilla I (eds) Historia del pensamiento iusinternacionalista español del siglo XX. Aranzadi/Thompson, Cizur Menor, pp 153–184

Fernández Rozas JC, Andrés Sáenz de Santa María P (2010) La aportación de la facultad de derecho de la universidad de Oviedo al progreso del derecho internacional. In: Coronas González SM (coord) Historia de la facultad de derecho. Servicio de Publicaciones de la Universidad de Oviedo, Oviedo, pp 495–570

Fernández Sánchez PA (2013) Spanish School of International Law (c. XVI–XVII). In: Carty T (ed) Oxford bibliographies in international law. Oxford University Press, New York

Fernández Sánchez PA (2015) From Totus Orbis to Global Law. Glob Commun Yearb Int Law Jurisprud, 113–124

Fidler DP (2001) The return of the standard of civilization. Chicago J Int Law 2(1):137–157

Finch GA (1944) James Brown Scott 1866–1943. Am J Int Law 38:183–217

Fiore P (1894–1895) Tratado de Derecho Internacional Público, aumentado con notas y un apéndice con los tratados entre España y las demás naciones por Alejo García Moreno, 4 vols, 2nd edn. Centro Editorial de Góngora, Madrid

Forcada I (2012) La influencia de la religión católica en la doctrina internacionalista española del período de entreguerras (1918–1939). In: Gamarra Y, Rasilla I (eds) Historia del pensamiento iusinternacionalista español en el siglo XX. Aranzadi/Thomson, Cizur Menor, pp 229–285

Gamarra Y (2011–2012) History of the historiography of textbooks and treatises on international law of the 19th Century in Spain. Span Yearb Int Law, 1–22

Gamarra Y (2012a) Los lenguajes del derecho internacional en la Constitución española de 1931. In: Gamarra Y, Rasilla I (eds) Historia del pensamiento iusinternacionalista español del siglo XX. Aranzadi/Thompson, Cizur Menor, pp 185–228

Gamarra Y (2012b) Rafael Altamira y Crevea (1866–1951). The International Judge as Gentle Civilizer. J Hist Int Law 2012(1):1–49

Gamarra Y (2016) Nacionalcatolicismo e internacionalismo en las cátedras de Derecho. Luís García Arias (1921–1973). e-Legal Hist Rev, nº 22. http://www.iustel.com/v2/revistas/detalle_revista.asp?id=15

Gamarra Y, Rasilla I (2012) Hacia una historiografía crítica del Derecho internacional en la España de los siglos XIX y XX. In: Gamarra Y, Rasilla I (eds) Historia del pensamiento iusinternacionalista español del siglo XX. Aranzadi/Thompson, Cizur Menor, pp 21–35

García Arias L (1947) Los internacionalistas clásicos extranjeros del siglo XVII que citan a Francisco de Vitoria. La Ciencia Tomista (Homenaje a Vitoria) LXXII(January–June):151–169

García Gallo A (1948) Hinojosa y su Obra. In: Hinojosa y Naveros E (ed) Obras completas. Instituto Nacional de Estudios Jurídicos, Madrid

Gascón y Marín J (1946) Fray Francisco de Vitoria, fundador del dercho internacional. In: Alonso Getino L et al (eds) Fray Fco. De Vitoria, fundador del derecho internacional moderno (1546–1946). Cultura Hispánica, Madrid, pp 191–123

González Campos J, Mesa Garrido R, Pecourt García E (1964) Notas para la historia del pensamiento internacionalista español: Aniceto Sela y Sampil (1863–1935). Revista Española de Derecho Internacional XVII(4):561–583

Haggenmacher P (1988) La place de Francisco de Vitoria parmi les fondateurs du droit international. In: Truyol y Serra A et al (eds) Actualité de la pensé juridique de Francisco de Vitoria: travaux de la journée d'études organiosée à Louvain-la-Neuve par le Centre Charles de Visscher pour le droit international le 5 décembre 1986. Bruylant, Brussels, pp 27–36

Hanke L (2002) The Spanish struggle for justice in the conquest of America. Southern Methodist University Press, University Park

Herrero Rubio A (1947) Don Joseph de Olmeda y León (1740–1805). Internacionalistas españoles del siglo XVIII. Prologue of Camilo Barcia Trelles. Seminario de Estudios Internacionales de Vázquez de Menchaca, Valladolid

Herrero Rubio A (1952) Le droit des gens dans l'Espagne du XVIIIe siècle. Recueil des cours - Académie de droit international 81:309–450

Herrero Rubio A (1953) Internacionalistas españoles del siglo XVIII: Pedro José Pérez Valiente (1713–1789). Universidad de Valladolid, Valladolid

Herrero Rubio A (1959) Historia del Derecho de gentes y de las relaciones internacionales, 2nd edn. Universidad de Valladolid, Valladolid

Hinojosa y Naveros de E (1889) Discursos leídos ante la Real Academia de la Historia en la recepción pública de D. Eduardo de Hinojosa, el día 10 de marzo de 1889. Tipografía de los Huérfanos, Madrid
Hinojosa y Naveros de E (1890) De la influencia que tuvieron en el Derecho público de su patria, y singularmente en el Derecho penal, los filósofos y teólogos españoles anteriores a nuestro siglo. Paper awarded by the *Academia de Ciencias Morales y Políticas* in 1889. Tipografía de los Huérfanos, Madrid
Kénovian D, Rygiel P (2015) Introduction. 'Faiseurs de droit': les juristas internationalistes, une approache globale située. Monde(s) 7:9–24
Koskenniemi M (2011a) Empire and international law: the real Spanish contribution. Univ Toronto Law J 61(1):1–36
Koskenniemi M (2011b) The Case for Comparative International Law. Finnish Yearb Int Law, 1–8
Koskenniemi M (2011c) Histories of international law: dealing with Eurocentrism. In: Duve T (ed) Rechtsgeschichte. Zeitschrift des Max-Planck-Instituts für Europäische Rechtsgeschichte Rg 19, pp 152–176
Koskenniemi M (2012a) A history of international law histories. In: Fassbender B, Peters A, Peter S, Högger D (eds) The Oxford Handbook of the History of International Law. Oxford University Press, Oxford, pp 943–971
Koskenniemi M (2012b) Imperio y Derecho internacional. In: Gamarra Y, Rasilla I (eds) Historia del pensamient Iusinternacionalista español del siglo XX. Aranzadi/Thompson, Cizur Menor, pp 37–77
Menéndez y Pelayo M (1890) Contestación del Ilmo. Sr. D. Marcelino Menéndez y Pelayo. Discursos leídos ante la Real Academia de la Historia en la recepción pública de D. Eduardo de Hinojosa, 10 Mar 1889
Menéndez y Pelayo M (1911) Historia de los heterodoxos españoles. La Editorial Católica, Madrid (1978)
Miaja de la Muela A (1934) Las ideas fundamentales del Derecho de Gentes en la obra de Fray Serafín de Freitas. Anuario de la Asociación Francisco de Vitoria V:171–222
Miaja de la Muela A (1945) Una sátira española contra los internacionalistas del siglo XVIII: la lección cuarta de los eruditos a la violeta. Colección de estudios en Homenaje al Profesor Camilo Barcia Trelles en sus bodas de plata de catedrático de Derecho internacional. Universidad de Santiago de Compostela, Santiago de Compostela
Miaja de la Muela A (1949) De la existencia de una Escuela española de los siglos XVI Y XVII. Anuario de la Asociación Francisco de Vitoria I:99–141
Miaja de la Muela A (1958) Perfiles humanos y científicos del professor Barcia Trelles. In: Estudios de Derecho Internacional. Homenaje al Profesor Camilo Barcia Trelles. Universidad de Santiago de Compostela, Santiago de Compostela, pp 15–66
Niemela P (2008) A Cosmopolitan World Order? Perspectives on Francisco de Vitoria and the United Nations. Max Planck Yearb United Nations 12:301–344
Nys E (1889) Les publicistes espagnols du XVIe siècle et les droits des Indiens. Revue de droit international et de législation comparée 21:532–560
Nys E (1890) Les droits des Indiens et les publicistes espagnols. Weissenbruch, Brussels
Nys E (1914) Le droit des gens et les anciens jurisconsultes espagnols. Weissenbruch, Brussels
Octavio R (1930) Les sauvages americains devant le Droit. Recueil des Cours de l'Academie de Droit International 32:177–292
Pagden A (1987) The languages of political theory in early-modern Europe. Cambridge University Press, Cambridge, 79–98
Pagden A (1997) Señores de todo el mundo, Ideologías del Imperio en España, Inglaterra y Francia (en los siglos XVI, XVII y XVIII). Península, Barcelona
Pasamar Alzuria G (1993) La configuración de la imagen de la decandencia española en los siglos XIX y XX (de la historia filosófica a la historiografía professional). Manuscrits 11:183–214
Pastor Ridruejo JA (2012) Francisco de Vitoria y la modernidad de sus enseñanzas: Ius Ad Bellum y Ius In Bello. In: Gamarra Y, Rasilla I (eds) Historia del pensamiento Iusinternacionalista español del siglo XX. Aranzadi/Thompson, Cizur Menor, pp 79–87

Peiró Martín I (2013) Historiadores en España. Historia de la Historia y memoria de la profesión. Prensas de la Universidad de Zaragoza, Zaragoza

Peiró Martín I, Pasamar Alzuria G (2002) Diccionario Akal de Historiadores españoles contemporáneos. Akal, Madrid

Peláez MM (2005) "Camilo Barcia Trelles" in Diccionario crítico de juristas españoles, portugueses y latinoamericanos (Hispánicos, Brasileños, Quebequenses y restantes francófonos). Editorial de Málaga, Zaragoza-Barcelona, pp 134–135

Pereña L (1992) La idea de justicia en la conquista de América. Mapfre, Madrid

Pérez González M (1988) El sentido de la perspectiva histórica. El País, 15 July

Petersmann E-U (2012) International economic law in the 21st century constitutional pluralism and multilevel governance of interdependent public goods. Hart, Oxford

Prashad V (2008) The darker nations: a people's history of the Third World. New Press, New York

Rodríguez-San Pedro Bezares LE, Polo Rodríguez JL (eds) (2008) La Universidad contemporánea. Miscelanea Alfonso IX. Ediciones de la Universidad de Salamanca, Salamanca

Rossi CR (1998) Broken chain of being: James Brown Scott and the origins of modern international law. Kluwer Law International, The Hague

Schröder G (2002) Progressive Governance for the 21st century. Beck, Munich

Schwöbel CEJ (2011) Global constitutionalism in international legal perspective. Martinus Nijhoff Publishers, Leiden/Boston

Todorov T (1987) La conquista de América: el problema del otro. Spanish translation by F. Botton Burlá. Siglo XXI, Madrid

Truyol y Serra A (1947) Doctrina vitoriana del orden internacional. La ciencia tomista 2:123–138

Truyol y Serra A (1993) El derecho de gentes como orden universal. In: Mangas Martín A (ed) La Escuela de Salamanca y el Derecho internacional en América. Del pasado al futuro. Asociación Española de Profesores de Derecho internacional y Reelaciones internacionales, Salamanca, pp 17– 25

Tuñón de Lara M (1982) Medio siglo de cultura española, 1885–1936. Bruguera, Barcelona

Verhoeven J (1988) Vitoria ou la matrice du droit international. In: Truyol y Serra A et al (eds) Actualité de la pensé juridique de Francisco de Vitoria: travaux de la journée d'études organiosée à Louvain-la-Neuve par le Centre Charles de Visscher pour le droit international le 5 décembre 1986. Bruylant, Bruxelles, pp 97–128

Villar G (2012) Fernando de los Ríos. Teoría y Realidad Constitucional 30:553–571

von Gierke O (1900) Political theories of the middle ages. Cambridge University Press, Cambridge

von Martens F (1882–1883) Derecho internacional contemporáneo de las naciones civilizadas, 2 vols. San Petersburg; Spanish edition, Tratado de Derecho internacional, with prologue and notes by Joaquín Fernández Prida, 4 vols. Madrid, undatted

Yanguas Messia de J (1933) El IV Centenario de las Relecciones de Vitoria. Acción Española I (25):6–7

Yanguas Messia de J (1958) Camilo Barcia. In: Estudios de Derecho Internacional. Homenaje al Profesor Camilo Barcia Trelles. Universidad de Santiago de Compostela, Santiago de Compostela, pp 11–14

Zapatero P (2009) Legal imagination in Vitoria. The power of ideals. J Hist Int Law 1(2):221–271

Zavala S (1971) Las instituciones jurídicas de la conquista de América Latina. Porrúa, México DF

Part II
Vitoria and the Jus Bellum Iustum

Chapter 7
Francisco de Vitoria on the "Just War": Brief Notes and Remarks

Mauro Mantovani

Abstract This contribution presents some notes on the theory of the law of war according to Francisco de Vitoria, an author who continues to generate interest and who is still the subject of various studies and several interpretations. The classical doctrine on the subject of war law addresses two fundamental questions: when is it permitted to make war? (*jus ad bellum*); what is permitted during war? (*jus in bello*). After some contextual notes, this chapter focuses on the development of Vitoria's perspective on these two questions, especially in his *relectiones De Indis* and *De iure belli*, considering above all his thought and his interpretation of the "*injuria*" according to the older law of war, and not taking directly into account the important and complementary issue of the "theology of conscience" of our Master. Vitoria's just war doctrine deals in fact with the relationship between "medieval" and "modern" and shows how this Spanish theologian is still current even in respect of new issues we face today.

1 Introduction

Set out below are some notes on the theory of the law of war according to Francisco de Vitoria, focusing especially in the classical discussion on the just cause for a valid war, reason that can be found—according to the previous Theologians—only in a suffered aggression (*injuria accepta*).[1]

[1]For further information, see Hamilton 1963; Brufau Prats 1989; Justenhoven 1991; Cruz Prados 1991; Hernández 1995a, b; Frayle Delgado 2007; Belda Plans 2000 (about Francisco de Vitoria: 313–398, 941–953); Janssen 2001; de Vitoria 2003, 2010, 213–229; Jericó Bermejo 2005; Tierney 2005; Maldonado Simán 2006; Muldoon 2006; Langella 2007, 2013; Aparisi Miralles 2007; Pena González 2009 (about Francisco de Vitoria, 25–53); Aspe Armella and Zorroza 2014. I would like to thank for their assistance Prof. David Johnson and Dr. Giulia Massazza Gal for this English text and for the discussion of some of the themes dealt with here. We have directly translated all the texts that are not currently available in English.

M. Mantovani (✉)
Salesian Pontifical University, Rome, Italy
e-mail: mantovani@unisal.it

J.M. Beneyto and J. Corti Varela (eds.), *At the Origins of Modernity*,
Studies in the History of Law and Justice 10, DOI 10.1007/978-3-319-62998-8_7

Regarding the right of making war and the concept of "just war" R.H.W. Regout wrote in his study (*The doctrine of just war by St. Augustine to the present day from the theologians and Catholic canonists*)[2] that the "doctrine did not reach its full extent until Francisco de Vitoria (†1546) and the greatest Spanish theologians of the late sixteenth century".[3] Is this true? If so, why? I will analyse Vitoria's thinking, considering also the most significant interpretations and making some comments on the subject, and at the end I will make a few concluding observations.

When is it permitted to make war? What is permitted during war? The former question concerns the right to resort to war, *jus ad bellum*; the latter the law during war, *jus in bello*.[4] In addition, the distinction between "defensive" and "offensive" war must be borne in mind. The first, considered as a response to an unjust offence suffered, is allowed unanimously by the classical doctrine: "every individual, every people has the right to defend their most precious property and to respond to violence within the limits of necessary protection: *vim vi repellere licet cum moderamine inculpatae tutelae* is the ancient axiom. It is fair to defend allies, friends; it is even a binding duty to come to the aid, if possible, of one's neighbour and in general to all the innocent victims of real injustice".[5] This theme, however, becomes more difficult and complex when the question is about "offensive war", because—as Regout affirms—"the expression *aggressive, offensive war* is not found in medieval authors [...]; it emerged in the sixteenth century (in Vitoria)".[6] As for the "offensive war", in fact, one must question in which cases it is permissible for a prince or a state to take justice in their own hands by taking the initiative against the opponent after suffering an offence and after this offence is repeated. On such occasions, "offensive" war may be allowed, and in this context:

> the famous conditions needed for the justification of offensive warfare appear. Most of the time, three or four of them are listed in the following order: (1) the prince's authority, "*auctoritas principis*"; (2) the just cause, that is to say the damage done, "*justa causa, scl. injuria illata*"; (3) the right intention, "*intenctio recta*"; (4) the permitted way to make war, "*justus modus*".[7]

In the classical doctrine, there is a correspondence between the *iusta causa* and the reason of the harm caused by the opponent. When considering the possibility of conducting a "just war", the conventional constraints are the following:

> "wrongdoing" means an injustice stubbornly perpetrated [...]; the use of armed force is permitted only if it is the only and ultimate way to repair the damage [...]; any persistent

[2]See Regout 1934 (about Francisco de Vitoria, 152–185).

[3]Regout 1934, 15.

[4]For further information, see Walzer 1976; Russell 1977; Dockrill and Paskins 1979; Johnson 1984; Miller 1991; Cahill 1994; Orend 2000, 2006; Mekonnen 2002; Robinson 2003; Zupan 2004; O'Donovan 2006; Simpson 2007; Brown 2008; Castaño 2010; Allman and Winright 2010.

[5]Regout 1934, 19.

[6]Regout 1934, 21, note 1. See also Del Vecchio 1964.

[7]Regout 1934, 20.

wrong that only war can stop is not enough to legitimize the beginning of hostilities; the severity of the harm and calamities involved with a war must be proportionate.[8]

When there is a just cause, it is only the prince, namely the authority, who has the power to declare an offensive war; this can be done provided there is the right intention; this means that the:

war must be undertaken and conducted with the intention of restoring the right, of punishing the guilty, of ensuring peace, that is peace in order. This pure intention is lacking if war is declared by greed, revenge, ambition, hatred, cruelty or other inordinate desire.[9]

Yet it is precisely the theme of the just cause—which "is for writers the damage caused by the enemy"[10]—to present some controversial points of interpretation:

some classic thinkers [...] insist forcefully on the guilt inherent in that damage, which deserves to be punished; war, in which the other party is always held guilty, has also for them a clearly vindictive character, that is to say punitive; other authors, on the contrary [...] rather see the legitimate cause of war in injustice itself, the "objective breach of law"; the element-fault is not considered essential for the justification of war.[11]

In this respect, some interpretations continue this doctrine (Regout), while others break away from this tradition (A. Vanderpol).[12] More recently many authors have discussed and developed this topic.[13]

Concerning the problem of the morality of participation in unjust war, J. McMahan writes, quoting Vitoria:

In the early, classical just war literature, "innocent" was often used to mean "not responsible for a wrong", and it was "this" that was supposed to confer moral immunity from attack in war. Writing in the first half of the sixteenth century, for example, Francisco de Vitoria argued that a political leader "cannot have greater authority over foreigners than he has over his own subjects; but he may not draw the sword against his own subjects unless they have done some wrong; therefore he cannot do so against foreigners except in the same circumstances". The implication here is straightforward: one may not attack ("draw the sword against") a person in war unless he has committed a wrong.[14]

As to the question concerning the right of a prince, a people, a state, with respect to the legitimacy of making war, one could say in general that:

medieval authors stick to some general principles: a prince, a people has the right to freedom, honour, its territory and its assets. But later writers [...] enter into more detail.

---

[8]Regout 1934, 21.

[9]Regout 1934, 23.

[10]Regout 1934, 25.

[11]Regout 1934, 25–26.

[12]See Vanderpol 1919.

[13]See, for instance, Haggenmacher 1983, and Whitman 2012. In his book *The Verdict of Battle. The Law of Victory and the Making of Modern War*, Whitman criticized Vanderpol's interpretation.

[14]McMahan 2009, 33. McMahan—continuing to quoting Vitoria—discusses the question of the moral equality of combatants, with an interesting distinction between *permissibility* and *justification*, as well as between *subjective* and *objective* versions of both. See 61–62 and 111–116.

> Their fundamental ideas then exert their influence: on the rights derived from the "*jus gentium*" and natural right, on the purpose of the State, on the rights and duties implied by the natural society [...]; they deduce their individual rights: the right to trade with foreigners, to have safe stay on foreign soil, to spread the Gospel freely, etc.[15]

Indeed, it is with the discovery of the Americas that "this theme had to cope with new needs, which forced people to change their minds on the notion of war".[16] As Hanke wrote:

> from this day of April 1495, when Queen Isabel asked if the first group of Indios shipped to Spain had been captured with a just war, the Spanish theorists began to discuss this topic. Some progressive thinkers like Juan Luis Vivés, claimed that all wars were illegal, inhumane and absurd. But most Spanish people believed that war was "right" under certain conditions. The war against the Indios was right, according to Alfonso Álvarez Guerrero, Juan Ginés de Sepúlveda and Bernardino de Arévalo, while Francisco de Vitoria, Bartolomé de Las Casas, Domingo de Soto and others objected vigorously to this opinion.[17]

Let us now analyse more deeply the figure of the Dominican Francisco de Vitoria. Regout, in his study, defined him the pioneer of a "new age":

> Faithful to tradition but attentive to the needs of his time, combining a bright and logical intelligence with a humanistic freedom and a psychological insight - it was thanks to his powerful impulse that the development of the theological science could take place in the sixteenth century. His treaties on the law of war essentially reaffirm the answer to all the key issues that will be discussed in detail later; we believe it is no exaggeration to say that if St. Augustine was the creator of the medieval doctrine of just war, Vitoria is the founder of the doctrine as it has developed since the sixteenth century and is almost wholly adopted by moralists and Catholic jurists.[18]

In fact, there are several and multiple interpretations of the thinking of the Spanish Master, for example, those of Schmitt (1950),[19] Villey (1975)[20] or Ferrajoli (1994),[21] who recognize, dealing with the theme of human rights, although with very diverse nuances, that the doctrine of war in terms of Vitoria means the development of a new concept of international law and international relations. In turn, Galli (2005) argues that the work of Vitoria on these topics is:

> a "*tertium genus*": that is an example of non-state-rationalist innovation, that the author reaches using in an original way the intellectual property offered by the ancient and Christian traditions.[22]

---

[15]Regout 1934, 22.
[16]Faraco 2013, 31.
[17]Hanke 1977, XV.
[18]Regout 1934, 150.
[19]See Schmitt 2006.
[20]See Villey 2013.
[21]See Ferrajoli 1994, 439–478.
[22]Galli 2005, VI.

The insight of Tosi (2006) is interesting; he encourages the avoidance of readings which are too *sub specie modernitatis* and which "project on the past the problems and the language that are typical of contemporaneity":

> Vitoria is a typical author of transition, who lives at a time of transition from one paradigm to another, from a political concept to another. He uses the old language, in an apparent loyalty to tradition, in order to solve new problems; this represents the ambivalence of his thought, which leads to multiple interpretations.[23]

Within the issue of the relationship between medieval and modern thought, concerning Vitoria's perspective, a fundamental issue that I don't consider here and that is a specific object of study in another chapter of this book is the question of the basic structure of moral decision-making, that in this way adds to the classical problem of establishing the rules for the conduct of war also the theological questioning about the "conscience" and the moral principles, counselling Christians on what sorts of actions might endanger their salvation.

In any case, the figure of the Spanish theologian continues to generate interest.[24] In fact the framework of the contemporary debate on just war is still furnished by the medieval and modern discussion, including late scholasticism. D. Fisher writes:

> Contemporary debates on war are being conducted employing a framework furnished by medieval theologians. […] The theory reached its zenith in the sixteenth and seventeenth centuries, with theologians such as Vitoria and Grotius. It was, however, then almost completely lost to sight. It was only rediscovered late in the twentieth century initially to help furnish a moral framework for the debate then raging over the morality of nuclear deterrence. The language of just war is now fashionably rolled out to provide a critique of all kinds of contemporary wars. But can such an antique theory really help us address our current security concerns?[25]

2 Contextual Notes

In order to focus on the specific situation in Vitoria's time, we have to take into account—as Hernández writes—that:

> in the political order, the confrontation between Christian princes, the interminable wars between France and Spain, and the conflicts in Italy, Germany and elsewhere in Europe, had never before acquired such intensity nor such sweeping proportions. The Ottoman Empire, at the height of its expansionist powers, represented another danger that led to war.

---

[23]Tosi 2006, 2.

[24]See, for instance, Ruede 1970; Wicker 1993; Dolan 1997; Smit 2005; Reed and Ryall 2007; Saada 2009; Manga 2010 [E. Manga proposes a kind of "critical analogy" between the concept of "just war" according to Vitoria and what it is possible to find about this topic in George Bush's writings and discourses]; Allhoff et al. 2013; Winright 2015.

[25]Fisher 2012, 158.

> There were also the wars in the Americas. When Vitoria ascended to his professorship, war appeared to be an invincibly malignant tumour that had infected all of Christendom.[26]

Vitoria tried to connect theological reflection with the problems of his time, and to provide keys and intellectual instruments for their possible solution. In this sense:

> his thinking is not subject to the facile historicism that measures and limits the import of a teacher's thinking by and to the time in which he lived, and scholars still study his works with the same fervour as in his time. Many of his writings and teachings speak to our time and our world with the same freshness that they had in the sixteenth century.[27]

The conventional canonical sources of Vitoria on the problem of war can be found in Augustine, the *Decretum Gratiani*, Thomas Aquinas and Cardinal Cajetan's interpretation of *Doctor Angelicus*. Closer to him, there was the work of canonists on just war (the *Summa Iuris* by Raimundo of Peñafort, Bartolo of Sassoferrato, John of Legnano, Conradus Summenhart), the *Summa Sylvestrina* by Silvestro Mazzolini of Prierio (*Prierias*) and the work of Alfonso de Madrigal, called "El Tostado", who was also a teacher at Salamanca.

When the discussion on the conquest of the New World arose, according to Tosi:

> the doctrine of just war was now consolidated by the scholastic tradition; the theory of necessary war, even if implicit, was present in those "realistic" thinkers such as Marsilio of Padua in the Middle Ages and Machiavelli in the 15th and 16th centuries, while there was a revival of both pacifism and Christian evangelism spread by Erasmus and More and – in a different and contradictory way – by Luther. The doctrine of Francisco de Vitoria [...] on war must be interpreted in this historical and conceptual context.[28]

The question of Spanish attitudes towards the Americas has always been very relevant for Vitoria:

> [it] had been burning within him for many years, and, in this connection, he considered the lawfulness of cannibalism in cases of extreme necessity. This was, of course, related to accounts from the New World concerning the existence of cannibals, the offering of human victims to the gods, and the eating of humans sacrificed in this manner. Could this be, he asked, a legitimate ground for war against these natives? On the basis of carefully crafted doctrine, Vitoria proceeded to define and establish limits that bound the power of Christian princes over the Indies, and that both strongly condemned abuses and called public conscience to account.[29]

The Dominican master therefore faces:

> on one side the conquest of the New World and on the other one the history of Europe of the first decades of the sixteenth century, divided on the inside by wars among Christian powers both because of religious conflicts and the struggle between the Emperor and the

[26]Hernández 1991, 1031.

[27]Hernández 1991, 1032.

[28]Tosi 2006, 2.

[29]Hernández 1991, 1040.

> rising national states [...] and threatened on the outside by the expansion of the Ottoman Empire. The two contexts are profoundly different and require a different approach.[30]

Regarding the question of war overseas, Vitoria is very critical of the idea of the inferiority of *Indios* supported by Sepúlveda and is against the general practice of the Spanish war. Cardinal Cajetan, in the role of General Master of Dominicans:

> had argued at the beginning of XVI century, in Rome, in the *Commentaria in II-II Sancti Thomae*, that the inhabitants of the New World had rights that the faithful could not deny. [He] was therefore the first theologian who applied the Thomistic theory to the inhabitants of America.[31]

The "Americanist" debate sought at the same time to face more openly the thorny issue of the cohabitation of the spiritual power with the temporal one, which had fascinated Europe. And in this context, Vitoria affirms that the power of the Pope was spiritual and was taking advantage of temporal powers only in this sense.[32]

Regarding the way to approach the topic of *Indios* and the war that divided the European Christianity and weakened its defences against the Turkish threat, the writings of Vitoria "are never systematic and organic treaties based on general principles, but rather the application of such principles to the solving of a specific case".[33]

3 The Development of the Concept of "Just War" in Vitoria's Works

Turning to the Master's work, it can be said that he devoted himself to the theme of war especially in the two *relectiones* dedicated to *Nuevo Mundo* (*De Indis*, 1539 and *De iure belli*, 1539),[34] in two other *relectiones* (*De civili potestate*, 1528, and *De temperantia*, 1537)[35] and in the comments to the q. 40 (*De bello*) II-II of *the Summa* by Thomas Aquinas.[36]

As Tosi remarks, "the classical text of reference remains the *Relectio de Jure Belli*, in which Vitoria briefly and clearly explains his position on the law of war".[37] Already in the *De Indis,* he had asserted that the one and only just cause for

---

[30]Tosi 2006, 2.

[31]de Gandía 1952, 14–15.

[32]See Zavala 1991, 27.

[33]Luppi 1988, 476.

[34]See de Vitoria 1981, 2007, 2009a; Pereña Vicente and Conde López 2002. Edition in English of the two *relectiones*: de Vitoria 1991a, b.

[35]See de Vitoria 2008, 2009b; Castañeda 2007.

[36]See de Vitoria 1932, t. II, 279–293.

[37]Tosi 2006, 2.

declaring war was suffering an offence. This does not mean that any offence of any kind is sufficient to declare a war. Our author speaks in this context of a just war within "the right of a people whose subjects are not individuals, but people who must maintain relationships for the exchange of goods, of individuals and ideas based on natural friendship and mutual interest".[38] From a moral point of view, those writings by our Spanish theologian show us the difficult question whether, and how much, he has translated counsel of conscience into something that we would recognize as law.[39] The more relevant questions were in fact those concerning the right choices preserving its own life, defending goods, territories and innocent people, inflicting harm to other persons, or killing someone in certain situations especially during a war. How, for instance, to solve the possible conflict between waging and winning a (just) war, and the moral principle to not to kill innocents?

In the *relectio* on civil power and authority, Vitoria started to develop his Americanist thinking; in the *relectio De temperantia,* he discussed the "apparently inoffensive topic" of moderation and linked this topic also to the question of the New World:

> Vitoria's presentation has an immediate impact. The news of its dissemination reached the royal court and caused concern that such matters should not be addressed in public again. Although Vitoria wanted to consider the matter in greater depth, he responded with his habitual prudence.[40]

The right moment to specifically consider the topic in a more profound way arrived two years later, in early 1539, when Vitoria presented his first *relectio* on the Americas, the *De Indis*, to the university community of Salamanca.

3.1 The de Indis

In this *relectio*, according to Hernández, Vitoria:

> established, first, the rights of the Indians to their freedom, their property, their territories, and self-governance. In the second part, he firmly denied the legitimacy of the then-reigning justifications for a just conquest of the Indies. While in the final part of his relection Vitoria set forth other grounds for his American expeditions, his rejection of the reigning ethic certainly disturbed many observers because Vitoria mediated and limited the omnipotent authority of the emperor by means of new arguments based on careful and precise definition. [...] Vitoria did not begin, as did many other authors of his time, from the basis of the universal authority of Pope or Emperor, because he denied the principle that either possessed universal authority. Nor, as did others, did he rely on certain opinions of civil or ecclesiastical law: the inhabitants of the Indies were ignorant of such laws, and they possessed their own. Vitoria would begin on the basis of natural right and *jus gentium*

[38]Tosi 2006, 3.

[39]See Haggenmacher, 1983.

[40]Hernández 1991, 1040.

implanted in the human nature that he saw as common to all peoples and as the sole basis of any sible dialogue with the New World.[41]

In the *De Indis,* it is stated that only if the "barbarians" do not allow free movement and trade and do not respect the right to preach the Gospel, then reverting to war will be recognized, once all forms of peaceful persuasion have been exhausted: it is therefore an *extrema ratio*, which at first is presented as defensive, although:

in the remainder of the argument the war is not only defensive but also offensive and preventive [...]. The war is justified only in case of aggression and objective impediment on the part of the natives to free trade, otherwise "*nullam possent ex hac parte hispani praetendere iustam causam occupandi bona illorum non quam christianorum*". It is significant to note the principle of reciprocity that Vitoria introduced (either *quam christianorum*) here and in other occasions (*non plus quam si illi invenissent nos*) without taking it to his ultimate conclusions.[42]

The Spanish Master argues indeed in *De Indis* that Spanish sovereigns can claim some legitimate titles of ownership of the lands of the *Indios:*

besides their possibility to choose freely to be governed by the Catholic king or to become allied with him [...] if the Indios deprive Spaniards of their natural right to pass through their lands [...] and to trade fairly with them [...] or if they persecute the converts; in the end, if they hurt the natural law and the law of nations – or the right of the Church of divine origin, to evangelization, which is not in contradiction with the equality of natural law among peoples, because it does not imply, according to Vitoria, equality of religions – then the Indios commit injustice, and they are liable to punishment, that can be the subject-matter of a just war, until the occupation of the lands and submission to the King of Spain [...], subject to the moderation of victors and the goods of the vanquished.[43]

In the *De Indis*, after having proposed the seven principles insufficient to justify the conquests [(1) *Imperator est dominus mundi*; (2) *Auctoritas Summi Pontificis*; (3) *Ius inventionis*; (4) *Barbari nolunt recipere fidem Christi*; (5) *Peccata ipsorum Barbarorum*; (6) *Electio voluntaria*; (7) *Speciale donum Dei*][44] Vitoria, on the basis of natural right and *jus gentium*, proposed eight principles that in his opinion were capable of justifying the conquest. Hernández comments:

We would do well to observe his arguments carefully. The adage, *summum ius, summa iniuria*, i.e., extreme law, or rigour of law is the greatest injury, was continuously present in his mind when dealing with the application of natural right to the Indians, as was the Pauline dictum, "all things are lawful for me, but not all things are expedient" (1Cor 6:12). As a result, his eight legitimate principles are not absolute nor incapable of prudent application.[45]

---

[41]Hernández 1991, 1040–1046.

[42]Tosi 2006, 3.

[43]Galli 2005, XII–XIII.

[44]See *De Indis* I, 2.

[45]Hernández 1991, 1047.

The first of these eight principles refers to the natural communication and sociability among peoples (*Primus titulus potest vocari naturalis societatis et communicationis. Et circa hoc sit prima conclusio: Hispani habent ius peregrinandi in illas provincias et illic degendi, sine aliquot tamen nocumento barbarorum, nec possunt ab illis prohiberi* [*De Indis* I, 3, 1]),[46] and the second is evangelization (*causa religionis christianae propagandae* [*De Indis* I, 3, 8]). Hernández notes: "Vitoria grounds each of these legitimatizing principles in natural right. He connects the second principle, which concerns evangelization, to the first and discovers in the propagation of the Catholic faith the rights to teach truth and fraternal redress".[47]

The third[48] and fourth[49] principles deal with the defence and protection of converts and are both related to the defence of religious freedom and the special fraternity that religious faith supports. The fifth concerns the defence of innocents or of the fundamental rights of human life against those who sacrifice and consume human flesh.[50] The sixth deals with the free choice of sovereignty, which is a natural right of all peoples.[51] The seventh principle concerns the defence of allies and friends, including those who do not share common traditions of faith: *alius titulus posset esse causa sociorum et amicorum* (*De Indis* I, 3, 16). Lastly, and with a particular reference to the civic and religious conditions in the Indies, Vitoria discusses (*de quo ego nihil affirmare audeo, sed nec omnino condemnare*) another (the eighth) principle, that addresses the protection and aid of the less fortunate.[52]

---

[46]"His presentation contains a rich international doctrine: free communication among peoples, the freedom of the seas, free commerce, trade, and contracting among civil societies, and even the freedom of information. Vitoria develops the content of each of these in the first four propositions of his first principle". Hernández 1991, 1047.

[47]Hernández 1991, 1048.

[48]"*Si quis ex barbaris conversi sunt ad Christum et principes eorum vi aut metu volunt eos revocare ad idolatriam, hispani hac ratione, si necesse fuerit, possunt, si alia* via *non possunt, movere bellum et cogere barbaros ut desistant ab illa iniuria et contra pertinaces iura belli prosequi, et per consequens aliquando etiam dominos deponere, sicut in aliis bellis iustis*". *De Indis* I, 3, 12.

[49]"*Si bona pars barbarorum conversa esset ad Christum, sive iure sive iniuria, id est, dato quod minis aut terroribus vel alias non servatis servandis, dummodo vere essent christiani, Papa ex rationabili causa posset, vel ipsis petentibus vel etiam non petentibus, dare illis principem christianum et auferre alios dominos infideles*". *De Indis* I, 3, 13.

[50]"*Alius titulus posset esse propter tyrannidem vel ipsorum dominorum apud barbaros vel etiam propter leges tyrannicas in iniuriam innocentium, puta quia sacrificant homines innocentes vel alias occident indemnatos ad vescendum carnibus eorum*". *De Indis* I, 3, 14.

[51]"*Alius titulus posset esse per veram et voluntariam electionem, puta si barbari ipsi intellegentes et prudentem administrationem et humanitatem hispanorum ultro vellent accipere in principem regem Hispaniae, tam domini quam alii. Hoc enim fieri posset et esset legitimus titulus etiam de iure naturali*". *De Indis* I, 3, 15.

[52]"*Alius titulus posset non quidem asseri, sed revocari in disputationem et videri aliquibus legitimus [...], et est talis: Barbari enim isti, licet (ut supra dictum est) non omnino sint amentes, tamen parum distant ab amentibus, ita ut non sint idonei ad constituendam vel administrandam legitimam et ordinatam rempublicam etiam inter terminos humanos et civiles*". *De Indis* I, 3, 17.

The last of these principles, according to Hernández, relates to the first part of the same *relectio*:

> Vitoria believed that Spain's mission was a limited one of protection and advancement until such time as the Indians could adequately govern themselves. This strict temporal limit to Spanish influence and domination was a central theme of his Americanist thinking. Thus, although Vitoria provided natural right and *jus gentium* justification for Spanish sovereignty over the Indies, there is no doubt that its application was frequently unjust and inhuman. The goal of colonization must be to prepare, in as short a period as possible, a people for a regime of self-governance that respects the fundamental rights of man.[53]

Hernández underlines also that in his *relectio* Vitoria recalls the ideas of friendship and fraternity that must exist among all persons,[54] and comments:

> It might come as a surprise that a friend of peace such as Vitoria would consider the defence of these rights to be a just basis for war and the removal of leaders. He addresses the question of war in his last three propositions, although each is subject to careful limits and conditions, and that in exercising the right of war moderation must be employed according to the nature and quality of the injury suffered.[55]

The three propositions are the fifth, the sixth and the seventh (*primus titulus*) of the third chapter,[56] opening the topics of the following *relectio*.

3.2 The De Iure Belli

Let us consider now the *relectio De iure belli*, which is to a certain extent an extension of what has already been dealt with by Vitoria mainly in the *relectio De Indis*. In fact, according to Galli, "as the Spanish possession of America can be seen as legitimate as a result of a just war, in this speech Vitoria wants to give a more argumentative and less brachilogical speech".[57] In this *relectio,* given in Salamanca on 19 June 1539, the Dominican Master talks about legality, ownership, cause, purpose and way of making war, and:

> fits into this debate a short and concise text, considered a classic of its kind, because of the new contributions that it introduces, and full of suggestions which aim to adapt the law of war to the new reality of emerging national states and characteristics of the law that Vitoria himself had sketched.[58]

---

[53]Hernández 1991, 1048.

[54]"All races are part of the human race, and each shares a natural right of friendship that demands a respect, love, and mutual assistance that civil authorities are obliged to support and further". Hernández 1991, 1047.

[55]Hernández 1991, 1047.

[56]See *De Indis* I, 3, 5–7.

[57]Galli 2005, XXII–XXIII.

[58]Tosi 2006, 4.

The Dominican Master here explicitly[59] analysed and criticized the right of waging war.

> The tenor of Vitoria's teaching could not fail to cause dissonance at the Spanish court which, at the time, was engaged in many armed conflicts in Africa, Europe and the New World. The Emperor himself, Charles V, wrote a letter, dated 10 November 1539, to the Prior of the Dominican monastery of Salamanca in which he expressed grave concern that some members of his community had called into question Spain's rights over the Indies. Charles V ordered the Prior to collect the various writings and copies in question, send them to the court for further study, and ordered that henceforth such matters were not to be raised or addressed in public "without our express permission".[60]

It is known also that:

> Pope Sixtus V tried to add the *Relectiones* of Vitoria to the Index of Prohibited Books, because it constituted an attack on the reputation of the Holy See. The Inquisition carried out a censure of the Spanish people that was harsher than any other modern political purges. In response to this attack Francisco de la Peña tried to demonstrate that the *Relectiones* were apocryphal.[61]

In the *De iure belli,* Vitoria considers directly the question of war affirming clearly that the only war that is just is a defensive war provoked by, and proportionate to, a grave injury. To this he adds, at the end of the *relectio*, his three main rules, resumed by Hernández in this way:

> Before war, nations must resort to all available peaceful means to resolve the dispute; during the war, nations must act without hatred and with a view to minimizing harm and casualties; and after the war, nations must be moderate and judicious in victory.[62]

---

[59]The Spaniards usually invoked in their American conquests the so-called *Requirimiento*. According to this document, "the Indians had to accept the sovereignty of the Spanish monarchs, and if they did not, they would be compelled to submit by force. The conquerors would preach the Christian faith, but they left the decision to assent to the Indians. Vitoria denied that this document possessed any legitimacy, and he refuted each of the seven grounds on which it sought to justify the conquests". Hernández 1991, 1046–1047.

[60]Hernández 1991, 1040–1041. See Alonso Getino 1930, 150.

[61]Pereña Vicente 1996, CXIX.

[62]Hernández 1991, 1048. "*Ex his omnibus possunt componi pauci canones et regulae belligerandi. Primus est: Supposito, quod principes habent auctoritatem gerendi bellum, primum omnium debent non quaerere occasiones et causas belli, sed, si fieri potest, cum omnibus cupiant pacem habere, ut Paulus praecepit* Rom *12,18. [...] Secundus canon: Conflato iam ex iustis causis bello oportet illud gerere non ad perniciem gentis, contra quam bellandum est, sed ad consecutionem iuris sui et defensionem patriae, ut ex illo bello pax aliquando et securitas consequatur. Tertius canon: Parta victoria et completo bello oportet moderate et modestia Christiana victoria uti. Et oportet victorem existimare se iudicem sedere inter duas res publicas: alteram, quae laesa est, alteram, quae iniuriam fecit, ut non tanquam accusator sententiam ferat, sed tanquam iudex satisfaciat quidem laesae, sed, quantum fieri poterit, sine calamitate rei publicae nocentis, et maxime, quia ut in plurimum, praecipue inter Christianos, tota culpa est penes principes. Nam subditi bona fide pro principibus pugnant*". *De iure belli, Conclusiones.*

About the just war and the essence of offensive war, commenting on the text, Regout notes that:

> according to the theory of Vitoria of the law of war, provided that it also meets the other conditions for justifying the war, it may be lawful to use the force of weapons in order to recuperate stolen goods, to take possession of what they are entitled to and, in general, to exercise certain rights, even "if we know that the enemy, who is opposed to this, is acting in good faith and without moral culpability". Or, in other words: as a justification of the use of war the certainty "of the wrong of the opposing party is not an essential requirement". Or: a just war that has all the appearances of an offensive war, since hostilities began that way, "is not necessarily a vindictive, punitive war".[63]

In the *De iure belli*, first Vitoria appeals to the theme of the compatibility of the war with the Christian religion and replies to the objections of evangelical pacifism, also in Lutheran form, relying on the traditional distinction between precepts and counsels for his main argument that war is lawful by natural law and for that reason the evangelical law cannot go against this. He then lists the reasons for why it is not possible to promote justice with war, since they are not sufficient; the diversity of religion or the extension of land or the glory of the prince:

> Vitoria – Tosi writes – denies that the mere desire to extend the land can be a good reason, for if it were, everyone would find good reasons to increase his/her own territory and there would be the situation of the innocence of both sides of the belligerents "*quia alia esset aeque iusta causa belli ex utraque parte, et sic essent omnes innocentes*". The just war theory, indeed, has the fundamental characteristic that one of the two opponents is right and the other one is wrong (except in the exceptional case of invincible ignorance). This is one of the discriminatory points by Carl Schmitt, that we can find in some of the theories, like those of Vitoria, which defend the just war in the double meaning of "*jus ad bellum and jus in bello*"; on the contrary, in the modern theories which are limited to the "*jus in bello*", that means to the offenses during the warlike conflict, we do not ask who is right and who is wrong, because we start from the assumption that both have their own reasons to promote a war, among which there may be also that of territorial conquest.[64]

In the *quarta propositio* of the *relectio,* it is stated that the only reason that determines whether a war is just is the repair of the damages received, "*ad vindicandum iniuriam acceptam*". Hereinafter in the *relectio,* the author develops the topic of the *jus in bello*, by first discussing what is lawful to do during a war and then the measurement and intensity of it. Finally, there is the presentation of doubts, both on the *ius ad bellum* and on the *jus in bello*.

In this *relectio*, with regard to the question of the permission for soldiers to fight under the command of a legitimate authority, provided they are not certain that the war is unjust, Vitoria affirmed that in defensive wars subjects are not merely permitted to follow their prince into battle even where the justice of the cause is in doubt, but are indeed bound to do so, and the same is true also of offensive wars. According to Vitoria, if subjects were unable to fight until they understood the justice of the war, the safety of the commonwealth would be gravely endangered;

[63]Regout 1934, 168.

[64]Tosi 2006, 5.

in cases of doubt, the safer course should be followed, but if subjects fail to obey their prince in war because of doubt, they run the risk of betraying the commonwealth into the hands of the enemy, which is much worse than fighting the enemy, doubts notwithstanding, therefore they had better fight. McMahan comments:

> By "the safer course", Vitoria seems to mean the prudentially safer course, the course that is most conductive to the security of the soldier's community, not the morally safer course, the course that involves the least moral risk. On this point he was at variance with some of the more eminent of his successors in the just war tradition, including Grotius, who, although he uses the same form of words as Vitoria, clearly means something quite different. He writes "that whoever hesitates, when reflecting, in his decision to act ought to choose the safer course. The safer course, however, is to refrain from war". That by the "safer course" Grotius means the one with the lesser risk of wrongdoing is evident [...] where he argues that "It is no objection that on the other side there is danger of disobedience. For when either course is uncertain that which is the lesser of two evils is free from sin; for if a war is unjust there is no disobedience in avoiding it. Moreover, disobedience in things of this kind, by its very nature, is a lesser evil than manslaughter, especially than the manslaughter of many innocent men".[65]

To summarize the positions,[66] we can say that according to Vitoria war is lawful for Christians (q. I);[67] its main protagonist is the political community or its prince (q. II);[68] that war is lawful only for a just cause, that is to say, if the war is the answer to a wrong suffered (q. III, 4),[69] never to extend the power and the glory of the prince (q. III, 2 and 3);[70] that the prince—under natural law (based on the Latinist principle of "*vim vi repellere licet*", q. I, 1) and the authority of all humanity (q. IV, II, 5)—leads the war both in a defensive and offensive form, such as fines for the infringement of natural right or the right of peoples (q. I, 2); that the goal of a just war is the defence and preservation of the political community and its common good, the recovery of assets unjustly stolen by enemies, the punishment of the latter, since the winner is the judge of the loser (q. IV, I, 2 and 5) and the restoration of peace and justice (q. IV, II, 5); manners and limits of war that derive from these purposes, i.e. the detailed cases of *licet et not licet*, not just in the *jus ad bellum* (q. IV, I), but especially in the *jus in bello* (q. IV, II), concerning the murders of culprits or innocents during the war and afterwards, seizures, repair of

---

[65]McMahan, 145–146. See Grotius 1625, *De iure belli ac pacis* (bk. II, ch. 26, § 4).

[66]See Galli 2005, XXIII.

[67]"*Sed relictis extraneis opinionibus respondetur ad quaestionem per unicam conclusionem talem: Licet Christianis militare et bella gerere*". de Vitoria 2005, *De iure belli*, q. I, 2.

[68]"*Pro qua sit prima propositio: Bellum defensivum quilibet potest suscipere, etiam homo privatus. [...] Secunda propositio: Quaelibet res publica habet auctoritatem indicendi et inferendi bellum. [...] Tertia propositio: Eandem auctoritatem habent quantum* ad hoc *principes sicut res publica*". de Vitoria 2005, *De iure belli*, q. II, 1–3.

[69]"*Quarta propositio: Una sola causa iusti belli est, scilicet iniuria accepta*". de Vitoria 2005, *De iure belli*, q. III, 4.

[70]"*Secunda propositio: Non est iusta causa belli amplificatio imperii. [...] Tertia propositio: Nec etiam est iusta causa belli gloria propria aut aliud commodum principis*". de Vitoria 2005, *De iure belli*, q. III, 2–3.

war damage and taxes, changes of political system, taking women and children hostage, the distinction between combatants and innocent civilians (peasants, clerics and intellectuals), conscientious objection, "parallel damage".

Tosi notices that the final conclusions of the *De iure belli* have Erasmians tones and represent an invitation to peace and moderation:

> quite abruptly, the Prince's adviser makes way for the preacher. Vitoria concludes with three "canons" which urge moderation and peace, and reminds princes that also they, as Christians, are obliged to follow the commandment to love one's neighbour and to abide by the concept of human brotherhood; "we must also consider that others are our neighbours, that we should love them as ourselves and that we have a single common Lord and before his tribunal we must all give an account of our actions". Vitoria ends, therefore, with a speech that returns to the area of charity, which he had earlier abandoned. In fact, with Vitoria and the Second Scholastics we have a shift to the *quaestio de bello*. While Aquinas, in the *Secunda secundae*, had placed the question within the discussion of vices contrary to charity, without treating them in a systematic and broad way and without any reference to the *justitia*, the Scholastics of Salamanca place it in the legal field (*De Justitia et Iure*) and insert it in a rather broad and systematic way into the debate on the law of peoples.[71]

War for Vitoria, as Galli writes:

> is a relationship between political entities, not between religions: the just war is not a holy war, nor an ideological war. And, despite its harshness, it does not aim to destroy the enemy's society, to eliminate certain peoples […], or to increase the power of the victors. Even if we consider war as intrinsic – *ratione peccati* – to the condition of humanity, we must not, in its commencement, continuation and completion, rely on blind natural highlights, mechanisms of games of power, a simple utilitarian evaluation, or the harsh tragedy of the exception. Also war must be placed within civilization that has evolved through religion, the idea of justice, rational morality, the law of people and politics concerned with the welfare of each state and the whole of mankind - namely a policy that wants peace, even if sometimes it has to go through a just war.[72]

4 Interpretations and Remarks

Although it is not our task here to examine the relationship between the *ius belli* and the *ius gentium* in greater depth, we can conclude by saying that the Spanish Master discusses just war with rational considerations inherent to the human condition in its natural, objective and historical objective structure; in this sense, he is deeply innovative, because this "changes the context of international law within which we accept just war. Indeed, […] Vitoria takes peoples […] at a level of fairness […] provided by the unity of humanity, created and redeemed by one God. […] Vitoria makes peoples the equal protagonists in international relations—these are the indigenous peoples who have rights and duties with respect to natural assets such as tranquillity and peace, namely the common assets of all humanity (q. IV, I, 4); so it

[71] Tosi 2006, 8.

[72] Galli 2005, XXIII–XXV.

is within the indigenous peoples that the political power grows naturally with society; it is they themselves who develop, on the basis of natural reason, the law of peoples; it is the peoples-nations, in a reciprocal communication among them and as parts of a single humanity (the theory of *cognatio*), who build the *auctoritas* of this world".[73] And therefore, war assumes a restorative function in the event of violation of the inalienable right of movement and expression of assets and ideas.

The influence of the doctrine of Vitoria was not immediate. We must wait for the final part of the XVI century to find renowned authors who have committed themselves, too, to comment on the q. 40 of the II-II of the *Summa Theologiae*. In addition to Suárez, these include Báñez, Molina, Bellarmine, Vázquez, Lessius and Gregory of Valencia. Vitoria's influence cannot be limited only to theological and ecclesiastical circles, but reached many great European thinkers of various ideological and philosophical perspectives. First of all, the Dutchman Hugo Grotius,[74] already mentioned, who in his *De iure belli et pacis* (1625) quotes Francisco de Vitoria many times and references many paragraphs of his *relectiones*.

On this subject, Regout states that:

> what is really original in the doctrine of the law of war of the great writers of the sixteenth century may be attributed to Vitoria. [...] The new vision of Vitoria, which is not simply postulated, but which in fact is the basis for various considerations, is the following: it recognizes as possible that the obstinacy of a prince or of a foreign people "in objectively unjust acts or failures does not necessarily imply a subjective guilt".[75]

According to Regout:

> the Vitoria's theory of the just war affirms a clear and continuing progress of the traditional doctrine and its theories show an acute and bright mind, which takes into account the subjective factors of "extenuating circumstances" for the offenders, but at the same time is careful to maintain the first need of objective justice: "to each his own dues".[76]

According to Tosi, instead, the doctrine of the war in Vitoria "remains in the field of language and traditional conceptuality: it reaffirms all elements of the doctrine of the just war and applies them to the new questions posed by the historical context".[77] We have to consider, in any case, the importance—in those Vitoria's writings—of theorizing the problem of the right choice, during a just war, between different rules that apparently look in the same time valid and contradicting, or when right moral actions have undesirable effects.

Despite all its limitations and conditionings, the Spanish Master:

> speaks to us too, which makes it a classic. And not just for his intellectually crucial role in early modernity and the strength of his return in the period of its the decline, but also for his sense of reality, which allows him to provide a view, which concerns us closely, on wars of

[73]Galli 2005, XXVII–XXIX.

[74]See Haggenmacher 1983.

[75]Regout 1934, 266.

[76]Regout 1934, 185.

[77]Tosi 2006, 11.

blinded peoples, on principles deceived by their own ideologies, and on bad counsellors who do not want or cannot understand the reasoning of right and wrong. In addition, the seriousness of his theories – especially the fact that there is not a *dominus orbis*, and that the peoples have no other guardianship than themselves – is at least a warning for those who, nowadays, wish to make a just war, because they must in any event appreciate the weight and stress of the harsh conditions (moral rigour, good faith, coherence, moderation) which the war imposes, not only on the vanquished, but also on the victors, not only on the "unjust", but also on the "just".[78]

We could also briefly say, with Galli, that

> *jus ad bellum* and *jus in bello* are deduced in Vitoria by a combination, that we shall not take to be contradictory, between faith and reason, between Scripture and Aristotle, between Fathers and Doctors of the Church, between the *Digestum* and the *Decretum Gratiani*, between lawyers, canonists, decretalists and theologians; Vitoria uses tradition with freedom and makes his texts say sometimes more and sometimes less than what they mean, within an argumentative strategy that seeks to recover as much as possible of tradition, to fit and harmonize it into a kind of Catholic critical rationalism open to new requirements.[79]

One of its undoubted merits with respect to tradition consists in moving from "the axis of the dissertation on just war at a moral level of the *culpa* [...] to a legal level",[80] showing at the same time the importance of some ethical questions like if, how and why it is morally permissible to kill someone, or like the validity of the principle of "double effect".

The fact of affirming the equality of peoples does not mean, according to Vitoria, equality among religions and civilizations. On the one hand, he prohibits the holy war, but on the other he strongly supports the right of Christian missionaries to engage in evangelization. In Vitoria, it is central, even in his relationship with Thomas Aquinas on the one side, and with Hobbes, Kant and modern thought on the other, to distinguish between "what is *medieval* and what is *modern*".[81]

5 Conclusion

Francisco de Vitoria's thinking tended to be more analytical and creative than focused on synthesis and on a system. He defined his thesis on colonization through direct contact with the very reality of the discovery of America. His love for truth and justice took precedence over every type of flattery or threat. Nevertheless the enemy of everything that is ostentatious, and also of risky innovations, he was able to attenuate his thesis, which was thoroughly original and revolutionary, in the bibliographic tradition of scholastic philosophy. He wished to soften his thesis due to political prudence, and for this reason only. Such was his scientific and human testimony.[82]

---

[78]Galli 2005, LVI.

[79]Galli 2005, XXIV.

[80]Galli 2005, XXVI.

[81]See Legaz Lacambra 1947, 195–211.

[82]See Pereña Vicente 1996, CXIX.

Galli writes:

Vitoria is not a "pre-modern" writer, that is to say "partially late" with respect to the criteria of laical rationalism (which also matures a century after his death); his positions are rather an example of modernization of Catholic political thought and are developed and developable in parallel guidelines – therefore they do not coincide – from the events of a "secular" modernity that revolves around the State and the subject. The modernity of Vitoria is at a low level of secularization: the transcendent has not changed into the transcendental, nor theism into deism, and God, more than a certainty, is still the foundation of the order of being and its objective rationality. From a spatial perspective, the New World is not, according to him, a conceptual and political revolution – the modern point of view centred on the difference and the balance between the European space, the extra-European space and free sea – but it is inserted in a sort of horizontal extension of *respublica christiana.*[83]

It could be argued—following Zolo—finally, with regard to the "just war", that:

in the intentions of its scholastic inventors, from Thomas Aquinas to Francisco de Vitoria [...], the distinction [between just and unjust war] should help to limit war by imposing on Christian princes the obligation to go to war only for good moral reasons and with lawful means [...]. The whole doctrine was within the political framework of the *respublica christiana* and involved the presence of an undisputed and stable *auctoritas spiritualis*, endowed with an international legal power: the Roman Catholic Church. [...] It was only with the abandonment of moral-theological and cosmopolitan premises of the medieval doctrine of *justum* bellum that "international inter-state law" could be established in Europe from the seventeenth century. Since it had been taken for granted by all opponents that war could be deemed "just" by a universal moral authority – *bellum utriquem justum* –international inter-state (and not cosmopolitan) law focused on setting rules that were exclusively formal and procedural in nature.[84]

This is an argument that deals with the relationship between medieval and modern not only as a specific topic of discussion, but also from the point of view of the "form" of rationality employed. This shows at the present time how Francisco de Vitoria remains current even in respect of new issues we are also facing today, especially—from a moral point of view—the process of our individual and social decision-making when the conscience (*conscientia*) and the ethical and legal reasoning are involved in difficult situations and conflicts, like before and during a war.

References

Allhoff F, Evans NG, Henschke A (eds) (2013) Routledge handbook of ethics and war. Just war theory in the twenty-first century. Routledge, New York, London

Allman MJ, Winright TL (2010) After the smoke clears. The just war tradition and post war justice. Orbis Books, Maryknoll

Alonso Getino LG (1930) El Maestro Fray Francisco de Vitoria. Su vida, su doctrina e influencia. Imprenta Católica, Madrid

[83]Galli 2005, L-LI.

[84]Zolo 1995, 98–99.

Aparisi Miralles Á (2007) Derecho a la paz y derecho a la guerra en Francisco de Vitoria. Comores, Granada
Aspe Armella V, Zorroza MI (2014) Francisco de Vitoria en la Escuela de Salamanca y su proyección en Nueva España. Pamplona
Belda Plans J (2000) La Escuela de Salamanca y la renovación de la teología en el siglo XVI. BAC, Madrid
Brown D (2008) The sword, the cross, and the eagle. The American Christian just war tradition. Rowman and Littlefield, Lanham
Brufau Prats J (1989) La Escuela de Salamanca ante el descubrimiento del Nuevo Mundo. San Esteban, Salamanca
Cahill LS (1994) Love your enemies. Discipleship, pacifism, and just war theory. Fortress Press, Minneapolis
Castañeda F (2007) Antropofagía y guerra justa en el *De temperantia* de Francisco de Vitoria in Francisco de Vitoria, Relección sobre la templanza. In: Castañeda F (ed). Universidad de los Andes, Bogotá
Castaño SR (2010) Guerra justa y criminalización del enemigo. De Carl Schmitt a la segunda escolástica. In: Actas de las Jornadas Nacionales de Ética, 2009. Conflictividad. UCES, Buenos Aires
Cruz Prados A (1991) Para un concepto de guerra en al filosofía de la *paz*. Actualidad del pensamiento de Vitoria. Anuario de Filosofía del Derecho 5:103–129
de Gandía E (1952) Francisco de Vitoria y el Nuevo Mundo. EKIN, Buenos Aires
de Vitoria F (1932) Comentarios a la Secunda secundae de Santo Tomás. In: de Heredia VB (ed). Biblioteca de Teólogos Españoles, Salamanca
de Vitoria F (1981). *Relectio de Indis*. In: Pereña Vicente L, Abril Castelló V, Baciero C, García A, Maseda F (eds). CSIC, Madrid
de Vitoria, F (1991a) On the American Indians. In: Pagden A, Lawrence J (eds) Vitoria, Political Writings. Cambridge University Press, Cambridge
de Vitoria F (1991b) On the law of war. In: Pagden A, Lawrence J (eds) Vitoria, Political Writings. Cambridge University Press, Cambridge
de Vitoria F (2003) Los derechos humanos. Antología. In: Hernández R (ed). San Esteban, Salamanca
de Vitoria F (2005) De iure belli. Laterza, Roma-Bari
de Vitoria F (2007) Sobre el poder civil, Sobre los Indios, Sobre el derecho de la guerra. Tecnos, Madrid
de Vitoria F (2008) Relectio de Potestate Civili. Estudios sobre su Filosofía Política. In: Pando JC (ed). CSIC, Madrid
de Vitoria F (2009a) Doctrina sobre los Indios. In Hernández R (ed). San Esteban, Salamanca
de Vitoria F (2009b) Sobre el poder civil. In: Pando JC (ed). San Esteban, Salamanca
de Vitoria F (2010) De Legibus (ed. José Barrientos García - Simona Langella). Ediciones Universidad de Salamanca - Università degli Studi di Genova, Salamanca
Del Vecchio G (1964) Le concept de la *guerre juste*. Théories de saint Thomas, F. de Vitoria, A. Gentilis, F. Suárez, etc. In: Le droit international et le problème de la paix. Caron et Cie, Caen, pp 75–95
Dockrill ML, Paskins BA (1979) The ethics of war. Duckworth, London
Dolan PJ (1997) Just war theory in the Gulf War debate. A review and assessment. Pontificia Studiorum Universitas a S. Thoma Aquinatis in Urbe, Romae
Faraco C (2013) Sul concetto di guerra in Francisco Suárez. Heliopolis. Culture Civiltà Politica 11:29–39
Ferrajoli L (1994) La conquista delle Americhe e la dottrina della sovranità degli Stati. In: Rigaux F (ed) 500 anni di solitudine. La conquista dell'America e il diritto internazionale. Tribunale Permanente dei Popoli - Bertani Editore, Verona, pp 439–478
Fisher D (2012) Can a medieval just war theory address 21st century concerns? Expository Times 4:157–165

Frayle Delgado L (2007) Estudio preliminar. In: de Vitoria F (ed) Sobre el poder civil, Sobre los Indios, Sobre el derecho de la guerra. Tecnos, Madrid

Galli C (2005) Introduzione. In: de Vitoria F (ed) De iure belli, V-LIX. Laterza, Roma-Bari

Grotius H (1625). De iure belli ac pacis. N. Buon, Parisiis

Haggenmacher P (1983) Grotius et la doctrine de la guerre juste. Presses Universitaires de France, Paris

Hamilton B (1963) Political Thought in sixteenth-Century Spain. A study of political ideas of Vitoria, De Soto, Suárez and Molina. Clarendon Press, Oxford

Hanke LU (ed) (1977) Cuerpo de documentos del siglo XVI sobre los derechos de España en las Indias y las Filipinas. Fondo de Cultura Económica, México

Hernández R (1991) The internationalization of Francisco de Vitoria and Domingo de Soto. Fordham International Law Journal 15:1031–1048

Hernández R (1995a) Francisco de Vitoria. Vida y pensamiento internacionalista. BAC, Madrid

Hernández R (1995b) Proyección internacionalista del jus belli de Vitoria y Soto. In: Soriano AH (ed) Mundo hispánico y Nuevo Mundo. Visión filosófica. Universidad de Salamanca, Salamanca, pp 31–68

Janssen D (2001) Die Theorie des gerechten Krieges im Denken des Francisco de Vitoria. In Grunert F, Seelman K (eds) Die Ordnung der Praxis. Neue Studien zur spanischen Spätscholastik. De Gruyter, Tübingen, pp 205–244

Jericó Bermejo I (2005) La Escuela de Salamanca del siglo XVI. Una pequeña introducción. Editorial Revista Agustiniana, Madrid

Johnson JT (1984) Just war tradition and the restraint of war. A moral and historical inquiry. Princeton University Press, Princeton

Justenhoven HG (1991) Francisco de Vitoria zu Krieg und Frieden. J.P. Buchen Verlag, Köln

Langella S (2007) Teologia e Legge naturale. Studio sulle lezioni di Francisco de Vitoria. Glauco Brigati, Genova

Langella S (2013) La ciencia teológica de Francisco de Vitoria y la Summa Theologiae de Santo Tomás de Aquino en el siglo XVI a la luz de textos inéditos. San Esteban, Salamanca

Legaz Lacambra L (1947) Horizontes del pensamiento jurídico. Bosch, Barcelona

Luppi S (1988) *Vis et auctoritas*: i paradossi del potere nella filosofia politica di Francisco de Vitoria. I diritti dell'uomo e la pace nel pensiero di Francisco de Vitoria e Bartolomé de Las Casas. Massimo, Milano, pp 463–496

Maldonado Simán B (2006) La guerra justa de Francisco de Vitoria. Anuario Mexicano de Derecho Internacional 6:676–701

Manga E (2010) Le retour de la guerre juste. Francisco de Vitoria et les fondements juridiques de la domination globale. L'Harmattan 1:13–38

McMahan J (2009) Killing in war. Clarendon Press, Oxford

Mekonnen T (2002) Analysis of the traditional just war theory in light of modern warfare and the changing attitude of the Catholic Church. Pontificia Università Lateranense, Roma

Miller RB (1991) Interpretations of conflict. Ethics, pacifism, and the just-war tradition. University of Chicago Press, Chicago, London

Muldoon J (2006) Francisco de Vitoria and Humanitarian Intervention. J Mil Ethics 5:128–143

O'Donovan O (2006) The just war revisited. Cambridge University Press, Cambridge

Orend B (2000) War and international justice. A Kantian perspective. Wilfrid Laurier Press, Waterloo

Orend B (2006) The morality of war. Broadview Press, Peterborough

Pena González MA (2009) La Escuela de Salamanca. De la Monarquía Hispanica al Orbe Católico. BAC, Madrid

Pereña Vicente L (1996) Il testo della *Relectio De Indis*. Introduzione storico-filologica. In: de Vitoria F (ed) Relectio De Indis. La questione degli Indios, ed. Ada Lamacchia, XCV-CXIX. Levante, Bari

Pereña Vicente L, Conde López J (eds) (2002) Corpus Hispanorum de Pace. Forum Hispanoamericano Francisco de Vitoria, Madrid

Reed C, Ryall D (eds) (2007) The price of peace. Just war in the twenty-first century. Cambridge University Press, Cambridge

Regout RHW (1934) La doctrine de la guerre juste de saint Augustin à nos jours d'après les théologiens et les canonistes catholiques. Pedone, Paris

Robinson P (ed) (2003) Just war in a comparative perspective. Routledge, Ashgate

Ruede E (1970) The morality of war. The just war theory and the problem of nuclear deterrence in R. Paul Ramsey. Pontificia Universitas Lateranensis, Romae

Russell FH (1977) The just war in the Middle Ages. Cambridge University Press, Cambridge

Saada J (2009) Pacifisme ou guerre totale? Une histoire politique du droit des gens: les lectures de Vitoria au XXe siècle. *Astérion* 6. http://asterion.revues.org/1508. Accessed Jul 2016

Schmitt C (2006) The nomos of the earth in the international law of the Jus Publicum Europaeum. Telos Press, New York

Simpson GM (2007) War, peace and God. Rethinking the just-war tradition. Augsburg Fortress, Minneapolis

Smit W (2005) Just war and terrorism. The end of the just war concept? Peeters, Leuven, Paris, Dudley

Tierney B (2005) Historical roots of modern rights: before Locke and after. Ave Maria Law Rev 3:23–43

Tosi G (2006) La teoria della guerra giusta in Francisco de Vitoria e il dibattito sulla conquista. Jura Gentium. http://www.juragentium.org/topics/wlgo/it/tosi. Accessed Jul 2016

Vanderpol A (1919) La doctrine scolastique du droit de guerre. Pedone, Paris

Villey M (2013) La formation de la pensée juridique moderne. PUF, Paris

Walzer M (1976) Just and unjust wars. A moral argument with historical illustrations. Basic Books, New York

Whitman JQ (2012) The verdict of battle. The law of victory and the making of modern war. Harvard University Press, Cambridge

Wicker B (1993) Studying war-no more? From just war to just peace. Kok Pharos, Kempen

Winright TL (2015) Can war be just in the 21st century? Ethicists engage the tradition. Orbis Books, New York

Zavala S (1991) Il pensiero politico nella Conquista d'America. Ponte alle Grazie, Firenze

Zolo D (1995) Cosmopolis. La prospettiva del governo mondiale. Feltrinelli, Milano

Zupan DS (2004) War, morality and autonomy. An investigation into just war theory. Aldershot, Ashgate

Chapter 8
Prevention and Intervention in Francisco de Vitoria's Theory of the Just War

Francisco Castilla Urbano

Abstract Francisco de Vitoria's doctrine of just war has two main objectives: to ensure that no war will start in the absence of very good reasons and, secondly, that if war is inevitable, its pursuance and, above all, its end will not cause new injustices which could lead to new wars in the future. This means that the imposition of measures by the winner must strike a balance that, on the one hand, makes good the damage with fairness and, on the other, does not generate a string of grievances that lead to a new confrontation. This means that the victorious prince must behave more like a judge than a party to the conflict. However, the doctrine of the prince as a judge is no more than a well-intentioned expression of intent on the part of Vitoria. There are no guarantees that the winner of the just war is the one who suffered injustice, or that the victor will behave like a judge. Herein lies the main problem of Vitoria's theory of just war: if indeed the winner behaves like a judge, the prevention that the theory presents and even war itself will probably be unnecessary; on the contrary, if the victor does not behave like a judge, the victory is at risk of being seen as a new injury that will generate a just war in the future.

This article has been written in the framework of the research project "Discursos legitimadores de la conquista y la colonización de América al norte y al sur del continente" (Franklin Institute-UAH 2011-007).

F. Castilla Urbano (✉)
Alcalá University (Spain), Alcalá de Henares, Spain
e-mail: francisco.castilla@uah.es

J.M. Beneyto and J. Corti Varela (eds.), *At the Origins of Modernity*,
Studies in the History of Law and Justice 10, DOI 10.1007/978-3-319-62998-8_8

1 Introduction

The work of Francisco de Vitoria (Burgos, 1483—Salamanca, 1546) culminates in his *relectiones*[1] (re-readings) of 1539, *De Indis* and *De iure belli*, the former probably delivered on 1 January, the latter on 19 June. Together with his *De potestate civili* (1528), they show us his thought at its best as he combines to greatest effect and with most originality the two subjects on which his contributions to the just war debate would lay their claim to fame, namely the New World and relations between communities.

Since the subject of war is central to the relection *De iure belli*, one can start by drawing attention to the paradox which runs through it. On the one hand, it has always been regarded as an Americanist text, a point reinforced by its continuation of *De Indis*. This can be demonstrated in at least three ways: firstly, the manuscripts refer to it as *Relectio secunda de indis* (Palencia) or *secunda pars* (Valencia); secondly, it was delivered less than six months after *De Indis*, at a time when Vitoria was finding it so difficult to fulfil the requirement of his university to deliver a so-called *repetition* each year, which is evidence that both were conceived together or very close to each other in the Dominican's thought; thirdly, the preamble stresses the purpose: "to round off the previous relection with a brief discussion of these laws".[2]

However, apart from this introductory reference, there is little or nothing in the contents which deals specifically with the Indies. Only at the start of the third article, the first question, which asks, "What are the permissible reasons and causes of just war?", is the answer given, "which brings us closer to the subject of our barbarians"; immediately afterwards, mention is made of the fact that religious difference is no cause for a just war which, we are reminded, "was amply proved in the previous relection, where I refuted the fourth title offered to justify the enslavement of the barbarians, namely, 'that they refuse to receive the Christian faith'".[3] Otherwise, only the final part of the relection and its statement that "so I end this whole disputation about the Indians, which I have undertaken",[4] hints once again at this alleged continuity. It seems to me that these references are too few for this lecture to be regarded, as is usually the case, as Americanist.

[1]A *relectio* was a conference of two hours that teachers in some colleges were required to give each year on non-school days on a subject that had been explored in the ordinary *lectiones* of the course. Because of his illness, Vitoria gave only fifteen of the twenty he was due to give, and the first and the last have been lost, leaving us with only thirteen. See Castilla Urbano 1992.

[2]Vitoria 2007 (*De iure belli*), 295.

[3]Vitoria 2007 (*De iure belli*), 302; (*De Indis*), 265-272.

[4]Vitoria 2007 (*De iure belli*), 327.

2 War and the Law of Nations

It is, then, a text whose arguments can be applied to war between states or communities worldwide, but which focuses above all on the relations between European countries, and between these and the Turks and Berbers. Therefore, Vitoria's theory of just war can be read most profitably in the framework of the law of peoples, a law created by a worldwide pact which grants it a power so far beyond that of its origin that it becomes a "force of law"[5] which "is or derives from natural law".[6] Vitoria's interpretation of the *ius gentium* is flexible enough to be transformed into a positive law based on agreement between men, without therefore forfeiting its authority, which puts it on almost the same level as natural law. This interpretation has been the subject of much debate.[7]

In Vitoria, the law of peoples has a clearly global scope: its obligations are the result of a global, or nearly global, pact. The Dominican's innovation with respect to tradition would appear to lie in this very transformation of a law of peoples, which subjects human beings to its provisions, into a *ius inter gentes*, which makes of nations the main players.[8] If the consent of the republics is the basis of the rules

---

[5]Vitoria 2007 (*De potestate civili*), 40: "the law of nations (*ius gentium*) does not have the force merely of pacts or agreements between men, but has the force of law (*vim legis*). The whole world, which is in a sense a commonwealth, has the power to enact laws which are just and convenient to all men; and these make up the law of nations. From this it follows that it is applicable to those who perpetrate crimes, at any rate in the case of the graver transgressions such as violating the immunity of ambassadors' sin mortally. No kingdom may choose to ignore this law of nations, because it has the sanction of the whole world". I have replaced "the validity of a positive enactment" (Pagden and Lawrance) with "the force of law".

[6]Vitoria 2007 (*De Indis*), 278.

[7]His disciples, beginning with Domingo de Soto, chose this interpretation, which was considered a deviation from the thought of St. Thomas by Father Ramírez (1955, 185), Urdánoz (1967, CXXIX, and 1960, 563), were of a similar opinion that Vitoria would "become the genuine concept of international law and natural law" in the *De Indis*, correcting the position taken in the *Comentarios a la II-II*; Villey (1987, 99), reiterating previous statements (Villey 1975, 362), not only noting a deep disagreement between St. Thomas and Vitoria, but considering that it has distorted the *Summa* to make of *ius gentium* "a *body of positive rules*, for the needs of construction of its new international law". An opposing appraisal is given by Menéndez-Reigada (1929, 1933), and Pereña (1952, 620), and also denies "that the thought of Vitoria on the positivity of international law defended in the readings of 1535 had changed in the Relectiones of 1539, when in explanations of 1543 it has the same principles", while Fernández-Largo (1984, 50) sees in the doctrine of Vitoria "the beginnings of a more current natural law more sensitive to history and to the increasing moral and legal consciousness of the people that what it was that logical and scientific synthesis of the formalist morality system of secondary, tertiary, etc. conclusions". See Pérez Luño 1995, Chaps. III and IV.

[8]Vitoria, a change which can only aim to highlight the new direction to be introduced, would have changed in the *De Indis* (Vitoria 1967, 78), the classic definition of Gayo, replacing *homines* by *gentes*: "*Quod naturalis ratio inter omnes gentes constituit, vocatur ius gentium*". This change does not seem as insignificant as Haggenmacher points (1998, 60), although it cannot involve either a foundation off international law; it is a change of hue, as so many others in the history of ideas.

underlying the international order, the original dependence of the *ius gentium* on the nations cannot be denied; however, this does not militate against its ontological priority with regard to the nations, not only because the pacts are incumbent on the parties, but also because their goal is to protect that totality which, in so far as it is composed of moral beings, constituted humanity before any nations came into being. At the same time, this accounts for the two sides of Vitoria's law of peoples, which also covers relations between individuals and aims to protect them from the excesses of states. Nonetheless, it is the states which most concern Vitoria and it is in his treatment of them that the greater part of his achievement lies.[9]

Vitoria's innovation cannot be viewed in isolation and unconnected from the crisis that had been besetting imperial and papal authority since the end of the Middle Ages. Both kinds of authority had been invoked by medieval thinkers as the only factors of power, but later they had become virtually honorary titles. In temporal terms, their authority did not exceed that of the governors of the most important republics of the Renaissance. Not only is Vitoria aware of that fact, but he takes pains to detach papal power from all that might be regarded as merely temporal; thus, his claim that "the Pope is not lord of the whole world",[10] an idea he returns to in the re-reading of *De Indis*.[11] Thereby, he denies that any such principle might justify Spanish domination of the New World; rather, even if it were the case, such power could not be transmitted to monarchs. In short, the ambition to make papal power an element of the temporal domination of the globe is neither supported by history, as humanist philology had taken upon itself to prove in its exposure of the falsity of the alleged Donation of Constantine,[12] nor by religion. What is more, a pope lacks temporal power over barbarians and other infidels because the temporal power he does have is exercised in relation to the spiritual but, given that he lacks spiritual power over non-believers, he cannot wield temporal authority over them either.[13]

Nor could imperial dominion of the world be advocated with any legitimacy: "the emperor is not master of the whole world", nor ever was.[14] But moreover, even if such dominion were to be recognised, it would be one of jurisdiction, not of

[9]Truyol y Serra 1987, 77. The controversy reflects on the meaning that can be given to the term *gentes*. His own intellectual trajectory is an example of the difficulty of choosing an unequivocal answer: in his (Truyol y Serra 1947, 126), the universal community of mankind "is not characterized by covering all men within it, but by embracing political societies as such", while Truyol y Serra (1967: CXLVII–CXLVIII note) says: "Having followed the first point of view, we have been moving closer to the second. The *ius gentium* is, of course, in part *ius inter gentes*, but at the same time, as a higher and broader reality, a common human right; moreover, the "gens" was not fully identified with the "State"".

[10]Vitoria 2007 (*De potestate Ecclesiae prior*), 83.

[11]Vitoria 2007 (*De Indis*), 260: "The pope is not the civil or temporal master of the whole world, in the proper meaning of *dominion* and *civil power*".

[12]Valla 2008. See Fryde 1983, 17.

[13]Vitoria 2007 (*De Indis*), 262.

[14]Vitoria 2007 (*De Indis*), 253.

ownership and accordingly the emperor could not dispose of territories for his personal benefit nor give them to others at will.[15]

There was to be, then, no resort to papal or imperial authority in order to establish the government of the world. If the growth of the Renaissance states made this state of affairs manifest, Vitoria's analysis cast it in iron. Yet that could not mean the abandonment of all order to the consequent detriment of mankind. What was required was the establishment of some foundation for the new reality of the different republics, and Vitoria's proposal took the shape of the law of peoples.

As we mentioned, the law of peoples was the result of an agreement between the nations, but its laws governed both relations between the republics and the relations established between these and men. However, the situations in which individuals found their rights impaired (tyranny, injustice, war, inviolability of legations and embassies, hospitality to strangers, recognition of properties, respect for trade and so on) were so many and could be the result of such powerful forces that it seemed their protection could only be guaranteed by republics and their governors.[16] Thus, communities were one rung above individuals when it came to attempting to establish universal rules of behaviour for particular situations.

The obligatory nature of the rules involved in the law of people should not entail one nation's advantage at the expense of another's. Vitoria considers that the *ius gentium* establishes law and justice between all countries and all humans without distinction: although the rules of the law of peoples are imposed by authority worldwide, they are not necessarily agreed to by the whole world and, therefore, no rule can be accepted as pertaining to the law of peoples—not even one which is fruit of an accord between various nations—if it is prejudicial or detrimental to another. Over and above the pact between nations, the common weal of the world was a demand that could not be relinquished when imposing rules of law which surpassed the former. In this regard, it should be remembered that the link between the law of peoples and natural law expressed so categorically in *De Indis* is no more or less than a guarantee of the validity of its rules, to the same extent as those of positive law, and a petition for universality. That is why any human law which, like the rules of the law of peoples, runs counter to natural law and, therefore, to the welfare of the world is lacking in value.[17] The goal of the law of peoples with respect to universal society is the achievement of mankind's common good. If this is affected by the action of one or various republics, the *ius gentium* stipulated the cessation of that action: "since any commonwealth is part of the world as a whole, and in particular since any Christian country is part of the Christian commonwealth,

[15]Vitoria 2007 (*De Indis*), 258.

[16]Vitoria 2007 (*De Indis*), 288. This does not mean a concern for individual salvation, but a standard of conduct between nations, which may therefore reach war.

[17]Vitoria 2007 (*De Indis*), 279: "if there were a human enactment (*lex*) which barred them without any foundation in divine or natural law, it would be inhumane and unreasonable, and therefore without the force of law".

I should regard any war which is useful to one commonwealth or kingdom but of proven harm to the world or Christendom as, by that very token, unjust".[18]

The common good of the world is the linchpin of interstate activities. Thus, when action taken by republics means that it cannot be achieved, solutions need to be found which impede the persistence of such actions. Vitoria found the best instance of this is the confrontation between Christian nations while the advancing Turk was threatening European territories: "if Spain declares war on France for reasons which are otherwise just, and even if the war is useful to the kingdom of Spain, if the waging of the war causes greater harm and loss to Christendom—for example, if the Turks are enabled in the meantime to occupy Christian countries—then hostilities should be suspended".[19]

What was called for was not civil war between Christian princes, but an alliance against the Turks. This view is a constant in Vitoria, resurfacing eight years later in his *Carta al Condestable de Castilla, D. Pedro Fernández de Velasco* (19. XI.1536), albeit in this case the enemy had grown to include heretics as well as Turks.[20]

The community of religion continues to be inscribed within the natural community formed by the human race, and it is this which legitimises both the recognition of the different forms of political organisation on a shared anthropological basis and different rights (right of society and communication, right of trade, right of hospitality and so on) contained in the *ius gentium*.

3 The Law of Nations and International Authority: The just War

Consequently, the rules of the law of peoples had to be kept for the good of the world. But what happened if that were not the case? Where could appeal be directed if rules were broken, as happens in any organisation? To avoid breaches from going unpunished, it was necessary to establish an authority which guaranteed respect for the rules as laid down. However, despite "having all the force of the law", the law of peoples was the outcome of a pact between nations and, over and above each nation's commitment to it, it made provision for no international authority that might be capable of abiding by and enforcing the agreement. It is here more than anywhere that the difference between the republic and the international order becomes most apparent: while in the republic it is the prince who guarantees obedience to the laws, there was no worldwide authority capable of accomplishing the same function. That explains Vitoria's insistence on the point that the world "is

[18]Vitoria 2007 (*De potestate civili*), 21.

[19]Vitoria 2007 (*De potestate civili*), 21–22.

[20]Vitoria 2007, 338: "are our wars for the good of Spain, or France, or Italy, or Germany? Or are they for their universal destruction, and the increase of Moordom and heresy?".

in a sense a commonwealth". The functions of an international authority should be performed by those who wielded authority in their own communities, not so much as representatives of those communities but as delegates of the world.

Vitoria views this authority delegated from the world as of a moral kind which legitimises the governor's action at the same time as it requires prudent conduct from him. Such conduct finds expression both in the preventive clauses that are introduced time and again in order to ensure that military action does not overstep the most reasonable limits, and in the esteem in which princes should hold their enemies, as if they were judges instead of interested parties.[21] However, Vitoria says nothing about this world authority invoking any material support from the rest of the countries for the injured party, with the result that that injured party would have to defend itself from the injuries received. This state of affairs is a long way from guaranteeing that the final outcome will be just. Thus, although Vitoria's ideas have an ethical basis and an internationalising outlook which anticipates the changes that proved to be necessary in a world of sovereign nations, they are not committed to their own implementation.

In short, the reparation of injustice between nations finds its utmost expression in the theory of the just war. But in Vitoria, the theory falls far short of offering effective support for the triumph of justice. This state of glimpsing evils and trying to remedy them but only ever getting halfway is typical of Vitoria's thought, for he reached a similar conclusion in relation to the rights of the Indians, as I shall show below.

Vitoria approaches war from the starting point of its legitimacy. Following a tradition which would continue to perpetuate a misunderstanding for some time yet, Vitoria attributes to Luther the rejection of Christians taking up arms,[22] while, oddly enough, he makes no mention of Erasmus, who was the most radical opponent of Christian involvement in war.[23] Vitoria follows the lead of Juan Ginés de Sepúlveda who, in his *Demócrates primero* (1535), deemed it legitimate for Christians to take part in war.[24]

In Vitoria's theory of war, a distinction should be drawn between the law for war (*ius ad bellum*), the law about how to conduct a war (*ius in bello*), and the law for the post-war (*ius post bellum*). Although the just war is always punitive by nature since it presupposes an order altered for no ethically justifiable reason, the existence of an injury and, in short, a punishable act, Vitoria fills the *ius ad bellum* with so many preventive measures that the chances of it ever being put into practice are inevitably limited. To begin with, at the outset of the just war, there must be some authority or other with capacity to declare it; that amounts to limiting the legitimacy

[21]Vitoria 2007 (*De iure belli*), 310–1: "Princes are the only judges in their own affairs, since they have no superiors; but it is clear that if anyone raises an objection to another's just title to his property, the judge is bound to examine the case, and therefore princes are similarly bound to examine their own title in cases of doubt".

[22]Castilla Urbano 2013, 76.

[23]Castilla Urbano 2014, 27–32.

[24]Vitoria 2007 (*De iure belli*), 297.

of armed intervention to a reduced number of protagonists, from which armed bands, warlords or any other group lacking political recognition were excluded as being invalid.[25]

Legitimate authorities do not fight on their own behalf but rather, in defence of their just cause, act in representation of the world. If the prince of a perfect republic, that is, "one which is not part of another commonwealth, but has its own laws, its own independent policy, and its own magistrates, as are the Kingdom of Castile and Aragon, and others of the same kind",[26] cannot tolerate that the territory he governs suffers abuses without intervening to correct the situation, neither can he accept that the world be steeped in disorder.[27] Vitoria does not appeal to the Holy Roman Empire for maintaining world order but to the states. Only states might engage in war, and statehood was a matter of the factual self-sufficiency of an entity.[28] In this case, rulers, not the emperor, act with the same capacity as when they intervene in their own kingdom in regard of any of its members. The law of peoples, whose rules make all humans equal regardless of their origin, and even natural law give princes sufficient authority to act as delegates of the world:

> The prince has the authority not only over his own people but also over foreigners to force them to abstain from harming others; this is his right by the law of nations and the authority of the whole world. Indeed, it seems he has this right by natural law: the world could not exist unless some men had the power and authority to deter the wicked by force from doing harm to the good and the innocent.[29]

Through its appeal to an authority which embodies national sovereignty, the theory of the just war formulates a solution to its non-existence in international relations. Of course, Vitoria knows that this delegation can be used to justify war, as can religion, territorial expansion, the prince's personal glory or any other excuse.[30]

---

[25]Haggenmacher (1992, 15): "dans la Leçon sur le droit de guerre, [qui] présente d'abord la *respublica* comme titulaire de la compétence de guerre plénière, mais ajoute aussitôt que sur ce point le *princeps* a le même pouvoir qu'elle, puisqu'il est élu par elle et qu'elle l'a investi de son autorité. Que Vitoria donne cependant le pas à la *respublica* sur le *princeps* est en soi significatif : c'est d'elle que dépend véritablement la compétence de guerre, celle du prince n'en est qu'un corollaire. Cela découle aussi des explications sur ce qu'est au juste une *respublica* aux fins du droit de guerre : Vitoria la définit par l'idée de «perfection» qui implique à ses yeux une triple connotation de totalité, d'autarcie et d'indépendance. Sans que la notion de souveraineté soit déjà articulèe, une étroite corrélation s'instaura ainsi entre l'indépendance et la compétence de guerre : la premiere conditionne la seconde, mais celle-ci révèle inversement la première. Cette circularité même est symptomatique du rôle catalyseur de la guerre dans l'émergence de l'Etat comme sujet du droit internationale".

[26]Vitoria 2007 (*De iure belli*), 301.

[27]Vitoria 2007 (*De iure belli*), 298: "Surely it would be impossible for the world to be happy—indeed, it would be the worst of all possible worlds—if tyrants and thieves and robbers were able to injure and oppress the good and the innocent without punishment, whereas the innocent were not allowed to teach the guilty a lesson in return".

[28]Koskenniemi 2011, 28.

[29]Vitoria 2007 (*De iure belli*), 305.

[30]Vitoria 2007 (*De iure belli*), 302–3.

That is why he insists that the only ground for a just war is reparations for the injury received. But immediately after stating this ground, Vitoria introduces new preventive clauses and starts to warn against a frivolous or partial interpretation. The first preventive clause has to do with the injury that may lead to the outbreak of war: the governor must be in absolutely no doubt regarding its justice, "the sole and only just cause for waging war is when harm has been inflicted".[31] The second preventive clause has to do with magnitude: only extremely serious injustices can justify resorting to war.[32]

Should there be doubts as to the legitimacy of war, in what amounts to a further restriction, the prince must seek the counsel of independent, judicious advisers who will state their opinions dispassionately; all of which is to ensure that such a sensitive decision as to whether or not go to war should not be taken without being absolutely certain of its justice and inevitability.[33] Vitoria even introduces an additional clause which is intended as a guarantee for those cases in which the drawbacks resulting from the just war would outweigh the advantages; in this case, war would be deemed inappropriate.[34] The chances of success and the correspondence between what can be gained from war and what is jeopardised in the conflict must also be borne in mind. Even if just, war is an evil and every attempt should be made to avoid it. In fact, the mere threat of war also performs a not insignificant preventive function.[35] However, once the injustice has been committed and there is no other means to obtain redress, the just war emerges in its true colours, its mission being to restore the situation existing before the law was violated.

---

[31]Vitoria 2007 (*De iure belli*), 303. Haggenmacher (1998, 67) points that this injury is an expression of a subjective right, while R. Tuck (46) finds in Vitoria "an objective definition", although he does not apply it to the theory of just war. The infringement of natural law should not be considered an example of infringement of a subjective right.

[32]Vitoria 2007 (*De iure belli*), 304: "Therefore, since all the effects of war are cruel and horrible—slaughter, fire, devastation- it is not lawful to persecute those responsible for trivial offences by waging war upon them. The wicked man shall 'be beaten… with the number of stripes according to his guilt' (Deut. 25: 2). Therefore it is not lawful to start war for every reason or injury".

[33]Vitoria 2007 (*De iure belli*), 307, note 24: "For in moral matters it is difficult to hit on the true and just course of action; if one proceeds without due caution, one can easily go astray. And a mistake of this kind cannot be used as an excuse, when the affair is of such importance as to concern the safety and destruction of many people, people who are after all our own neighbors, whom we are supposed to love as ourselves".

[34]Vitoria 2007 (*De iure belli*), 314: "War in itself is just; it is unjust and unlawful only in its accidents. But it is clear that one may have a right to reclaim a city or province, and yet find that right nullified by the danger of provoking greater conflict. As I have said, wars should only be waged for the common good (1.3§12); if the recovery of one city is bound to involve the commonwealth in greater damage, for instance the devastation of several cities, heavy casualties, or rivalry between princes and the occasion of further wars, there can be no doubt that the prince should cede his right and abstain from war". See Vitoria 2007 (*De potestate civili*), 21.

[35]Vitoria 2007 (*De iure belli*), 298: "the purpose of war is the peace and security of the commonwealth [as Augustine says in *De civitate dei* XIX, 12, and in his *Ep.* 189, 6 to Boniface. But there can be no security for the commonwealth] unless its enemies are prevented from injustice by fear of war".

When there is a legitimate authority, a just cause, proportionality in the actions to be undertaken and a chance of success, the question of the *ius ad bellum* is resolved and intervention becomes inevitable. What can we say about the *ius in bello*? What is permitted in a just war and to what extent? Vitoria's answers leave nothing to doubt: "in the just war one may do everything necessary for the defence of the public good".[36] We should not forget that "the whole commonwealth may lawfully be punished for the sin of its monarch", which corroborates the right of the injured party to recover any goods it has lost, to be compensated for any expenses incurred, and even take hostages or requisition vessels, weapons and, in general, anything that might be deemed necessary to avoid new menaces, including to "plunder and pursue all the other rights of war against that sovereign's subjects, even if they are innocent of offence".[37]

It might be argued that such a categorical statement as this one leaves no room for any prevention at all. So does Vitoria contemplate any limit to what is permitted in a just war? Despite his statement just quoted, there seems to be no simple answer. On the one hand, Vitoria's characteristic humanity steps in to warn against any needless excess:

> "If the war can be satisfactorily waged without plundering farmers or other non-combatants [innocents], it is not lawful to plunder them"[38]; on the other hand, a war which seeks to establish justice is still a war and as such is liable for reparation at any cost for the harm done[39] and may lead to episodes which may be regarded as cruel: "If necessary, when the war is over one may take prisoners, even innocent women and children, but not to enslave them, only to hold them to ransom".[40]

Vitoria, then, does not refer solely to accidents in which civilians may suffer the consequences of actions targeting combatants,[41] which in modern parlance is euphemistically termed collateral damage; innocents suffer the consequences of war as if they were participants in it because otherwise it would not be possible to achieve the goals required by victory and, with victory, justice:

> It is occasionally lawful to kill the innocent not by mistake, but with full knowledge of what one is doing, if this is an accidental effect: for example, during the justified storming of a fortress or city, where one knows there are many innocent people, but where it is impossible to fire artillery and other projectiles or set fire to buildings without crushing or burning the innocent along with combatants. This is proven, since it would otherwise be impossible to wage war against the guilty, thereby preventing the just side from fighting. Similarly, on the other hand, if a town is unjustly attacked and justly defended, it is permissible to fire

---

[36]Vitoria 2007 (*De iure belli*), 304.
[37]Vitoria 2007 (*De potestate civili*), 21.
[38]Vitoria 2007 (*De iure belli*), 317.
[39]Vitoria 2007 (*De iure belli*), 318.
[40]Vitoria 2007 (*De iure belli*), 319.
[41]Vitoria 2007 (*De iure belli*), 316.

artillery and other projectiles at the besieging enemy encampments, though there may be children or non-combatants among them.[42]

Viewed in this light, the underlying principle governing Vitoria's *ius in bello* appears to be that any action is legitimate if undertaken in the interests of justice and peace, in other words, if it serves the purposes of the just war, but only provided that there is no less cruel alternative. In addition to the preventive clauses already mentioned, intervention in a just war must always be with good intentions, but some of these may be sacrificed if the goal of victory so requires. Once all the preventive arguments have been taken into consideration, it seems that intervention aimed at righting a wrong that has been committed need stop at nothing.

4 Limitations of the Doctrine of the Prince as Judge

Nonetheless, prevention is never entirely exhausted. It should not be forgotten that compensation for the injury received can never consist solely in the defeat of the aggressor if what is really at stake is the achievement of the world's good. If the punitive action is carried out by delegation of the world, victory must also be administered under its supervision. This means that in the *ius post bellum* the implementation of measures must strike a balance between just restitution for damages caused and taking care not to set in train such actions that might lead inevitably to a new confrontation. It is therefore necessary for the prince to constantly bear in mind that he is acting as a delegate of the world and that he must deal with the defeated more as a judge than as an injured party, above all in the knowledge that many combatants place their trust blindly in their leaders, taking for granted that the war is justified since their leaders have approved it:

> Once the war has been fought and victory won, he must use his victory with moderation and Christian humility. The victor must think of himself as a judge sitting in judgment between two commonwealths, one the injured party and the other the offender; he must not pass sentence as the prosecutor, but as a judge. He must give satisfaction to the injured, but as far as possible without causing the utter ruination of the guilty commonwealth. Let him remember above all that for the most part, and especially in wars between Christian commonwealths, it is the princes themselves who are completely to blame; for subjects usually fight in good faith for their princes. And it is most unjust that, as the poet (Horace, Epistles, I, 2, 14) puts it, the Greeks must suffer for every folly of their kings.[43]

---

[42]Vitoria 2007 (*De iure belli*), 315; 319: "In the actual conflict of battle, or during the storming or defense of a city, in short so long as matters hang dangerously in the balance, *it is lawful to kill indiscriminately all those who fight against us*".

[43]Vitoria 2007 (*De iure belli*), 327. Vitoria holds that citizens can participate in the war trusting their leaders, unless the evidence of injustice was so clear that there was no excuse not to consider its legality.

In case they judge the war as unfair, he considers they should not obey, whether they are wrong or not.

However, Vitoria does not fully work out the doctrine of the prince as judge and this amounts to little more than wishful thinking on his part. There is no guarantee that the victor in a just war will behave like a judge and there is certainly nothing, not even the authority of the world, that compels him to do so. It is moreover possible that victory falls on the side of the unjust aggressor, which would not only rule out the idea of the victor as impartial judge, but would also make any restoration of justice impossible. Of course, if the unjustly injured party emerges victorious, its moral duty is to act with equity, to take into account the extent of the wrong, the damage caused and the crimes committed, but without any resort to cruelty or acts of vengeance.[44] It is, of course, possible both to exact tributes from the defeated to indemnify the damage caused and also to punish the unjust action.[45] It is also legitimate to take all necessary precautions to avoid something similar occurring in the future: "to protect life and safety where there is danger from the enemy, *it is lawful to occupy and hold any enemy fort or city which is necessary for our defence* or to deprive the enemy of a base from which they may harm us".[46]

Yet it would be out of all proportion for the victor in the just war to receive compensation in great excess of the damage and harm done,[47] or for the measures imposed such as "to depose the enemy's princes and set up new ones in their place, or take over the government ourselves"[48] to be grossly inhumane.

The fact is that when Vitoria considers the war's victor as judge, he seems to come close to conceiving of him as a prince who behaves as a true Christian. That would explain his belief in the justice of his actions and the piety with which he should treat the vanquished. If this is the case, the question is how often would a prince take all the preliminary steps required by just wars? Except in one-off cases, would he not seek to stop any armed action from the start? The same doubt applies to many other dilemmas posed by Vitoria's theory of the just war, since it is a theory which relies on the good intentions of the interested parties. Let us set out some of these: Can princes sacrifice their own interests in order to subject their rights to a just war to objective examination? Can a prince's advisers be sufficiently detached from their monarch to argue against his wishes? Can even his subjects refuse to take part in a war they consider unjust? In practice, Vitoria's thinking about the just war seems to follow a vicious circle: in order for it to make sense, it requires of those who practise it a moral stature which, if it existed, would render unnecessary the theory's guarantees; on the other hand, without any such moral stature, his proposals would have no chance of ever prospering.

[44] Vitoria 2007 (*De iure belli*), 320–321.

[45] Vitoria 2007 (*De iure belli*), 325.

[46] Vitoria 2007 (*De iure belli*), 324.

[47] Vitoria 2007 (*De iure belli*), 323.

[48] Vitoria 2007 (*De iure belli*), 325.

References

Castilla Urbano F (1992) Francisco de Vitoria, una biografía de sus ideas políticas y religiosas. In: Humanismo y visión del otro en la España moderna. CSIC, Madrid, pp 13–135

Castilla Urbano F (2013) El pensamiento de Juan Ginés de Sepúlveda: vida activa, humanismo y guerra en el Renacimiento. CEPC, Madrid

Castilla Urbano F (2014) "Concordia y discordia en el Renacimiento: el pensamiento sobre la guerra en la primera mitad del siglo XVI", Araucaria. Revista Iberoamericana de Filosofía, Política y Humanidades 32:25–52

Fernández-Largo AO (1984) De la idea del Sacro Imperio al Derecho Internacional. El pensamiento político de Francisco de Vitoria. Ciencia Tomista 111(1):29–60

Fryde EB (1983) The Revival of a 'Scientific' and Erudite Historiography in the Earlier Renaissance. Humanism and Renaissance Historiography. The Hambledon Press, London

Haggenmacher P (1992) L'Etat souverain comme sujet de droit international, de Vitoria a Vattel. Droits 16:11–20

Haggenmacher P (1998) La place de Francisco de Vitoria parmi les fondateurs du droit international. Actualité de la pensée juridique de Francisco de Vitoria, Bruylant, pp 27–80

Koskenniemi M (2011) Empire and international law: the real Spanish contribution. University of Toronto Law Journal 61:1–36

Menéndez-Reigada IG (1929) El sistema ético-jurídico de Vitoria sobre el derecho de gentes, La Ciencia Tomista XXXIX, pp 307–330

Menéndez-Reigada IG (1933) El derecho de gentes según el P. Vitoria, Anuario de la Asoc. de F Vitoria IV, 37–69

Pereña L (1952) El concepto del derecho de gentes en Francisco de Vitoria. Revista Española de Derecho Internacional V, 603–628

Pérez Luño A-E (1995) La polémica sobre el Nuevo Mundo. Los clásicos españoles de la Filosofía del Derecho. Trotta, Madrid

Ramírez Santiago (1955) El derecho de gentes. Studium, Madrid

Truyol y Serra A (1947) Doctrina vitoriana del orden internacional. La Ciencia Tomista 223:123–138

Truyol y Serra A (1967) Vitoria en la perspectiva de nuestro tiempo. In Edón. Pereña l (ed) Vitoria Francisco de: Relectio de indis. CHP-CSIC, Madrid

Truyol y Serra A (1987) De la notion traditionnelle du droit des gens a la notion moderne de droit international public. Concepts-clefs de la pensée de Vitoria. Le Supplément. Revue d'Éthique et de Théologie morale 160:73–91

Tuck R (1998; orig. 1979) Natural rights theories. Their origin and development. Cambridge University Press

Urdánoz T (1960) Introduction to F. de Vitoria. Obras. Relecciones teológicas. Edón. Urdánoz T. BAC, Madrid

Urdánoz T (1967) Síntesis teológico-jurídica de la doctrina de Vitoria. In: Edón. Pereña l (ed) Vitoria Francisco de. Relectio de indis. CHP-CSIC, Madrid

Valla L (2008) On the donation of Constantine. Trad. Bowersock GW. Harvard University Press, Cambridge

Villey Michel (1975) La formation de la pensée juridique moderne. Montchrestien, París

Villey M (1987) Saint Thomas d'Aquin et Vitoria. Le Supplément. Revue d'Éthique et de Théologie morale 160:93–100

Vitoria F de (1967) In: Edón. Pereña L (ed) Relectio de indis. CHP-CSIC, Madrid

Vitoria F de (1991) In: Pagden A, Lawrance J (ed) (2007) Political writings. Including: on the law of war (De iure belli), On the American Indians (De Indis), On civil power (De potestate civili), On the power of the Church (De potestate Ecclesiae prior). Cambridge University Press, Cambridge

Chapter 9
Francisco de Vitoria on Self-defence, Killing Innocents and the Limits of "Double Effect"

Jörg Alejandro Tellkamp

Abstract This article aims to analyse some aspects of Francisco de Vitoria's moral arguments with regard to the principle of self-defence. It will first trace the reasons for saying that the intended aim of self-defence, being an evident moral principle, is self-preservation, which, however, often results in choosing means that harm or kill the aggressor. Although Vitoria introduces a series of practical limitations that limit the harm done, the case of self-defence is nonetheless a clear instance of the doctrine of double effect. A case that mirrors the arguments set forth in the discussion on self-defence is the killing of innocents in the course of a just war. It will be argued that Vitoria can obviously not morally justify the death of innocents on the grounds of an aggression, and this calls into question the validity of his overall argument. It will finally be shown that for Vitoria a way to morally justify the deaths of innocents is in fact not compatible with the doctrine of double effect and that it should rather be seen as the consequence of an early form of probabilistic reasoning, which in the end endorses less certain moral principles over more certain rules. Thus, killing innocents, although undesirable, can be justified on moral grounds.

1 Introducing Vitoria's Theory of Collateral Damage

When it comes to morally relevant dilemmas, everyone would appear to want to make the right choice, which is especially significant when the options chosen imply inflicting harm on other persons. In his *Relectio de iure belli* from 1539, Francisco de Vitoria discusses at length cases designed to show that in certain situations, such as in a war, it is morally permissible to kill someone. Considering that self-defence is legitimate, because "force can be repelled by force",[1] the death of

[1]de Vitoria 1981, 110. The translations from *De iure belli* are my own.

J.A. Tellkamp (✉)
Universidad Autónoma Metropolitana, Mexico City, Mexico
e-mail: tlkp@xanum.uam.mx

J.M. Beneyto and J. Corti Varela (eds.), *At the Origins of Modernity*,
Studies in the History of Law and Justice 10, DOI 10.1007/978-3-319-62998-8_9

the attacking person can be justified because the end intended is not per se that of causing his or her death, but of preserving one's own life. The argument—which *in nuce* contains the principle of double effect—could be summarised as follows (*argument I*):

(1) It is a moral obligation for *A* to preserve her own life.
(2) The aggression of *B* is designed to shorten the life of *A*.
(3) In order to comply with (1) *A* proceeds to defend herself.
(4) The unintended, but foreseeable, side effect is the death of *B*, which, however, is permissible, because otherwise (1) could not be achieved.

This is a clear case of the principle of double effect, which will be spelt out below. A seemingly related situation is that under certain circumstances, people not actually involved in an aggression can justifiably be killed, when this serves a main objective, such as restoring peace. A stripped-down version of this argument could be as follows (*argument II*):

(1) It is a moral obligation for *A* to preserve her life. The same could be said of groups of people or communities.
(2) Victory is the intended end of warring.
(3) Victory, and therefore peace and social stability, often cannot be obtained without killing innocents, e.g. when a besieged town can only be captured by violent means.
(4) Although killing innocents is not the intended end, it is a morally justifiable side effect in the light of (1).

Argument I and *argument II* rest on the underlying premise that preserving one's own life has to be seen as the overarching reason to determine the validity of moral arguments. There are, however, significant differences between both arguments, the most obvious of which is that *argument II* attempts to justify the death of persons that play no active role in an actual aggression and who cannot be considered to be directly endangering anyone. This article will build on the apparent contradiction that arises from contrasting the foreseeable side effect of killing people unrelated to the aggression with the moral principle which forbids the killing of innocent people, whose death, however, is instrumental in achieving the principal purpose of a war, i.e. victory.

The main question this paper intends to address is whether Vitoria is inconsistent regarding the issue of the moral justification of killing innocents or whether alternative forms of moral argumentation have to be explored in order to justify the death of innocents. In this respect, it will be important to enquire whether Vitoria's theory of moral choice is compatible with the idea that less certain normative principles, e.g. principles that allow the killing of innocents, could be chosen under given circumstances, even though more certain moral principles, e.g. not killing innocents, would per se exclude such a choice. More specifically, the difficulty in question arises with a clash of principles of which the first is seemingly stronger and more general than the second:

(1) General principle: The content of natural law is identical with universal and unchanging moral guidelines, in this case the prohibition of killing people.
(2) Subordinate principle: Under certain circumstances, this general principle cannot be applied without leading to morally undesirable consequences, such as killing someone in self-defence or killing innocent people if their deaths avoid a greater evil.

I will argue that this second principle is only meaningful if approached from a probabilistic perspective and not primarily from the point of view of the doctrine of double effect.[2] I will also take for granted that moral decision-making generally occurs from a position of epistemic disadvantage. This means that our assessment and application of the principles at stake can only be made once we have adequate knowledge of the relevant information about the action, its recipient, its end, its means, etc. But as we shall see, the empirical data we need to make a decision is in itself morally ambivalent, leading to doubt, and it is therefore necessary to strike a balance between conflicting views. This in turn implies that our reasons for applying principle (1) or principle (2) are based on probable or dialectical arguments and not demonstrative ones.[3]

In order to show that Vitoria's view is, in fact, not inconsistent, the broader context of his moral theory of justified killing has to be set out. (1) In the first place, his general ideas regarding the intrinsic value of human life will be discussed. (2) Then, a short account of the principle of double effect will set the stage for (3) a discussion of morally different kinds of killing, thus showing that homicide or justified killing are only two cases among many. (4) Finally, the case of killing innocent civilians as part of a just war will conclude the paper. I will suggest that Vitoria's account of killing non-combatant civilians should be read from a probabilistic perspective, thus hinting that the theory of double effect is insufficient to cope with this specific problem if, as Vitoria thinks, the killing of innocents can be morally justified.

2 The Broader Context: The Moral and Legal Value of Human Life

The point of departure for Vitoria's discussion about killing is that human life (a) has an intrinsic value that does not depend on human conventions and (b) it cannot be disposed of freely by other human beings, i.e. it is not subject to human ownership in the sense of unrestricted possession. The main reason for this assertion is based on Scripture: God created man according to his image. Being an image has to be understood as being a copy of sorts of the original, which means that the image,

---

[2]See MacIntyre 2014 for a short, if sympathetic, discussion of this doctrine.

[3]There is not space here to delve into the structure of 16th century probabilism, but one may consult Schüssler 2004 and Hacking 2006, 18–30.

i.e. man, is imperfect with respect to the original, i.e. God. The ontological inferiority of man also indicates a hierarchical top-down relation with God. The hierarchically superior (God) is causally and logically prior to the inferior, and hence, the reason for the latter's existence has to be the former. If the inferior depends on the superior, then the inferior is not, as it were, self-dependent in order to exist.

This is the model Vitoria uses in order to introduce relations among humans, thinking mainly of ownership and property, for which the generic Latin term is *dominium*. *Dominia* only hold between ontologically unequal *relata*, e.g. between father and son. If there are no ontological differences between the *relata*, then there would be no *dominium*. In particular, since being human is essentially equivalent to being alive, there would be no ontological difference between oneself and one's life. From this, it follows that humans do not own their lives in the proper sense of the word. Excluding such a *dominium* among humans, if ownership over human life is to be maintained, it must be God who owns it in the strictest sense of the word *dominium*.[4]

A basic moral directive is the consequence: if the intrinsic value of human life is the result of creation itself and if God is the true *dominus* of human life, it must be an absolute moral imperative not to kill anyone or to kill oneself, because it would have to be seen as an offence against God himself who is, as it were, the rightful owner thereof. However, humans are copies of sorts of the divine original, and it seems therefore that they can exert some sort of analogical, but not true and proper, ownership over their own life. This basic moral directive is intertwined with idea that preserving one's life constitutes a natural inclination, the cause of which is God himself: "[…] Human inclination as such is good. And therefore, it inclines to nothing evil or opposed to virtue".[5] The reason for this is simple enough: since God's act of creation is because of his all-encompassing goodness, there are no inclinations in nature that could possibly contradict his general design. This means that ultimately harming oneself and, by extension, someone else runs counter to the natural inclination of self-preservation.

Given that everyone uses his or her body basically for the business of being alive, it follows that the use of something entails certain rights over it. In fact, with the analogical conception of *dominium* in mind it can said that everyone has power (*potestas*) over his or her own body and its faculties. And following the almost canonical definition of *dominium* as a power or faculty regarding the rightful use of something,[6] one might conclude that everyone has a legitimate claim to preserve the physical integrity of what is being possessed, be it a material object, be it one's own body and its members. The two arguments, i.e. (a) that God is properly the true owner of human life and (b) that humans exert rightful powers over their lives, lead to the conclusion that taking someone's life has to be unlawful and immoral unless there was a very good reason to do so, e.g. a just cause. This point will be addressed below.

---

[4]See Brufau Prats 1989, 38–41. See also Tellkamp 2009.

[5]de Vitoria 1997, 63.

[6]Brufau Prats 1989, 38–41.

3 The Broader Context: Different Ways of Killing

Killing someone is not the clear-cut affair it might seem at first glance. The mere physical fact of causing someone's death, which in principle is open to public observation and scrutiny, is, as strangely as it may sound, morally ambivalent. This is due to the opaque nature of the intentions that specify a given action. Subject *A* could be the killer of *B*, because he had the intention of doing so, i.e. having the goal (*finis*) of killing *B* in mind. In this case, he would be committing homicide, which clearly runs counter to the general prohibition of killing. But *A* could kill *B* in a case of self-defence, which is a case that justifies killing an aggressor as a means of self-preservation, and therefore, the proper end of the act of killing is not per se killing someone, but self-preservation.

While it is clear that the intention of actively killing someone constitutes a morally reprehensible act, one should also think of other morally relevant cases. When Thomas Aquinas, for instance, discusses the importance of ignorance in relation to voluntary actions, he thinks that not having the explicit intention of killing someone might be morally dubious even if it was not intended. The case in point is that of someone who is chasing deer in the woods and accidentally kills his worst enemy without knowing that he was hiding there. Aquinas says that the fact of not being aware of his presence is irrelevant, because *ex post* the shooter agrees with the result of the unintended outcome, concluding that he would have shot him anyway had he known that he was hiding there.[7] Knowledge or the lack of it does not necessarily exculpate, and in fact it plays an important role in assessing the moral value of an action. When it comes to the moral worth of killing, it also seems to be essential to think of the passive and active components involved in voluntary action. While actively killing someone might be morally evil, not preventing someone's death, i.e. not actively bringing it about, but passively permitting it, might be equally evil. Yet the arguments regarding the active and passive causation of someone's death are weighted differently. In the *Relectio de homicidio*, which in fact is mostly about suicide, Vitoria notes that killing oneself is always wrong, because in such case the intention consists in ending one's life. Yet not seeking to prolong one's life or not preventing one's death, e.g. not wanting to take preventive measures, might be excusable, because doing whatever is necessary to live longer is not necessarily better than living a meaningful, but shorter life:

> I say that it is in no way lawful to shorten one's life. But it should be taken into account that […] it is one thing to shorten life and another thing not to prolong it. Second, it should be noted that although a man is obliged not to shorten his life, he is not however obliged to seek all means, even all lawful means, to lengthen it. This is very clear: for granted that

[7]Aquinas ST I-II q. 7 a. 8 c.: *Concomitanter quidem, quando ignorantia est de eo quod agitur, tamen, etiam si sciretur, nihilominus ageretur. Tunc enim ignorantia non inducit ad volendum ut hoc fiat, sed accidit simul esse aliquid factum et ignoratum, sicut, in exemplo posito, cum aliquis vellet quidem occidere hostem, sed ignorans occidit eum, putans occidere cervum. Et talis ignorantia non facit involuntarium […] quia non causat aliquid quod sit repugnans voluntati, sed facit non voluntarium, quia non potest esse actu volitum quod ignoratum est.* I will use the canonical custom of quoting the *Summa theologiae*.

> someone knows with certainty that the air in India is more healthful and temperate, and that he would live longer there than in his homeland, he is not obliged to sail to India. Indeed, he is not obliged to go from one city to another more healthful. Neither, indeed, did God intend us to be so worried about a long life.[8]

In stressing the difference between the obligation of not interrupting anyone's life and the right to not extend it beyond its natural course, Vitoria seems intent on showing that the *dominium* exerted over someone's life is limited by what the natural course of life indicates. Not being a precise boundary, Vitoria also supposes that everyone ought to be able to carry on with their business in an unimpeded manner.

War, however, stands in a clear contradiction to that idea, since in wars people almost necessarily are maimed and killed. The apparent conflict between the moral imperative to not to kill and the established practice of waging wars makes the call for good reasons all the more pressing. Vitoria thinks, and this topic has been dealt with in great detail in the literature, that the one good reason or just cause to accept the validity of a war, and hence killing and maiming people, is an aggression (*iniuria*) suffered, which in turn justifies self-defence with violent means: "[…] There is only one just cause for a war, namely when an aggression has been suffered (*iniuria accepta*)".[9] Analogous to the case of personal self-defence, the aggression a country or nation suffers, which Vitoria also calls *iniuria*, is a valid reason for it to defend itself, thus foreseeing the deaths of the ones attacking. Here, the death of members of the attacking party is the means or side effect of the process of re-establishing the original peace.

Personal or collective self-defence is, then, an action that aims at preserving one's own life; this constitutes the proper purpose of self-defence, while inflicting harm or causing death to members of the attacking party is not its proper end, but rather a means to an end or a side effect. In this short account, the venerable theory of double effect seems already to be implicit and it would be rewarding to briefly analyse Vitoria's stance regarding this, mostly with reference to his commentary on Aquinas's *Secunda Secundae* question 64 article 7, which deals with the question as to whether it is legitimate to kill someone while defending oneself.

4 Vitoria on Double Effect

In general, the doctrine of double effect is designed to come to terms with the fact that occasionally actions which are morally required can have an undesirable outcome. In particular, it establishes reasons to show that those outcomes can be morally permissible, although they are neither intended as such or even mandatory. Vitoria's commentary on Aquinas's passage of the *Secunda secundae* rests on some

[8]de Vitoria 1997, 103.
[9]de Vitoria 1981, 126.

of the principles laid out in *Summa Theologiae Prima secundae* in which the basic elements for moral conduct are outlined. In exploring the psychology of human choice, Aquinas himself arrives at an account that posits the bases of what ought to be done in order not only to act in a morally correct way, but also to provide the necessary conditions for salvation. Standard cases of moral conduct encompass moral actions as put forward in the Ten Commandments (notably not to kill) and those required to live a worthy life (e.g. giving alms). The basic structure of moral decision-making, however, has to come to terms with the fact that more often than not, morally required actions do have undesirable effects; this is an aspect that those actions share with moral prohibitions whose aim it is to avoid undesirable consequences.[10] As to the ambivalent character of moral actions, Aquinas in *Summa Theologiae Secunda secundae* q. 64 a. 7 states the following:

> A single act may have two effects, of which one alone is intended, whilst the other is incidental to that intention. But the way a moral act is to be classified depends on what is intended, not on what goes beyond such an intention, since this is merely incidental thereto […]. In the light of this distinction we can see that an act of self-defence may have two effects: the saving of one's own life, and the killing of the attacker. Now such an act of self-defence is not illegitimate just because the agent intends to save his own life, because it is natural for anything to want to preserve itself in being as far as it can. An act that is properly motivated may, nevertheless, become vitiated if it is not proportionate to the end intended. And this is why somebody who uses more violence than is necessary to defend himself will be doing something wrong. On the other hand, the controlled use of counter-violence constitutes legitimate self-defence, for according to the law *it is legitimate to answer force with force provided it goes no further than due defence requires*. Moreover a person is not obliged under pain of loss of eternal life to renounce the use of proportionate counter-force in order to avoid killing another, for a man is under greater obligation to care for his own life than for another's.[11]

The argument itself seems to be straightforward.[12] The intended end that leads to an action of self-defence is the preservation of one's own life, yet under certain circumstances this aim can only be achieved by harming someone else. That, however, is not the intended effect, but it is seen as *per accidens* regarding the end of self-preservation. Killing is not desirable in itself, because no human being can freely dispose of the life of someone else, but it can be justified as a side effect of the intended action. In this case, the action of self-defence has one main effect, i.e. self-preservation, and one accidental effect: killing someone. Intentionally killing someone (homicide) or doing so accidentally (self-defence) has the same observable outcome (the death of one person), but the intention that led either to commit homicide or to killing someone as a means of self-defence is not morally equivalent.

One salient aspect of this passage is that Aquinas introduces practical constraints on the theory of double effect, the most important of which is the principle of commensurability (*proportionalitas*), i.e. the idea that excessive force can render an action

[10]See also Boyle 2015, 465.

[11]Aquinas ST II-II a. 64 a. 7 c. transl. Aquinas 2006, 41–43.

[12]For a contemporary reading of war and self-defence in the light of Aquinas's theory, see Porter 2015.

illegitimate even if its purpose is morally acceptable. Another aspect is where killing in self-defence is legitimate by virtue of some kind of public authority, such as when a war has been declared or when a public person is being jeopardised. This constraint is apparently necessary so as to avoid a kind of slippery slope, since it would be possible to argue that any given morally valid end implies the justification of the means that lead to it. But this is clearly a consequence that Aquinas rejects.[13] To be sure, if someone is wielding a knife threatening to kill me, it would be permissible to defend myself, thus killing the attacker. If, however, someone were merely trespassing with no obvious threat to my life, the same action would certainly be excessive.

There seem to be several obvious complications with Aquinas's attempt to limit the scope of the theory of double effect. (a) The first is the difficulty of establishing excessive force or the lack of it. (b) The second is probably more relevant. Aquinas wishes to exclude the non-intended effects as a means to an end, saying they are accidents of the action. But, from a metaphysical point of view, accidents are always predicated of a substance, which means that they do bear a relevance on the description of it and, in this case, on the description of the substance of the action.[14] It seems therefore that foreseeable side effects, which are mainly seen as means to an end, do play a role in the process of deciding for or against a given course of action. Clearly, the unintended effect cannot be simply deemed beyond the scope of any intended outcome; rather, it must be a crucial part of the moral decision-making process. After all, self-defence would appear to imply the possibility of harming or even killing an aggressor, which albeit not necessary, is certainly foreseeable.

Francisco de Vitoria, in commenting on these very passages of the *Secunda Secundae,* is very well aware of some of the problems just mentioned, and in fact, his analysis of double effect leads to a form of moral argumentation that emphasises the foreseeable and morally justifiable side effects of an action. Since this article is concerned with the killing of innocents in the course of a just war, it is crucial to first point out the basic arguments concerning the question whether it is legitimate to kill in self-defence. In this respect, Vitoria intends to elucidate the following three conclusions:

(1) "It is not unlawful to kill an attacker".
(2) "It is lawful to kill another in self-defence".
(3) "It is not lawful to kill a man in revenge (*tamquam in vindictam*) while defending oneself".[15]

As to (1), Vitoria, as did Aquinas, immediately sees this basic moral principle in the light of the distinction between intended ends and non-intended effects. Only self-preservation has to count as the intended essential effect of self-defence, but not

[13]Aquinas ST I-II q. 13 a. 6 ad 1.

[14]The metaphysics of the moral action is laid out in detail in Aquinas ST I-II qq. 18–21. Here, he distinguishes the species of the act in virtue of its object and its concomitant aspects which he calls the circumstances.

[15]de Vitoria 1997, 193.

per se the death of the aggressor. Since such an outcome would be *praeter intentionem*, the action leading to the death of the aggressor would not be imputable from a moral point of view. In this respect, Vitoria seems to conflate the distinction between killing someone as a means to an end and killing someone as the unintended outcome while striving for an end. The reason for this conflation is that choosing ends and means always implies intention and voluntary action, which means that the unintended outcome would have to be a part of the rational decision-making regarding a particular action.

Insofar as killing is considered a means for self-preservation, another question arises, namely whether the means to an end are necessary in order to obtain it or whether they are merely contingent. Non-necessary means would point to a range of possibilities that lead to the intended end, so that, in the case of self-defence, there would not be only one way to achieve the end, but potentially many. It appears that Vitoria has this in mind when discussing various scenarios that relate to the choice of the means for an intended end, thus encompassing the need to think about the reasonably foreseeable consequences of the means.

Vitoria uses the principle of commensurability under the assumption that it is generally difficult to establish excessive force. If it is possible to use less force to achieve an end, then this has to be preferred. Hence, the question arises as to whether it would be better to flee in the face of an aggression rather than to actively engage in self-defence:

> If I can defend myself by fleeing from an attacker, am I obliged to flee or can I stand fast and kill him? The doubt is evident, because if I can save myself and him without either of us dying, it seems uncharitable to kill and send him to hell, and thus it seems that I am obliged to flee.
>
> The answer is that when by fleeing a person would suffer harm, in such a way that, if he were to flee, he would lose something great, for example, honour, 'as [would be the case] if he were a knight,' then he is not obliged to flee. Especially if he is a man of honour whose honour is in question, and it would be a great stain on his reputation were he to flee. It seems certain that he would not be obliged to flee, because dishonour to a nobleman is a greater harm than the loss of his home.[16]

There is, then, neither an obligation to flee from the aggressor nor an obligation to kill him, all of which highlights a major point: that the means for an intended end can be modified and that a consideration of the broader picture of what is at stake is required, for example when fleeing would stain the honour of the one being attacked.[17] Ultimately, it seems that for Vitoria the non-intended and nonetheless willed effect of an action, such as the death of an attacker, is mostly an issue related

[16]de Vitoria 1997, 201.

[17]This line of argument is also applied to the apparently unrelated question as to whether it is legitimate to pre-emptively kill enemies. This is an interesting case analogous to the killing of innocent people insofar as neither is actively involved in an aggression that would justify killing in the name of self-defence. Preventive killing of enemies is contrary to self-defence "within the bounds of blameless defence" (*cum moderamine inculpatae tutelae*), cf. de Vitoria 1997, 148.

to moral decision-making inasmuch as he sees this outcome as a non-necessary means to an end and because he clearly applies certain epistemic conditions in probabilistic terms. Hence, if the reasonable course of action could exclude the death of the attacker and still preserve one's life, then, in the light of the relevant information, it would be unlawful to kill him.

5 Epistemic Constraints

The preceding remarks which relate to Vitoria's *Commentary on the Secunda Secundae* are only clear at first glance, in that they suggest that in any given instance the defender somehow knows how to proceed. Under real-world conditions, however, clear-cut judgments regarding observable facts are quite hard to come by, mostly because of certain epistemic constraints every agent is usually faced with whenever an observable fact has to be interpreted with regard to its moral value. Relevant questions would, for instance, involve the following:

(1) Is what the agent observes in fact a case of aggression?
(2) If so, is it possible to predict its outcome? That is to say, is it possible to know, before it actually happens, whether the aggression will endanger the defender's life?
(3) Assuming that it does endanger his or her life, is it possible to foresee whether killing the attacker is the only way to avoid harm? This question points at the need to posit criteria that would help to reasonably anticipate future events as a consequence of a present action.[18]
(4) Another question deals with the normative apparatus that underlies moral decision-making. Although self-preservation overrides the life of the attacker, killing that person would still require a thorough explanation as to why killing him had to be preferred over, say, immobilising him.

The epistemic constraints in the process of moral decision-making highlight at least two underlying issues. Firstly, such decision-making is dependent on a structured set of information on the context and the agent's motivation in bringing about the action. Secondly, such actions are based on the certainty of moral rules. Since the epistemic component of moral decision-making involves facing uncertainties in order to comply with objectively valid rules, it seems that an additional principle is required that would assist in making tough choices. Vitoria does in fact provide a principle that offers certainty when it is hard to come by through regular moral and legal reasoning: it is the inner court of conscience (*conscientia*).

[18]Cf. de Vitoria 1934: 304.

6 Conscience and Justified Scruples

Conscience delivers an answer to epistemic constraints that usually make the application of objective standards difficult or even impossible. Given this kind of uncertainty, it follows that moral choices can be doubtful even if they seem to be based on a clear set of rules. Also, when doubts arise, choosing between alternative scenarios appears to imply a choice between contradicting moral rules even if both are viewed as valid. The main question is how to decide between one set of rules or another, if (a) they are equally convincing or if (b) one is morally more certain than the other. The need to identify relevant rules and to decide which one to apply is more likely to leave the agent confused and perplexed. One such case is, for instance, the fulfilment of marital duties in the event that the husband doubts whether it is in fact his wife he is dealing with.[19] Fulfilling his marital duties would be a sin if she is not his wife, and not fulfilling them would also be sin if she is in fact his wife.

One way to solve this impasse is to ask whether both alternatives are equally doubtful from the point of view of stating the facts. It is probably within the husband's power to confirm that the woman next to him is actually his wife. More important, however, is to decide whether the moral principles at stake are of equal value, which in the present case might not be as problematic as in others. But if one has to lie in order to prevent a murder, the lie is morally more acceptable than the murder itself, since the first is a venial and the second a mortal sin.[20] However, if both alternatives were equally challenging, e.g. if both were to lead to mortal sins, then credence should be given to a deciding authority, such as a prelate, because obeying him is more certain than not obeying him.[21] Even so, it is possible to cast doubts on the prelate's judgment, when, for instance, he is known to be forgetful thus not remembering that on a specific day it is mandatory to fast.

It is, then, possible to understand the validity of one of the alternatives based on judgement or authority, but matters are more problematic when neither is certain. In this case, Vitoria puts the emphasis on the foreseeable effects of doing one thing or the other:

> The danger has always to be considered and whether it is greater and more severe in one case, such as when someone doubts whether today eating meat is not permitted, while

[19]de Vitoria 2015, 234: *Si autem neutra pars sit tuta, v. g. maritus dubitat hanc haec sit uxor eius et dubitat quia reddo debitum pecco, si non reddo etiam pecco; et supponamus quod iste non scit deponere dubium, quid tune est faciendum cum non debeat esse perplexus?".*

[20]de Vitoria 2015, 234: *[…] Tunc magis debeo inelinare in partem illam ubi minus periculum est, quia esse homicidam est peceatum mortale, mentiri autem veniale, si mentiret ut non pecearet quia ex alia parte incurreret peccatum mortale.*

[21]de Vitoria 2015, 234–235: *Sed si ex utraque parte sit periculum mortale, tunc comparanda sunt peccata inter se et declinandum esset in minus, v. g. si aliquis religiosus videt quod iste homo moritur fame et praelatus iubet sub pracepto quod non dem illi panem sunt illi pro utraque parte dubia. Sed tamen magis credo quod teneor oboedire praelato, tunc dico quod potest.*

> fearing that he will die [i.e. when he does not eat–J.T.] In this case he should bow to his fear and eat rather than abstain.[22]

Fear (*formido*) is a powerful factor that can cast doubt (*scrupulus*) on one's own moral judgements, and it can change the process of moral decision-making so as to morally justify it. This means that a less certain principle can be chosen even if a more certain principle is apparently required.[23]

Those examples suggest that Vitoria to some extent anticipates the probabilistic method which was famously advanced by the Dominican Bartolomé de Medina (1528–1580) a few decades later, which, in a nutshell, states that "if there is a probable opinion, it is legitimate to follow it, even though the opposite [opinion] is more probable".[24] Since in a given situation two alternatives might be equally certain or equally uncertain, the deciding element is the doubt regarding the moral viability of one course of action over another, e.g. if I have justified doubts as to whether someone has committed a crime, I should treat him as if he had not committed it.[25]

7 Combatants and Non-combatants

So far it has been shown that the principle of self-defence justifies the killing of an aggressor when certain caveats are taken into account, especially the principle of commensurability which requires the defending party to ponder whether killing is the only alternative in the face of an aggression. It has also been shown that the reasons that would justify the attacker's death are not a necessary consequence of objective standards, such as laws, taking into account instead the inner court of conscience, which establishes an instrument for moral decision-making based on epistemic and moral certainties. The standard cases Vitoria discusses in this respect deal with issues that are a matter of public rules (such as fasting during Lent) and which can be verified

---

[22]de Vitoria 2015, 238: *[...] Semper est considerandum periculum et si pro una parte sit maius et gravius, ut si quis dubitat quod hodie non licet comedere carnes, sed habet formidinem quod moriretur tunc potius debet inclinari in formidinem, et comedere quam abstinere. The translations of this text are my own.*

[23]From Vitoria's perspective, another interesting case is that of prostitution, which requires the pondering of various moral alternatives; cf. de Vitoria 1934, 163: *[...] Dare stipendium scorto non est malum nisi ex fine, quia datio de se est bona, nec illa ideo quod sit meretrix perdit jus* ad hoc *quod non possit sibi aliquid dari. Unde si datio fiat ad movendum illam ad fornicationem, est mala, et argente peccat mortaliter; sicut si diceret, veni in domum meam, et dabo tibi duos argenteos; etiam quidquid aliud faciat, est malum si propter talem finem faciat. Secundo dico, quod peracta re, id est post fornicationem, si dat aliquid tamquam mercedem, bene potest ei licite dare, et non est peccatum, quia jam illic finis non est malus.* See also Decock 2013, 432–457.

[24]de Medina 1586, 179a. For a thorough analysis of probabilistic moral reasoning, see again Schüssler 2004.

[25]This type of argument proved to be quite important regarding the legitimacy of the conquest of the American continent. de Vitoria 1934, 101: *[...] Melior est conditio possidentis in dubiis.* See also Schüssler 2006.

even if contradicting information comes into play. The role a publicly trusted authority plays in resolving eventual conflicts should be recalled, as well as the possibility of rejecting reasons given in favour of apparently less certain principles.[26]

A special case which differs from the cases discussed above is the justification of killing innocents in the course of a just war. Again, killing is generally admissible only if based on sound reasons, a just cause, and public authority. Although it seems to be an essential characteristic of wars that people are killed, killing in a war is morally justified only if it occurs in a just war, i.e. if it has a just cause, which is when a nation has suffered an aggression. This assumption leads to the further supposition that during a war someone can only be killed if he or she has played an active part in the aggression, e.g. a commanding officer or the soldiers who obey his orders. In any case, the non-combatant part of the population of the nation that carried out the aggression has explicitly to be left alone. They have not, as Vitoria says, done anything wrong, and hence, they play no active part in the aggression: "The reason for a just war is an aggression (*iniuria*) […]. But the innocent has done nothing wrong. Therefore [it is not appropriate to wage war against them]".[27]

The distinction between combatants and non-combatants—Vitoria uses the terms *nocens* and *innocens*—is of the utmost importance, since it establishes who is an actual attacker and who is not. Yet this distinction—here the evil combatants, there the otherwise blameless civilians—is not primarily moral; it serves instead as a way to distinguish that part of the population that actively participates in combat and that carries weapons from the part of the population that does not. *Innocentes* are persons who, as a matter of fact, do not or cannot carry weapons and who, consequently, do not fight, such as women and children. Non-combatants by definition play no active role during the aggression, and hence, they do not cause *iniuria*, which is the main reason to justify killing someone. Consequently, it seems that no argument can be put forward in order to justify the death of innocents, even if the war itself is being regarded as just.

The argument presupposes that the justice of a war can be established, even though the epistemic constraints mentioned above regarding the assessment of an aggression are basically the same. More often than not, the reasons (*causae iustae*) are not easy to assess and they might even be based on fallacious arguments. Given this uncertainty, the presumed rightful actions during a war (*ius in bello*) are doubtful whenever they have an impact on the civilian population. For instance, when you come to think of recent debates about drone strikes, which have killed scores of civilians, the almost intuitive reaction is that something unjust has happened when people unrelated to combat die. Vitoria certainly does not rely on this sort of moral sentiment; instead, he wishes to establish grounds that would show under which circumstances the death of innocents can be considered as morally

[26]Vitoria thinks that priests are a more trusted source of normative certainty than are jurists; see de Vitoria 1952, 364: *Profecto opinio est verissima, et ita quod opposita, quantumcumque omnes canonistae convenirent in illam opinionem, esset falsissima, quia in his quae sunt in foro conscientiae, standum est opinioni theologorum, et non canonistarum.*

[27]de Vitoria 1981, 164: *Fundamentum iusti belli est iniuria […]. Sed innocens nihil malum fecit. Ergo [non licet bello uti contra illum].*

justifiable. The following points are taken from *Relectio de iure belli* and the *Commentary on the Secunda Secundae*:

(1) It is per se inadmissible to kill an innocent, non-combatant person directly and intentionally, and Vitoria stresses that "it is obvious that against those who do us no harm, it is not legitimate to draw the sword against them, because killing innocents is against natural rights". Exercising its political authority, the republic itself is not justified to take action against innocents, even if they happen to be on the side of the enemy: "The republic is not allowed to punish innocents for the crimes of the enemies (*malorum*). Hence, based on an aggression of the enemy, killing the innocents among the enemy is not permitted".[28] This holds true also in any post-war order in the sense that retaliating against the civilian population is out of the question once victory has been achieved.[29]

(2) Yet it is a matter of fact that in wars innocent people often die, probably, as Vitoria would argue, as the unintended outcome of fighting the enemy. This, however, raises the related question as to the moral justification of their deaths, whether or not in the course of a just war. Since, as the previous quote shows, innocents cannot be targeted directly and intentionally, it is again clear that their death is potentially justifiable within the framework of the theory of double effect, i.e. if it is an accidental and not intended consequence of battle. There are according to Vitoria two ways to morally justify such outcome:

    (a) When it is impossible to distinguish between combatants and non-combatants, e.g. when the use of heavy artillery is advised in order to conquer a city.[30]
    (b) When this kind of warfare quite generally leads directly to military victory.[31]

[28]de Vitoria 1981, 300: *Non licet in republica pro delictis malorum punire innocentes. Ergo etiam nec pro iniuria malorum non licet interficere innocentes apud hostes.*

[29]de Vitoria 1981, 300: *Licet fortasse posset defendi quod in tali casu licet eos interficere, tamen credo quod nullo modo licet, quia non sunt facienda mala ut vitentur etiam alia mala maiora. Et intolerabile est profecto quod occidatur aliquis pro peccato futuro. Et primum sunt multa alia remedia ad cavendum in futurum ab illis, ut captivitas, exilium,* etc. *item non licet hoc in propriis civibus, occidere aliquem pro peccato futuro. Ergo non licet in extraneos. Non dubito de hoc.*

[30]de Vitoria 1981, 166: *Per accidens autem etiam scienter aliquando licet interficere innocentes, puta cum oppugnatur arx aut civilas iuste, in qua tamen constat esse multos innocentes nec possunt machinae solvi vel alia tela vel ignis aedificiis subici quin etiam opprimantur innocentes sicut nocentes.* Obviously the issue of using the civilian population as a human shield springs into mind.

[31]de Vitoria 1981, 166: *Et tandem nunquam videtur licitum opprimere innocentes etiam per accidens et praeter intentionem, nisi quando [ad] bellum iustum expedit et geri aliter non potest [...].*

8 Probabilism and the Limits of Double Effect

The preceding remarks point at a fundamental drawback in Vitoria's argumentation, and hence, the validity of double effect theorising has to be called into question, especially with regard to the moral justification of killing innocents in a just war. In particular, if spelt out, the problem is as follows:

(1) Killing innocent people, i.e. non-combatants, in a just war cannot be justified, because they do not fulfil the requirement of having provided legitimate reasons for self-defence.
(2) Therefore, if they have not done any harm, no action can be taken against them.
(3) Yet, and contrary to (1) and (2) Vitoria claims, and apparently, this is in agreement with the theory of double effect that innocents can justifiably be killed if their deaths are not the intended but rather the accidental consequence of waging a just war.

In order to see what is wrong with (3), it is useful to revisit the theory of double effect, which "is often invoked to explain the permissibility of an action that causes a serious harm, such as the death of a human being, as a side effect of promoting some good aim".[32] As discussed above, Thomas Aquinas considers self-defence as an action that can have such a double effect: in intending to preserve one's own life (which is a moral obligation), it is permissible to take the life of the attacker (which is undesirable and yet permissible).[33] Clearly, the proper intention of preserving one's life makes the side effect morally acceptable.

From the point of view of Aquinas's moral theory, there are reasons to believe that the doctrine of double effect as such is flawed, mainly because it quite generally runs counter to his own theory of the goodness of the moral act, which, in order to be emphatically good, has to be completely good, i.e. all of its constitutive elements have to come together: the intention, the means, the circumstances, the external, observable action and the real, observable outcome. If only one of those aspects does not obtain, the action cannot be considered as morally good, at least not emphatically.[34] In his lectures on those very passages from *Summa theolgiae Prima secundae* question 19, Vitoria stresses the idea that the morality of the intended aim is the overarching criterion, while the means that lead to it also play a pivotal role. Both the end and the means have to be the result of rational choice, and hence, both have to be susceptible to being evaluated from a moral point of view. From a normative perspective, situations may be solved by recurring not only to one, but to two moral principles, which, however, contradict each other:

---

[32]MacIntyre 2014.

[33]Aquinas ST II-II q. 64 a. 7.

[34]In ST I-II q. 19 a. 6 ad 1 Aquinas quotes Ps.-Dionysius's famous saying from *De divinis nominibus* IV that "good is caused by a complete cause, while evil [is caused] by particular defects" (*bonum causatur ex integra causa, malum autem ex singularibus defectibus*).

> Let us assume that Peter now loves God above all else and that he thereafter judges that he has to love his neighbour and that he has to steal for that end. Therefore, it is argued: the love of God is a present good. Consequently, a volition in accordance with that judgment is good. From the love of God follows the love for the neighbour, which is good and from that love follows the theft.[35]

The consequence is that stealing is admissible based on the love for God, but Vitoria cannot endorse such a conclusion, mostly because the moral action has to be evaluated in its entirety and not only with regard to the intended end:

> What do we say to this argument? Answer: supposing there is a distinction between the volition of the means that somehow are necessary and somehow not, [it follows that] the good volition of the end is good, [even] if the means are not necessary; but if it leads to the volition of bad means, then it is bad [i.e. even if the intended end is good-J.T.]. This is obvious, because it [i.e. the volition-J.T.] necessitates knowingly and it cannot remain without sin.[36]

From this, Vitoria concludes that, even if the end intended necessitates the corresponding volition, the means that lead to it are not themselves as necessary, and hence, choosing one means or another can equally lead to the end, while one may be regarded as morally bad and the other not:

> [...] One might say that from the intention which necessarily leads to an end, no [necessary] election of the means is the consequence, because those means contain the roots of evil and hence they are not necessary.[37]

One of the main issues that the preceding quotes address is a dialectical process of sorts that helps to clarify the moral principles at stake. Vitoria himself often considers practical moral issues to be problematic—in fact he often refers to *dubia* —and that they can be resolved by recurring to what is most probable (or plausible) in a concrete situation. As Aristotle already pointed out in *Topics*, *éndoxa* or probable arguments are not per se true, but they are made plausible by the fact that many or the wisest endorse them.[38] The relevant point in trying to resolve a moral dilemma is that it is possible to entertain various probable arguments simultaneously regarding the evaluation of one and the same action so that, in the end, one

---

[35]de Vitoria 2015, 244–246: *[...] Ponamus quod Petrus nunc diligat Deum super omnia et postea iudicat quod est diligendus proximus et quod subveniendum est illi et quod* ad hoc *oportet furari. Tunc arguitur: diligere Deum est bonum nunc. Ergo volitio conformis illi iudicio est bona. Et ex illa dilectione Dei sequitur dilectio proximi quae est bona, et ex illa dilectione sequitur furtum.*

[36]de Vitoria 2015, 246: *Quid ergo dicemus ad argumentum? Respondetur quod, supposita distinctio quod volitio medii aliquo modo necessitatur et aliquo modo non, volitio finis bona, si medium non necessitat, est bona; si autem necessitat ad volitionem mali medii, est mala. Patet quia necessitat scienter et non potest stare sine peccato [...].*

[37]de Vitoria 2015, 246: *[...] Potest dici quod forte ex intentione necessaria finis non sequitur electio medii, quia in tali medio apparet ratio mali, et sic non necessitor.*

[38]Aristotle, *Topics* 100b20. See also Schüssler 2015.

opinion might be endorsed, not because it is more probable than another, but because it does not go against one's conscience.

Since Vitoria's arguments regarding the justified killing of innocents mirror his general stance on killing intentionally—be it directly, be it as the side effect of an intended act—this point becomes especially relevant. On the one hand, it is imperative to recognise the overarching, general moral principle that intentionally killing people is inadmissible. This is to say that it is unacceptable to just walk around killing people. Yet Vitoria thinks that there are certain conditions under which killing someone can be justified, e.g. when justice has to be restored, such as in the case of a publically sanctioned death penalty (which Vitoria endorses), or when it is a clear case of self-defence. These cases do not present intrinsic problems for Vitoria, and they are compatible with his overall idea that *iniuria* to the community or to the individual morally justifies the killing of the aggressor.

This, however, cannot be said of the non-combatant part of a nation that has caused *iniuria* to another and against which the attacked nation wages a just war. As we have seen, for Vitoria it is a given that all individuals not participating actively in battle are beyond the scope of a justified reprisal, which applies only to soldiers and commanders. Again, in no case is it legitimate or moral to kill innocents, i.e. civilians, because the conditions established by the causes for a just war cannot be applied to them, quite simply because otherwise they would not be innocent. And yet Vitoria admits that innocents can be targeted accidentally during a bombardment, for instance in order to secure military victory.

The tension in this account is obvious, and it raises the equally obvious question as to whether Vitoria's theory of justified killing is inconsistent, for at least two reasons:

(1) First, to what extent can the death of innocents be described as accidental, when it is explicitly assumed that victory cannot be obtained otherwise? Contrary to Vitoria's arguments, bombardments seem to play an essential role in military strategy, and hence, it can be reasonably foreseen that civilians will come to harm, when a town is subjected to indiscriminate shelling.
(2) Second, even if it is assumed that the death of innocents is indeed accidental, it still is difficult to understand how it cannot be part of military planning. Every country and every city has inhabitants that are not actively involved in fighting, and military strategy has to take this into account and try at least to mitigate the impact on the civilian population.

As it is, one might still be tempted to solve this problem by applying the doctrine of double effect. In order to do good, some evil has to be done as well, and given the morally right intention, the negative effects are justifiable, although are not in themselves desirable. It would seem to be a case of ends justifying the means. Yet Vitoria endorses Aquinas's integral view of the moral act and, hence, that no intention, however good, should contravene the revered principle that no evil

should be done in order to bring about a good.[39] If the foreseen negative side effect is considered as a means to an end, then it should in fact be avoided.

At this point, it would be possible to construe Vitoria's theory of moral decision-making differently: if the subjects involved in an action have adequate knowledge of the concrete situation as well as an adequate knowledge of the general moral principles at stake, then they should be able to weigh up whether one moral principle or another is applicable, even if the both are not strictly equivalent. If this is so, Vitoria would seem to endorse a view according to which the general moral principle (not to kill innocents) is superseded by another principle (to obtain military victory for the sake of the common good, thus requiring the killing of innocents). This shift of principles can help explain how, under given circumstances, the harm done to civilians would be the lesser evil, i.e. vis-à-vis not killing them.

Yet again this argument is problematic, because it might lead to some sort of moral laxism: every time a general and more certain principle fails, it would be possible to come up with another principle that, under the current circumstances, is more plausible. As to this objection, two points have to be made. The first is that all moral rules which are valid in the court of conscience also have to be congruent with natural law. This, however, can be said of both principles, i.e. (a) not killing innocents and (b) preserving the common good which, in the light of the first, is a less certain and derivative moral principle. Second, this less certain moral principle can be construed from the point of view of utility; as Vitoria seems to imply, a quantitative criterion can be chosen, such as harming the fewest number of people, even if harming innocent people has to be chosen as well. Assuming that in a war the civilian population will always be affected, it might therefore be reasonable to introduce the idea that the number of those affected should be kept small and that if a certain number of people are in fact affected, the greater benefit of the community has to outweigh the damage inflicted. It seems, then, that Vitoria wishes to endorse a view according to which the greatest good for the greatest number is a certain moral guideline amidst the murky choices warring nations are faced with.

This is not to say that we should view Vitoria as a moral consequentialist; he is not. Yet his theory allows for the possibility of positively assessing the principle of utility, abandoning the more certain general rule of not killing innocent people. It is important to note that the principle of utility does not invalidate the general rule of not killing innocent people; rather, it gives way to a theory of moral choice that, by taking into account probabilistic reasoning, is more complex than the unequivocal application of general rules. In the end, if the less certain moral principle of utility leads to anything, it should help us reassess Vitoria's theory of moral choice in the sense that not only the acknowledgement of universal principles is needed, but also —crucially—the need to refrain from using those principles in favour of less certain moral principles.

---

[39] In reference to Romans 3, 8 Aquinas discusses the related issue of suicide; cf. Aquinas ST II-II q. 64 a. 5 c.: "[...] Nobody is entitled to kill himself for fear of consenting to sin, because *evil may not be done that good may come* [...]". Trans. in Aquinas 2006, 35.

References

Sources

Aquinas T (2006) Summa Theologiae, vol 38: Injustice (2a2ae. 63–79) (trans: Marcus Lefébure OP). Cambridge University Press, Cambridge

de Medina B (1586) Expositio in Primam Secundae Doctoris D. Thomae Aquinatis. Typis Comini Venturae et Sociorum, Bergomi

de Vitoria F (1934) Comentarios a la Secunda secundae de Santo Tomás, tomo III: De Justitia (qq. 57–66). In: de Heredia VB (ed). Biblioteca de Teólogos Españoles, Salamanca

de Vitoria F (1952) Comentarios a la Secunda secundae de Santo Tomás, tomo VI: De virtute temperantiae-De prophetia-De vita active et contemplative-De statibus hominum (qq. 141–189). In: de Heredia (ed). Biblioteca de Teólogos Españoles, Salamanca

de Vitoria F (1981) Relectio de Iure Belli o Paz Dinámica. Escuela Española de la Paz primera generación 1526–1560. In: Pereña L et al (eds). CSIC, Madrid

de Vitoria F (1997) Relection on Homicide and Commentary on Summa theologiae IIa-IIa q. 64 (Thomas Aquinas) (trans: Doyle JP). Marquette University Press, Milwaukee

de Vitoria F (2015) De actibus humanis. Sobre los actos humanos. In: Sarmiento A (ed). Frommann-Holzboog, Stuttgart/Bad Cannstatt

Secondary Literature

Boyle Joseph (2015) Intention, permissibility, and the structure of agency. Am Catholic Philos Q 89:461–478

Brufau Prats J (1989) La Escuela de Salamanca ante el descubrimiento del Nuevo Mundo. Editorial San Esteban, Salamanca

Decock W (2013) Theologians and Contract Law. The Moral Transformation of the Ius Commune (ca. 1500–1650). Nijhoff, Leiden

Hacking I (2006) The emergence of probability. A philosophical study of early ideas about probability, induction and statistical inference. Cambridge University Press, Cambridge

MacIntyre A (2014) Doctrine of double effect. Stanford Encyclopedia of Philosophy. http://plato.stanford.edu/archives/win2014/entries/doubleeffect/. Accessed 10 July 2016

Porter J (2015) Choice, causality, and relation: aquinas's analysis of the moral act and the doctrine of double effect. Am Catholic Philos Q 89:479–504

Schüssler R (2004) Moral im Zweifel. Vol. 1: Die scholastische Theorie des Entscheidens unter moralischer Unsicherheit. Mentis, Paderborn

Schüssler R (2006) Moral self-ownership and ius possessionis in late scholastics. In: Mäkinen V, Korkman P (eds) Transformations in medieval and early-modern rights discourse. Springer, Dordrecht, pp 149–172

Schüssler R (2015) Probability in medieval and renaissance philosophy. Stanford Encyclopedia of Philosophy. http://plato.stanford.edu/archives/spr2015/entries/probability-medieval-renaissance/. Accessed 10 July 2016

Tellkamp JA (2009) Ius est idem quod dominium: Conrado Summenhart, Francisco de Vitoria y la Conquista de América. Veritas 54:34–51

Part III
The Ambiguous Modernity of Vitoria's Theological and Economical Thoughts

Chapter 10
Francisco de Vitoria and the Postmodern Grand Critique of International Law

Pablo Zapatero Miguel

Abstract Although quasi-hagiographic studies of Francisco de Vitoria are, fortunately, longer in fashion, the standardization of historiographical analysis regarding Francisco de Vitoria is as yet incomplete. Postmodern critics of international law are currently proposing an alternative history of international law, using Francisco de Vitoria extensively as a springboard for a new grand and overarching narrative of international law. Within such narrative, international law was a mere instrument of colonial oppression invented by Vitoria and others at the time of the encounter of the Old and New Worlds and continues to be so to the present day. This article aims to contextualize the ideas of Vitoria and take issue with this argument, framing Vitoria as an honourable moderate thinker of his time.

1 Framing a Black Friar

Two centuries after Charles V adopted the motto *Plus Ultra* (1516), foreshadowing the extension of his rule beyond the "Pillars of Hercules" (Gibraltar) to the New World, Giovanni Battista Tiepolo painted *The Apotheosis of Spain* (1764) on the ceiling of the Throne Room at the Royal Palace in Madrid.[1] The fresco allegorically depicts the Spanish monarchy as a voluptuous woman with the Pillars of Hercules on one side and a hooded man on the other, along with other elements including Moors and American Indians. The painting ostensibly celebrates the glory of Spain.

Almost two centuries later, the ceiling of one of the Halls of the *Palace des Nations* (Geneva) was painted by Jose María Sert with a decidedly different take: *The Lesson of Salamanca* (1935–1936). The mural depicts five colossi (the five continents) uniting their hands. On one side of the mural, some professors are in discussion surrounded by attentive and studious disciples. In the classic Spanish

[1]See, for example, Rosenthal 1971, 204–228.

P. Zapatero Miguel (✉)
Carlos III University of Madrid, Getafe, Spain
e-mail: pablo.zapatero@uc3m.es

J.M. Beneyto and J. Corti Varela (eds.), *At the Origins of Modernity*,
Studies in the History of Law and Justice 10, DOI 10.1007/978-3-319-62998-8_10

tradition of burlesque, the composition includes a considerable number of donkeys standing amongst the scholars, by which we are meant to understand that some did not adequately grasp the lesson.

This later mural was unveiled in October 1936, three months after the Spanish Civil War had begun as the prelude to World War II. After the nightmare of the worldwide conflict and the fall of fascism in most parts of Europe except Spain, a radical revamping of the institutional structures of international law was sought. At that moment, the idea of a world political community with common rules for all shone brightly as a necessary collective project for a post-war world. And here, the figure of Francisco de Vitoria (1483–1546) became a political and moral reference for a whole new generation called on to construct a new international legal order. As a result, a significant portion of early contemporary studies on Francisco de Vitoria focussed on the international law aspects of his thinking. However, this has too often meant simply adapting doctrines of the past to present-day categories of international law.[2]

There is a risk of decontextualization when classifying circumstances of the past under concepts and measures pertaining to the modern legal culture. Paraphrasing Pagden:

> by re-describing the battles of the early modern world in modern terms, by making Francisco de Vitoria the remote ancestor of the Charter of the United Nations or the Bill of Rights, the specificity of the conflict is lost, and with it the possibility of its significance as a process over time.[3]

Certainly, some of these early contemporary studies seriously called for a new wave of research perspectives on the Black Friar. As a result, nowadays, there is a healthy amount of work being currently done on Vitoria with more nuanced visions. In this regard, after the period of quasi-hagiographic studies, work on the Black Friar finally appears to have entered the realm of standard historical analysis. However, although eulogies may be over, the standardization of historiographical approaches to the study of Vitoria is still incomplete.

2 The New Revisionism

Currently, a new trend of historical revisionism produces studies that frame Vitoria in a diametrically opposite vein to those previous exercises. In these studies, the Black Friar is used as the springboard for an "alternative history of international law". The idea behind this new interpretation is simple but quite telling: Francisco de Vitoria is, it is argued, the first legitimizer of *colonialism* and a key intellectual figure behind the "colonial origins of international law". This approach has been taken by several studies, particularly in the postmodern academic orbit. Henry

---

[2]See particularly Pérez Luño 1992, 31.

[3]Pagden 1994, x.

Mechoulan, for example, argues that all of Vitoria's arguments can be summarized by two imperatives: (1) that the Spanish have exclusive title to the despoilment of Amerindian wealth and (2) that there is a right and a duty to see to the salvation of Amerindian souls. In the striking words of this author, the Dominican′s "real genius" is the "art of camouflaging" the justification of a fact—colonization—by appealing to "interhuman sociability".[4]

Other highly critical arguments on Vitoria can be found in the field of American Indian legal studies. For example, in his book *The American Indian in Western Legal Thought*, Richard Williams defines "Victoria" (sic) as "the first articulator of a European discourse of conquest founded on secularly rationalizable norms and values". In the opinion of this author, the Black Friar "justified the extension of Western power over the American Indians as an imperative of the European's vision of truth".[5] However, it is easy to agree with Cavallar that this totalizing "Western legal discourse" assumed by Williams incurs "the fallacy of *another great narrative*" by constructing "a meta-narrative of modern history".[6] Interestingly, some of these studies are connected with the literature of the so-called Third World Approaches to International Law (TWAIL).[7] As Mutua points out, the *raison d'etre* of TWAIL is founded on, among other sources, a much quoted passage by Mohamed Bedjaoui, a judge of the International Court of Justice[8]: "classical international law…consisted of a set of rules with a geographical bias (it was a European law), a religious-ethical aspiration (it was a Christian law), an economic motivation (it was a mercantilist law), and political aims (it was an *imperialist law*)".[9] Under this rationale, international law is "premised on Europe as the centre, Christianity as the basis for civilization, capitalism as innate in humans, and imperialism as a necessity".[10]

The broad argument of these studies is that international law is an inherently imperialist construct which stretches from the sixteenth century to the present day. The works of Antony Anghie are perhaps among the most interesting and sophisticated examples of this postmodern narrative. This former research assistant of Christopher Weeramantry began writing on the colonial origins of international law in an article (*The Heart of my home* 1993 resulting from participation in the Nauru Commission of Inquiry 1986[11]:

> Colonialism…reproduces itself through its victims and continuously creates and represses new subjects. In this way, colonialism is like sovereignty itself. This is a challenge for international lawyers, whose craft inevitably demands the articulation and reproduction of

[4]Mechoulan 1988, 25.

[5]Williams 1992, 106–107 (emphasis added).

[6]Cavallar 2008, 207.

[7]Snyder and Sathirathai 1987.

[8]Mutua 2000.

[9]Bedjaoui 1985, 153 (emphasis added).

[10]Mutua 2000, 33 (emphasis added).

[11]Weeramantry and Berman 1999, 1565.

> the language of sovereignty and with it, perhaps, the suppressions and exclusions that characterize its history.[12]

Searching for a strong thesis regarding international law, as candidate for SJD at that time, Anghie was perhaps overreaching in his use of the Black Friar's texts: "Vitoria's work illustrates the centrality of the colonial encounter for the formation of international law and its key doctrines, showing the ways in which international law characterizes, excludes and disciplines peoples and societies understood as different and alien".[13] Thus, starting as the subject of an article on the "colonial origins of international law",[14] Vitoria became the key intellectual figure in a full monograph on the issue entitled *Imperialism, Sovereignty and the Making of International Law*, with the above-mentioned article as its first chapter and theoretical foundation. The central idea of the book is that both the invention and the universalization of international law have been instrumental to an imperial expansion that subordinated non-European peoples to European powers and their interests. In this book, we read, for example, that: "colonialism was central to the constitution of international law in that many of the basic doctrines of international law—including the doctrine of sovereignty—were forged out of the attempt to create a legal system that could account for the relationship between the European and non-European worlds in the colonial confrontation".[15]

Underlying this grand new narrative is the contention that the history of the relationship between international law and colonial peoples cannot be properly analysed under the "traditional historiographical parameters", which focus on how to achieve governance among autonomous sovereign states. Instead, the history of international law "must recognize" according to Anghie, "the *underlying assumptions* of its foundational texts" such as the texts of Vitoria.

This line of reasoning is of course appealing to those TWAIL scholars familiar with the postmodern critic's work. Bret Bowden, for example, has reiterated the idea of international law as an instrument of the "Western imperial project" in the European Journal of International Law.[16] Interestingly, other scholars seem eager to push the argument even further. For Leslye Obiora, for example, Anghie's thesis identifies the seminal works of Francisco de Vitoria as "a watershed that engendered juridical techniques and institutions manifestly appropriated as license to live by plunder". In her opinion, it copiously depicts "the chameleonic persistence *of Vitorian epochs* belied by rituals of innovation in the international legal framework".[17] It might reasonably be said, however, that in selecting Vitoria for the

---

[12]Anghie 1993, 505–506.

[13]Anghie 1998, 375.

[14]Anghie 1996, 321–336.

[15]Anghie 2005, 3.

[16]Bowden 2005, 1–23. See also Bowden 2006, 689–692.

[17]Obiora 2006, 729.

construction of alternative postmodern histories of international law, these authors seem to have chosen the wrong person.[18]

3 Praise for Context

In essence, the traditional postmodern critique of international law (international law as the main tool of imperialism/colonialism) is currently proposing an alternative history of international law, using certain scholars (read Vitoria) as framework for a new great overarching postmodern narrative. This approach basically sustains that international law was (and is) a mere instrument of colonial oppression invented by Vitoria and others at the time of the encounter of the New and Old World and continues to be so to the present day. However, in order to defend such a conclusion, standards of historiographical analysis such as contextualization are abandoned. Thinkers of the past have to be read in their context, not ours.

The encounter stands out as one of the most important events of the transition to modernity. It marks a watershed in the history of ideas, and it changed the way mankind sees the world. From the 1530s on, the conquest became a subject of heated debate in universities: the complex intellectual challenge of understanding the encounter would produce several new legal and political ideas. This issue was certainly not within the natural realm of a traditional academic mind of the period. New paths had to be opened, and not without difficulty. In this context, compelled by dramatic events and aware of the moral dimension of his work, Vitoria and other scholars were among the first to enter the debate. As Villey puts it, a great deal was expected from these theologians at this crossroads and the friar felt the need to participate by counselling the men of action in Spain, such as the missionaries and bishops in America.[19] In short, the theologians fuelled the debate.

But who were these men? Francisco de Vitoria is together with Domingo de Soto and Francisco Suarez among the foremost representatives of the so-called *Seconda Scolastica*. Their effort produced a “revamped Scholasticism”, different from that of the early Middle Ages which showed a preoccupation with trivial distinctions, classifications and the inflation of abstraction at the expense of reality.[20] On the contrary, Vitoria and his colleagues developed and disseminated their new ideas by guiding and nurturing this academic current with a characteristically direct concern and contact with the issues of the time.[21] In essence, they basically rejected the “flight from reality” of previous Scholasticism,[22] and abstract speculation, in favour of analysing social life with an abundance of data, erudition…and imagination.

---

[18]Cavallar, 184.

[19]Villey 1968, 357.

[20]Truyol 1999, 70–71.

[21]Hamilton 1963.

[22]Truyol 1999, 71.

A broad conception of theology allowed Vitoria to examine a wide range of social issues, which he approached with a significant critical sense for his time. Some of his key theses bear witness to that; "I can defend nothing other than what I have said" (*Sed ego hactenus non possum aliud intelligere, nisi quod dictum est*). As a result, in fact, his ideas drew the attention of Charles V himself, strongly displeased that doctrines contrary to his interests were being taught at the University of Salamanca. In this regard, the Black Friar was overtly critical of some decisions taken by the monarch concerning the *res publica* of Spain, but also expressed concerns and disagreed on the American Indies.

Being an eminent theologian, Vitoria was in a privileged position to explore the relationships between moral concerns, secular ideas and reason under the authoritative framework of theology, the "Supreme Science". Taking advantage of his position, he made some major intellectual leaps. Only a favoured court jester such as the unfortunate Francesillo (1480–1532)[23] would have dared to express himself so critically with respect to issues such as the just titles of the Emperor. In this regard, Vitoria was among the first Europeans who publicly disseminated his serious doubts and concerns on the affairs of the American Indies as well as to publicly and critically examine, in relation to it, the proper limits of the secular and spiritual legal instruments of dominion employed by the great powers of his time: the Emperor and the Pope. And by doing so, as we know, the Black Friar developed the idea of the *res publica* of the whole world (as an overarching world political community called to bring together all peoples), and the idea of the law of peoples (as a set of shared rules regulating that community). In sum, by stretching his political and legal imagination to challenging new events of his time, he sketched the idea of one world under a common system of rules.

Therefore, portraying such ideas as the mere legitimation of imperialism is arguably going too far. In this regard, some contextualization is thus required. Vitoria gave form to his ideas within a vibrant cultural *acquis* that mixed humanism with the intellectual legacy of the Middle Ages. By crossing the Ocean Sea, an entirely New World was revealed to the European mind. In essence, the discovery of an entire continent populated by *infidels* made the old paradigms unworkable. Tested to their limits, conventional ideas collapsed, opening the gate to new mentalities: here began the long and slow demise of the tortuous dualistic logic that had put the Christian on one side and the *infidel* on the other. Thus, critical old questions together with entirely new ones needed to be addressed, as the European mind was gleaning for the first time the reality of a larger world in which the Old Continent was a mere unit of the aggregate whole.

Vitoria took on the challenge, gave it thoughtful consideration and publicly disseminated his conclusions. The nucleus of his philosophy for tackling this major issues lies at the intersection of the doctrinal tradition of the Middle Ages and the budding phenomenon of Humanism. In this regard, he made his contribution by applying both reason and imagination to the wealth of both classical and Christian

[23]Zúñiga 1981. See also Bouza 1991.

culture.[24] With this combination, he managed to go beyond the limits of conventional thinking, the geographical borders of his political community and the legal prerogatives of the European power structures of his time.

The *Seconda Scolastica* was essentially a group of men reengineering law and theology (the authoritative sources of the *statu quo*) to find answers to some of the questions of their time. These men were necessarily children of two modes of conception, faith and reason, in search of a compromise, however complex; besides being scholars, they were members of an order (*Ordo Praedicatorum*) devoted to preaching the gospel around the world. In this regard, Francisco de Vitoria and his colleagues, being friars and theologians of the sixteenth century, could hardly have avoided applying the cultural parameters and values of Western (Christian) civilization to the Amerindians.[25] However, paraphrasing Cavallar, Vitoria's moral cosmopolitanism, while incomplete, was still an impressive feat.[26]

The geographical and social reality of the American Indies posed an urgent *quaestio facti* and *quaestio iuris*. Moving beyond the intellectual frontier of the Old World, the modes of conventional thinking had to be abandoned. Naturally, theologians such as Vitoria and other members of the Salamanca School were not free of doubts, vagueness and self-contradiction, as their texts evidence. However, it is precisely this process of formal "doubting" that provided an important intellectual contribution in the history of ideas, especially in the questioning of the worldwide exercise of power using the (de)legitimizing vehicle of the then so-called supreme science (read theology). In essence, from this questioning of power, a new concept was developed to deal with an unexpected New World: universalism.

From that conceptual stance, the Black Friar developed a wide variety of philosophical and theological ideas of universal applicability. In practice, he was cleaving a wedge into conventional thinking with new doubts and questions. Interestingly, even legal titles such as those concerning the tutelage of the Amerindians (widely acknowledged by postmodern studies on Vitoria) were, in his own words, mentioned for the sake of the argument but not asserted with confidence: "this is another title which indeed cannot be confirmed, but rather brought up for discussion, and some think it a lawful one. I dare not affirm it at all, nor do I condemn it entirely".[27] In sum, the emergence of doubts connected to facts (*versus* beliefs) is a critical step towards modern thinking; and this intellectual process is certainly present, here and there, in the *lectios* (regular lectures) and *relectios* (public lectures) of Vitoria. In this regard, Friar Vitoria's philosophy exemplifies a subtle and important shift in the evolution of modern thought: expressing personal doubts and engaging in rational questioning.

[24]Truyol 1998, 80.

[25]For both the protestant and "Norman Yoke" discourse on the American Indians, see Williams 1992 (parts II and III).

[26]Cavallar, 188.

[27]de Vitoria 1960.

4 Personal Engagement

Francisco de Vitoria raised doubts on both the theocratic and imperialist theses nurtured in the late Middle Ages. First, his ideas questioned the Empire of Charles V, a unique power structure that, together with the Holy Church, had nurtured aspirations towards unlimited expansion. Secondly and directly connected to this, his ideas put powerful concepts into circulation that would help others to conceive of an alternative legal world within a single *secular and consensual* framework: the idea of international law. The universalist ideas of Vitoria ultimately refuted the claims to universal jurisdiction of both the Emperor and the Pope. At that time, it was argued that the papal bull *Inter Caetera* of 1493 (covering the territorial and evangelization disputes of Spain and Portugal in the American Indies) granted dominion to the Crown of Spain over the newly "discovered" territories. However, the bull issued by Pope Alexander VI did not precisely establish whether it provided strictly for a territorial dividing line for evangelization between the two peninsular powers, or for a division of temporal/civil jurisdiction in those territories as well. Certainly, Isabel of Castile had an interest in interpreting the bull in the latter sense; as she stated clearly in her *Codicilio*, she believed she had obtained dominion.

The legal elites' attendant on the Crown used a clear line of argument to legitimate the king's dominion of the New World: the Pope, by his *Plenitudo Potestatis* had granted the lands of the "barbarians" to the Crown of Castile. However, for Vitoria, papal bulls did not constitute solid legal grounding. The friar was not ignorant of the fact that members of the Roman Curia were all too familiar with the practice of selling political favours, in the same manner as those electors who had granted Charles V the title of Holy Roman Emperor (thanks to the letters of credit from the Fugger bankers).[28]

Francisco de Vitoria's main arguments challenging the supreme power of the Pope in the Indies are as follows: (1) the Pope has no universal dominium by natural, divine law, or human law; (2) even if he had such a dominium, he could not transfer it to a secular power; (3) the Pope's temporal power is restricted to purely spiritual matters; (4) the Pope has no temporal power over the Indians. In short, Vitoria rejected, in the first two *Relectios*, the claim that the Pope had temporal jurisdiction above all princes, and declared, in his fifth *Relectio*, that the Pope was not the temporal master of the world.

Yet for obvious reasons, the idea of "Empire" was particularly appealing to some of the most powerful families (dynasties) controlling politics of Old Europe. For the Habsburg, the Valois and other dynastic European families, the expansion of the Roman Empire and the imperial coronation of Charlemagne (800) had nurtured a dream of power and dominion. However, it was the Habsburg dynasty that won the greatest prize of all: the *Monarchia Universalis*. In the words of Lesaffer, "Charles

---

[28]For a detailed study of the relationship of Charles V with the financial community, see Carande 1990.

V may have been the last emperor to be able to aspire to secular supremacy over the other *sovereign* princes".[29]

The monarch had managed to be appointed successor to the Roman Caesars and, thus, the secular leader of Christianity. The legal basis for this grand plan could only be gradually delegitimized by institutions such as universities, and the Chair of Theology at San Esteban was among those scholars who first and publicly opposed that unlimited concentration of power. Vitoria's lecture entitled *De potestate civili* (1528) is particularly direct in this regard. But it is a letter to a friend of his that best captures his strict position in regard to unchecked power: "To the King … Don Fernando was called simply *Your Mercy*; but now [Charles V] is called *Your Majesty* and *Holy Caesar*; *nothing remains but to say he is God*".[30]

The impetus for his theorization of the law of war in the second *De Indis* was the Dominican's particular concern over the actions of the Spanish in the American Indies but also over the devastating religious wars in Europe. In particular, Francisco de Vitoria strongly opposed the struggle between the Habsburg and Valois-Angoulême dynasties and thus Charles V's entire policy towards France. As he stated in his private correspondence, "wars were not invented for the good of princes but rather of their peoples; and if this be true, as it is, consider well men of good will, if our wars be for the good of Spain, or France, or Italy or Germany, and not to the destruction of them all".[31]

Not only did Vitoria express his critical ideas in the *Relectios* concerning this state of affairs, but he personally advocated for peace in his contact and correspondence with the notables of Spain. The correspondence between the friar and his friend Don Pedro Fernandez de Velasco, the influential *Condestable* of Castile and Count of Haro, is illustrative in this regard; Vitoria writes in 1538:

> It is well-known how little heed princes pay to anyone's recommendations, especially if they lie not within their inclination, but if any might occasion his Majesty, none more than [your Lordship] by your many titles…I think it may go hard, but if a way could be found to give some pause between his Majesty and the King of France, I believe that would be an even greater victory than the battle of Tunis.[32]

Interestingly, that same year, at the Courts of Toledo, his friend Don Pedro responded to the imperial demands that a general tax be approved to fund the wars in Europe with these bold words, publicly addressed to the Emperor himself: "it is of the utmost importance … that you likewise be entreated to work towards universal peace with all for a time. For be the war upon the infidels ever so just, peace is often to be had with them, as was had by the kings of Castile with the kings of Granada". As might be expected, the *Condestable* of Castile's speech enraged Charles V so much that he suspended the sessions and even threatened to throw Don Pedro into the corridor with his own hands; the answer of Don Pedro was

[29]Lesaffer 2004, 32.

[30]Vitoria 1935, 61.

[31]Getino 1930, 218.

[32]Getino 1930, 220–221.

audacious: "*Mirarlo ha mejor Vuestra Majestad, que si bien soy pequeño peso mucho*".[33] Not incidentally, that was the last time that notables and prelates would be represented in the Courts of Toledo.

In considering the limits of public power, Francisco de Vitoria admitted several valid and legitimate forms of dominion (*dominium*): *unde illa distinctio iuristarum, dominium altum bassum, directum utile, merum mixtum*. But while accepting these, the Black Friar rejected the idea that Charles V was Emperor of the All the World: *imperator non est dominus totius orbis*. And even if Charles V were indeed *Emperor of All the World* (*dato quod imperator esset*...), he could not in any case abrogate the Amerindians' rights.

It can be said that the position of Vitoria in these and other issues was challenging. His intellectual stance gave shape to potentially dangerous ideas for the *statu quo*. In consequence, the censoring of these ideas, so explicitly mandated in an imperial letter to the Prior of San Esteban (1539), would be enforced by the state apparatus and the power elites of the Court. As a result, the *Relectios* of Francisco de Vitoria would have to wait to see the light of day in print until Charles V had died and, even then, the first edition had to be printed in France; thus, the first edition of his lectures came to light in Lyon (1557) at the publishing house of Jacques Boyer. After that, there was a succession of editions disseminated all around Europe, in Salamanca (1565), Lyon (fourth edition, 1587), Antwerp (1604), Venice (1626), Salamanca (1680), Cologne (1696), etc.

The prohibition, in any case, was not able to contain the spread of these ideas but only to slow it down. In fact, the ideas were widely disseminated by the spoken word and transcripts. Although Charles V had tried to inhibit this, he obviously lacked the means to prevent the informal transmission of these ideas through the dissemination of manuscript copies by his disciples and students. In short, the classroom provided the Black Friar with a uniquely powerful channel of communication with the future elites of Spain, many of whom were educated in the University of Salamanca and had later informal access to those ideas.

The political importance of these *Relectios* in delegitimizing the *statu quo* is thus self-evident. The power elites made several efforts to contain their impact (particularly that of *De Indis*); from Charles V's prohibition on expressing these ideas in public to the later process aimed at including Vitoria's works in the Index of Forbidden Books by Pope Sixtus V (1521–1590).[34] Also interestingly, there was an additional subtle action taken that deserves to be mentioned: the *authorship* of the texts was later questioned, as there was no formally published version of *De Indies*. Thus, a formal Memorandum was written in 1608 by Francisco de la Peña, a member of the influential Faculty of Law at Bologne, questioning the authenticity of the words attributed to the Black Friar.[35] The argument was easy to devise: a great master such as Vitoria could not have written these words.

[33]de Sandoval 1614, n. VIII.

[34]Godman 2000, 136–138.

[35]Pereña 1979, 36–37.

5 Moral Concerns and Doubts

Notwithstanding some new contemporary studies, it is fair to argue that Francisco de Vitoria was not a cynic. Because the Dominicans (*Ordo Praedicatorum*) had been the first to join the project of the new evangelization in America, the friars in San Esteban would be amongst the first to learn of the crude realities in the accounts of their brothers in the New World.[36] Before Vitoria's famous lectures of 1535 and 1536, the Black Friar had already written the following lines in a private letter to his friend Manuel de Arcos, Prior of the College of San Gregorio (Valladolid): "the things that I learn [concerning the events involving the peoples of Peru upon the arrival of Spanish] no longer horrify or embarrass me, except the trickery and profiteering and things of the Indies [(*trampas y beneficios y cosas de Indias*)], which make my blood freeze on just hearing of them" (1534).[37] In his letter, Vitoria acknowledged that there may be people who would excuse and praise these "events, killings and spoils". He, on the other hand, refused to defend the men he labelled with the derogatory term *peruleros* and expressed consternation about excusing them:

> I contrive to do likewise with the peruleros, although they are few, yet some come by here. I do not declare nec excito tragoedias against the ones nor against the others, but rather, since I cannot pretend, nor say nothing more, but that I do not understand it, and scarce can see the justice or certainty in it, that they consult with others who might better comprehend it.

His objection was manifest: "May my tongue and my hand wither if I speak or write anything so inhuman and apart from all Christianity".[38]

These private reflections expressing concerns, doubts and perplexities on the information reaching San Esteban would later give shape to the two *De Indis*. Interestingly, one year later, in 1535, Vitoria's favourite disciple Domingo de Soto (1495–1560) presented a first *Relectio* entitled *De Dominio* where the first doubts concerning the affairs of the Indies are raised: "By what right do we take possession of the transatlantic Empire so recently discovered? In truth, I know not". It would take Vitoria two more years to present his first formal statements on the question in a *Relectio* entitled *De Temperantia*. In that lecture of 1537, Vitoria first tackled the thorny issue of the conquest of the Indies.

De Temperantia (On Moderation) is essentially a prologue to his thoughts on the issue, later developed in his two *De Indis* (January and June, 1539). The *lectio* was given in a very politically complicated year for Charles V: it was the same year that Pope Paul III issued the bull *Sublimis Deus* (May, 1537), in which the Church declared that grave offences were being tolerated (slavery and forced conversion) under the rule and dominion of the Holy Roman Emperor. The wording of the papal bull was certainly a warning sign for Charles V: "Indians are truly men" and "not

---

[36]Baciero 1984, 416.

[37]de Vitoria 1967, 137.

[38]de Vitoria 1967, 138.

only capable of understanding the Catholic Faith but, according to our information, they desire exceedingly to receive it". For the Church, the Indians "are by no means to be deprived of their liberty or the possession of their property, even though they be outside the faith of Jesus Christ" notwithstanding "whatever may have been or may be said to the contrary". *Sublimis Deus* was precise in this regard: "they may and should, freely and legitimately, enjoy their liberty and the possession of their property; *nor should they be in any way enslaved*; should the contrary happen, it shall be null and have no effect".

Interestingly, the Emperor began requesting Vitoria's counsel just after the issuance of the bull. Twelve months afterwards, Charles V wrote to the friar requesting a *Parecer* (recommendation) on the issue of "the education and conversion of the Indians to the holy faith". The letter was written in Toledo on 31 January 1539 and refers expressly to concerns raised by the Bishop of México, Juan de Zumárraga, to the Council of the Indies.[39] One month before, on 1 January 1539, Francisco de Vitoria had already presented the first *De Indis* as a general public lecture (*Relectio*) in Salamanca University: the main theme was whether or not it is lawful to baptize the children of unbelievers against the wishes of their parents.

The text condenses Vitoria's main ideas on the Amerindians, their relations with the Spanish and the Crown's titles to the New World. The Dominican would comment on the newness of these questions in the first *De Indis* (1539): "It must be kept in mind that I have seen nothing written on this question". His rejection of the doubtful titles concerning the alleged incapacity of the American Indians was among the first times in modern history in which moral arguments were taken into consideration when dealing with relations between peoples. For this analysis, Francisco de Vitoria made a full anthropological sketch of the Amerindian communities on the purely rational basis.

The lecture propounded a series of natural law foundations questioning the expansion of power and authority of both the Emperor and the Pope, while on the other hand formalized *just titles* to protect the channels of interaction of the Spaniards with the Amerindians. In this intellectual process, the rational capacity that Vitoria attributed to the American Indians led him to defend their public dominion and natural property rights. The viewpoint he expressed was structurally paternalistic, and although connected to the idea of equality among men, it is biased in favour of those "civilized" (read Europeans), who must care for and educate the Amerindians. His position is illustrated with an artificial construct: a land in which all adults have perished and only children and adolescents have survived. In this scenario, the European princes should care for and govern them while they are in such a state.[40] By analogy, the same treatment should be afforded to the Indians.

In this context, certainties coexist with doubts in the mind of the Black Friar. Interestingly, Vitoria does not assert the "possible title" with confidence: "this is another title which indeed cannot be confirmed, but rather brought up for

[39]Charles 1914, 427.

[40]de Vitoria 1960.

discussion, and some think it a lawful one. I dare not affirm it at all, nor do I condemn it entirely".[41] We can guess that Charles V was aware of that lecture. In any case, six months later, on June 18, the friar would present his second *De Indis* at Salamanca, in the most formal and highly visible university lecture of the year (*relectio*).

It is safe to say that presenting these ideas to the most learned audience of his time—the university community—was a display of audacity for a scholar of the sixteenth century. The Emperor, being in questionable possession of the Indies and engaged in several wars in and around Europe as well as the New World, was severely irritated by these lectures. His famous letter to the Prior of San Esteban dated 10 November 1539 expressed consternation that members of his monastery were calling into question Spain's rights to the Indies, and delivered a warning:

> I have been informed that some religious men of this house have put to discussion and treated in their sermons and in relectios, on our right to the Indies, Islands, and terra firma of the Ocean Sea… [I] charge and order that thereafter, without any delay, you call before you the said teachers and religious men…and obtain from them sworn affidavits that they declare at what times and places and before what persons they have discussed and affirmed the aforementioned.

In addition, as above mentioned, the Emperor ordered the Prior to collect the manuscripts and send them to the Royal Court and also forbade addressing such matters in public, "without his express permission".[42]

Not incidentally, half a year later, Charles V continued to request the advice of the friar on particular issues, probably as a lesser evil to keep this prominent member of the Salamanca School under a close eye: on 18 April 1539, another imperial letter was sent, also at Bishop Zumárraga's suggestion, requesting that Vitoria select twelve clergymen of good reputation to be sent as missionaries to New Spain (México).[43] In addition, on 31 March 1541, Charles V formally requested (*Real Cédula*) that the friar form a committee of theologians, under his tutelage, to make a judgement on the baptism of the Indians.[44] As a result, on July 1 of that year, Vitoria and other eight theologians signed their formal opinion (*Parecer*) recommending preliminary instruction before baptism.[45] Reasonably, these requests for counsel on specific issues were a pragmatic policy of the Emperor towards San Esteban: at that time, "theological hegemony" was unquestionably vested in Spain by the Chair of Theology in Salamanca and, as explained, theology was the supreme science in Europe.[46]

European scholars at that time were not able to freely express themselves against the interest of an Emperor or a Pope and expect that there would be no consequences.

---

[41]de Vitoria 1960.

[42]Getino 1930, 150.

[43]Charles 1928, 163.

[44]Charles 1914, 428.

[45]de Vitoria et al. 1967 (*Parecer*), 158.

[46]Getino 1930, 67.

Early modern academia was greatly constrained in this sense. Hence, the above-mentioned facts suggest that Vitoria tested the "limits of the system" with *De Indis*. For the rest of his years (1539–1546), he was prevented from publicly exploring other major critical issues. Arguably, the imperial requests for counsel on issues strictly related to missions (preliminary instruction of the Amerindians, etc.) were merely small consolations for the enforced silence of the theologian. In this connection, a reasonable interpretation is that an eminent scholar was basically and aseptically silenced by an Emperor.

Interestingly, at the end of his life, the Dominican was invited by Charles V to assist as imperial Theologian to the Council of Trent (1545–1563); due to his advanced illness, he declined in a formal letter to the King and his son Phillip (April or May 1545), expressing a preference for his disciple Domingo de Soto. In fact, Vitoria died on 12 August 1546, while the Council was still in its first round of sessions. After the *De Indies*, he did not enter in any major intellectual debate, nor further explored or developed his early challenging legal visions. However, some of his disciples managed to open fronts in several "policy battles". The appearance of some of Vitoria's ideas in the negotiations of the Council of Trent is a clear example. A narrator presents at the event, Astrain, describes these sessions of intense debate. From what he recalls of the discussions, in which Domingo de Soto participated, the Spanish theologians at Trent tenaciously defended the opinion that Bishops (e.g. Zumárraga) received their *potestas* directly from God and thus referred to a so-called divine right of Bishops. In writing that these "theologians fought for their opinions as knights fight for their dames",[47] Astrain suggests that these theologians were idealists removed from reality. However, this was not the case; what has been described as no more than an "obscure theological question" was directly linked to the ideals of the Salamanca School: the education of the American Indians. As we know, San Esteban had strong connections with some Bishops in the New World. Thus, the *Seconda Scolastica* was perfectly aware of the practical relevance of this theological question to the fate of its ideas concerning the education of the Amerindians (i.e. preliminary instruction previous to baptism).

It can be said that the School of Salamanca is an interesting early case study on the impact of schools of thought on the evolution of public policy. Twenty-four of Vitoria's his disciples held chairs at Salamanca and around five thousand students passed through the lecture rooms.[48] Over the following decades, their students, pupils, colleagues and successors disseminated ideas that influenced public decision-making both in Spain and the Indies.[49] Their critical voice in the Old World, together with that of the orders in the New World, influenced to some extent the redesign of some policies.[50] Thus, the *Junta* convened by Charles V to

[47]Astrain, 319.

[48]Hamilton 1963, 175.

[49]For a detailed list of professors and students from Salamanca in the Indies (1534–1585), see Pereña 1986, 216–255.

[50]Williams (1992) (see Chap. 2 in particular).

promulgate the New Laws of Indies took place three years after De *Indis* (1542), and four years before Vitoria's death. According to Pagden, the "changing tone" of this legislation regulating the Crown's relationship with both the colonialists and the Amerindians, and "the numerous, if ultimately ineffective attempts to curb activities in order to prevent further atrocities", suggests that the Salamanca theologians "voiced their views to some effect in the influential circles in which they moved".[51] In sum, there was some major doubting and questioning among the elites of a society on how to manage their relationships with other peoples, in particular the encounter with the New World. It is reasonable to affirm that a significant role in this regard was played by Vitoria and his colleagues from San Esteban. Thus, depicting the Black Friar as a founding father of imperialism and colonialism, as some contemporary literature does nowadays, is quite a stretch.

6 Sense of *Temperantia*

Let us now briefly contextualize the individual rather than the intellectual figure. The Flemish humanist Nicolaus Clenardus (Cleynaerts), a professor of Greek at the University of Salamanca from 1531 to 1537, offers us a good portrait of Francisco de Vitoria.[52] In his collected correspondence published in 1566 (Antwerpen), Cleynaerts describes the respect that Vitoria enjoyed among his academic peers. In one of these letters, from 1534, Cleynaerts writes to Johannes Vaseus about Vitoria: "[a man] of admirable simplicity; he has a singular love for scholars…You may not easily glean all of his qualities, because his erudition is quite vast, and yet, he does not glory in it".[53] Vaseus agreed, describing him as a man of "incredible erudition and almost unlimited reading", concluding with this reflection: "this would he have left in evidence, had he been as zealous to write as he was capable of extraordinary mastery to do so" (1540–1541).

One last appraisal also deserves transcription:

> the fame of his erudition is great in France and Spain… know no one, even among those who have spent their life writing in Latin, whose letters have given me so much pleasure as the many [I have] received from Vitoria. If one day, he finally decides to write, this man's fame will encompass the scholarly world. Salamanca is ignorant of the treasure she has in our Vitoria.[54]

Being such a respected intellectual figure, even before *De Indis,* it is puzzling that he never published his work, except for some prefaces from his early years in Paris. The Black Friar certainly had nothing against publishing; in fact, he actively participated in procuring one of the first university presses in Spain, and many of his

[51]Pagden 1990, 25.

[52]Klucas 1992, 87–98.

[53]Roersch 1940–1941.

[54]Roersch 1940–1941, 133.

disciples did publish their works during his lifetime. We can only guess that Vitoria was simply dedicated exclusively to his teaching, a vocation that he performed with outstanding success.

According to Melchor Cano, "Master Vitoria may have disciples wiser than he, but ten of the most learned cannot teach like him"[55]; or even in the friar's own words, "Master Astudillo knows more than I, but he cannot sell it as well as I can". The friar's was a unique academically driven personality. Characterized by hard work and austerity, this disposition appears to have been formed in his early years as a student and professor in Paris. In a preface to the works of Peter Crockart, in 1514, Vitoria reveals his devotion to the academic life: "after many years spent in writing, in teaching, in debating, when by surplus of rights you could have chosen a more restful life".[56] This praise for Crockart would be fitting to his own later life. In fact, on several occasions, his health broke down from working so hard that his superiors had to make special arrangements for his classes due to his deteriorating health. A remarkable illustration of both his devotion for teaching and his students' respect for him is the fact that in his last days, due to illness, he was carried from San Esteban to the university lecture rooms on his students' shoulders.

This man, committed to academia, was an example of moderation for his time and place: the Post-*Al Andalus* Spain. In this regard, it is reasonable to depict him as an early moderate. In fact, he taught the value of moderation to his pupils and disciples and even expounded on its importance in a *Relectio* under the title *On Moderation* (*De Temperantia*); as referred to above, a public lecture concerned in part with the affairs of the Indies and presented to the academic community two years before *De Indis* (1539). As a direct result of his personal advocacy for intellectual temperance, moderation has been one of the underlying values permeating the work of the School of Salamanca.

Interestingly, Melchor Cano himself expressly refers to the learned friar as "a moderate" in his ten sources of theological proof: *vir erat ille natura ipsa moderatus*. In this contribution to theological *positivism*, *De Locis Theologicis Libri XII* (1563), Cano reflected on the need to limit the weight that authority is given in academic thought. To support this point, Cano, who became the Chair of Theology after the death of Vitoria, recalled that his Master taught his disciples not to take Thomas Aquinas' own words at face value without proper analysis: "and though he was a man of moderate character, he at times dissented from Thomas Aquinas, and garnered greater praise in his dissenting than in consenting".

In essence, Francisco de Vitoria was concerned with finding answers to the urgent questions of his time. To paraphrase Hamilton, he had a characteristic tendency to consider speculative moral issues in the light of their practical, everyday applications and contexts.[57] In order to do so, the Black Friar had to confront and clarify some of his intellectual doubts on the one hand, and to question certain

---

[55]Getino 1930, 66.

[56]Getino 1930, 31.

[57]Hamilton 1963, 174.

elements of the *statu quo* on the other. Indeed, this probing spirit is remarkable for a man who was born in the time of the *Reconquista* of *Al Andalus*, raised in the culture of the Catholic Kings, attached to a religious order (*Ordo Praedicatorum*) and trained as a theologian in the old scholastic tradition.[58]

As the progressive legal philosopher and minister of education of the Spanish Republic, Fernando de los Rios pointed out in his 1927 conferences at Columbia University, the battle between Catholicism and Protestantism (and its concomitant religious wars) impinged severely on the objectivity of the writing of European history.[59] In fact, Francisco de Vitoria vanishes from the history of ideas for three centuries, in part due to the distorting effect in academia of the wars of religion, the notorious practices of Empire and the resulting construction of the so-called black legend. Fortunately, this rich and influential intellectual figure was recovered by the seminal works of the Belgian Ernest Nys (1851–1920), and the American James Brown Scott (1866–1943), among many others. Nowadays, however, a new blend of misinterpretations of both his ideas and context have currently gone beyond the old traditional protestant–catholic split to create a new artificial north–south divide fuelled by postmodern approaches to international law, in which Vitoria is taken out of context to mould his ideas to a particular world vision: modern and contemporary international law as colonialism.

Not surprisingly, being identified as one of the so-called founding fathers of such a big idea as international law, many past and present researchers use his intellectual figure as a framework to depict their personal vision of the world and, not incidentally, international law. As a result, as mentioned, the ideas of the Black Friar have been the subject of an enormous amount of secondary literature often swinging from one extreme to the other, from neo-hagiography to postmodern historical revisionism. Leaving aside extreme interpretations, it is reasonable to argue that Francisco de Vitoria was basically a moderate of his time, as this article suggests. Depicting him as intellectually responsible for legitimizing colonialism and imperialism is certainly placing an unreasonable burden on the shoulders of this friar.

Reframing the ideas of a man of the sixteenth century within such a scenario is perhaps useful for some critics of international law. Certainly, by structurally questioning its early framers, international law as an idea (a world under common rules) casts a very different light; not incidentally, contemporary international law is also structurally delegitimized. However, changing the world for good and for all requires changing the rules, not taking down the very idea of international law, and here, it is reasonable to argue that the scholar from San Esteban, with all the self-evident biases of his age and environment, was basically an honourable man who began the exploring and rationalizing of one of the greatest ideas, namely the existence of certain common rules for the entire world, in the interest of all peoples.

---

[58]For a depiction as an early "intellectual", in Gramscian terms, see Barbier 1999, 100–101.

[59]De los Rios 1997, 485.

References

Anghie A (1993) The heart of my home: colonialism, environmental damage, and the Nauru case. Harvard Int Law J 34:445–506

Anghie A (1996) Francisco de Vitoria and the colonial origins of international law. Soc Legal Stud 5:321–336

Anghie A (1998) Reading international legal texts: on the Indians lately discovered and sixteenth-century international law. American Society of International Law Proceedings, April 1–4, 375

Anghie A (2005) Imperialism, sovereignty and the making of international law. Cambridge University Press, UK

Astrain A "Los españoles en el Concilio de Trento", Razón y Fe IV

Baciero C (1984) Conclusiones definitivas de la segunda generación. Vitoria, La Etica de la conquista de America, Corpus Hispanorum de Pace, vol 25. CSIC

Bedjaoui M (1985) "Poverty of the international order". In: Falk R, Kratochwil F, Mendlovitz S (eds) International law: a contemporary perspective. WestviewPress, Boulder

Barbier M (1999) "La notion de respublica chez Vitoria". In: Zarka YC (ed) Aspects de la pensée médiévale dans la philosophie politique moderne. PUF, Paris

Bouza F (1991) Locos, enanos y hombres de placer en la Corte de los Austrias. Oficio de burlas. Temas de Hoy, Madrid

Bowden B (2005) The colonial origins of international law: European expansion and the classical standard of civilisation. J Hist Int Law 7:1–23

Bowden B (2006) European Journal of International Law 17:689–692

Carande R (1990) Carlos V y sus Banqueros (3 volumes). Crítica, Madrid

Cavallar G (2008) Vitoria, Grotius, Pufendorf, Wolff and Vattel: accomplices of European colonialism and exploitation or True Cosmopolitans. J Hist Int Law 10:207

Charles V (1914) Real cédula del emperador Carlos V en que consulta al maestro fray Francisco de Vitoria sobre asuntos de Indias (Toledo, 31 de enero de 1539). In: Esperabé de Arteaga, E. Historia pragmática e interna de la Universidad de Salamanca, vol II. Imprenta y Librería de Francisco Nuñez, Salamanca

Charles V (1928) Real cédula de Carlos V al maestro fray Francisco de Vitoria, en que le ruega escoja de entre sus discípulos doce sacerdotes de buena vida y doc-trina para enviarlos a Nueva España (Toledo, 18 de abril de 1539). In: de Heredia VB (ed) Los manuscritos del Maestro Fray Francisco de Vitoria. Santo Domingo del Real, Madrid

de Sandoval P (1614) Historia de la Vida y Hechos del Emperador Carlos V, Libro 24, Año 1538, n VIII

de Vitoria F (1935) De Justitia, quaestio 94, articulus 4. In: de Heredia VB (ed) Comentarios a la Secunda secundae de Santo Tomas, vol 5. Universidad de Salamanca, Salamanca

de Vitoria F (1960) De Indis recenter inventis, proposition 18, Teófilo Urdanoz (annotated edition) Obras de Francisco de Vitoria. Relecciones Teológicas. Editorial Catolic, Madrid

de Vitoria F (1967) Carta de Francisco de Vitoria a Manuel de Arcos sobre negocios en Indias. Corpus Hipanorum de Pace, vol 5. CSIC, Madrid

de Vitoria F et al (1967) Parecer de los teólogos de la Universidad de Salamanca sobre el bautismo de los Indios. In: Vitoria F (ed) Relectio de Indis, Corpus Hispanorum de Pace, vol 5. CSIC, Madrid

de Zúñiga F (1981) Crónica burlesca del emperador Carlos V, edited with comments by Diane Pamp de Avalle-Arce. Crítica, Barcelona

De los Rios F (1997) Religión y Estado en la España del Siglo XVI (1926), Obras Completas, vol 2. Anthropos, Barcelona

Getino LA (1930) El Maestro Fr. Francisco de Vitoria: Su vida, su doctrina e influencia. Imprenta Católica, Madrid

Godman P (2000) The saint as censor: Robert Bellarmine between inquisition and index. BRILL, Leiden–Boston–Cologne

Hamilton B (1963) Political thought in sixteenth-century Spain: a study of the political ideas of Vitoria, De Soto, Suárez, and Molina. Clarendon Press, Oxford
Klucas J (1992) Nicolas Clenardus: a pioneer of the new learning in Renaissance Portugal. Luso-Brazilian Rev 29:87–98
Lesaffer R (2004) Peace treaties from Lodi to Westphalia. Peace Treaties and International law in European History. Cambridge University Press, Cambridge
Mechoulan H (1988) Vitoria, pére du droit international?. In: Truyol y Serra A (ed) Actualité de la pensée juridique de Francisco de Vitoria. Bruylant, Bruxelles
Mutua M (2000) What is TWAIL? Am Soc Int Law Proc 94:31–40
Obiora L (2006) "Book review", 40. Law Soc Rev 40:729
Pereña L (1979) Relectio de iure belli o Paz dinámica. CSIC, Madrid
Pereña L (1986) La Escuela de Salamanca. Proceso a la Conquista de America. Caja de Ahorros y Monte de Piedad de Salamanca, Salamanca
Pagden A (1990) Spanish Imperialism and the political imagination. Studies in European and Spanish-American Social and Political Theory 1513–1830. Yale University Press, New Haven
Pagden A (1994) The uncertainties of empire: essays in Iberian and Ibero-American History. Hampshire, Aldershot
Pérez Luño A (1992) La polémica sobre el Nuevo Mundo. Los clásicos españoles de la Filosofía del Derecho. Trotta, Madrid
Roersch A (1940–1941) Correspondance de Nicolas Clénard. Palais des Académies, Bruxelles
Rosenthal E (1971) Plus ultra, non plus ultra, and the Columnar Device of Emperor Charles V 34. J Warburg and Courtauld Institutes 34:204–228
Snyder F, Sathirathai S (eds) (1987) Third world attitudes towards international law. Martinus Nijhoff, Dordrecht-Boston-Lancaster
Truyol A (1998) Historia del derecho internacional público. Técnos, Madrid
Truyol A (1999) Vitoria et la tradition scolastique. In: Zarka YC (ed) Aspects de la pensée médiévale dans la philosophie politique moderne. PUF, Paris
Villey M (1968) La formation de la pensée juridique moderne. Éditions Montchrestien, Paris
Williams RA (1992) The American Indian in western legal thought. The discourses of conquest. Oxford University Press, Oxford
Weeramantry C, Berman N (1999) The Grotius lecture series. Am Univ Int Law Rev 14:1565

Chapter 11
Francisco de Vitoria and the Nomos of the Code: The Digital Commons and Natural Law, Digital Communication as a Human Right, Just Cyber-Warfare

Johannes Thumfart

Abstract This chapter concentrates on a contemporary reading of Vitoria's *De Indis* for the digital age, employing Skinner's method of contextualization by critically extending it to contemporary contexts, as a form of "intended prolepsis" that generates a coherent system of international digital legal thought. The systematic importance of the commons in Vitoria's thought is first underlined and then applied to current issues, for example cyber-wars, post-humanism and copyright, whilst giving a critical new reading of a broad range of Vitoria's texts, such as *De indis*, *De iure belli*, *De homicidio*, *De potestate civili* and his commentary on Aquinas.

1 Introduction

Vitoria, previously referred to rather imprecisely as the "father of international law", is important today because of those aspects of his thought that transcend—in Vitoria's time: precede—the classical Westphalian model of sovereign nation states. This has, for example, often been noted in relation to Vitoria's concept of the *res publica totius orbis* ("republic of the whole world").

Although for Vitoria the *res publica totius orbis* is more an analogy than a developed systematic concept—and not even one that he employs in *De Indis*, which is considered the first teaching on modern international law, but rather in *De Potestate Civili*[1]—it can be argued that with this idea, Vitoria foresees the kind of

http://www.spiegel.de/impressum/autor-23613.html.

[1] de Vitoria 1995 (*De potestate civili*), 21.

J. Thumfart (✉)
Der Spiegel, Hamburg, Germany
e-mail: johannes_thumfart@gmx.de

J.M. Beneyto and J. Corti Varela (eds.), *At the Origins of Modernity*,
Studies in the History of Law and Justice 10, DOI 10.1007/978-3-319-62998-8_11

close post-Westphalian international collaboration that is working more or less well today in agreements such as the Hague Conventions, the UN, international trade treaties, the EU, and, also, the Convention on Cybercrime.

In our age of digital networks—which can be dubbed, following Lessig[2] in a Schmittian way, the age of "the nomos of the code"—Vitoria's concepts of *communicatio* (communication) and *res communes* (commons) seem even more important. In Vitoria's *Relectio de Indis,* they serve as anthropological, customary (*communicatio*) and material (*commons*) underpinnings of international political collaboration. In this way, as manifestations of global flows and transpersonal streams, they form the material base for Vitoria's concept of the "republic of the whole world". The common air and seas were globally connected, and common gestures travelled over cultural borders through mimesis, both long before the nation states even emerged.

Both ideas, the idea of common goods and the idea of global communication, have long been thought to be merely idealistic or simply outdated, especially concerning arguments along the lines of *The Tragedy of the Commons*[3] and the deconstruction of Kantian public discourse as a world of "transcendental" illusions and make-believe that masks the significant asymmetry in public spheres in terms of power, capital and gender.[4]

Both ideas, however, are being revived in the age of digital networks, in relation to questions of intellectual property and a new kind of global interconnectedness that actually—and not only transcendentally—grants the same possibilities of participation to everyone. In our digital world, commons and global communication are no longer ideals, but, rather, at least de facto realities of our everyday lives, on which global political agreements can and must be built, if we want to avoid the worst possible outcomes of a neighbourship in a state of anarchy.

Another aspect covered by Vitoria that seems to be predestined for reinterpretation in every historical period is his application of the concept of the *bellum iustum* (just war) to problems of international relations. This also applies to our digital era of the nomos of the code. The difficulties concerning cyber-wars—foremost of these, how to detect and to define cyber-wars and to retaliate against cyber-aggressors—have already led some cyber-war theorists[5] to go back to thinkers such as Vitoria and Grotius.

Clearly, pre-Westphalian models such as Vitoria's are helpful in providing orientation in our age of "planetary-scale computation", which "distorts and deforms traditional Westphalian modes of political geography, jurisdiction and sovereignty, and produces new territories".[6] There cannot be, however, an understanding of Vitoria's normative demands concerning just wars without first

[2]Lessig 1999.

[3]Hardin 1968.

[4]Dean 2003.

[5]Giesen 2014, Solis 2014, Hildebrandt 2013.

[6]Bratton 2014.

understanding Vitoria's concept of the commons and of the common good, since these are the moral fixed points starting from which all normative demands are developed in Vitoria's Thomistic thought.

The different sections of this chapter therefore deal with separate aspects of how Vitoria can facilitate our understanding of digital commons, digital communication and cyber-warfare, but they do so within a rather systemic reading of Vitoria that might be frustrating to those only interested in questions concerning digital networks. However, in Sects. 4 and 5, there is a bullet point presentation that should be of assistance.

As will be clarified in a short methodological preface—which I encourage readers not interested in subtleties of intellectual history to skip—it is not only my aim to provide orientation to those scholars occupied with contemporary problems regarding digital networks, but also to clarify aspects of Vitoria's teachings themselves by relating them to the contemporary context—especially the loose bundle of ideas in Vitoria's teachings that has been labelled the *ius communicationis*, the "right to communicate".[7]

Only such a systematic reading of Vitoria can provide the orientation that we need today concerning questions of digital international relations. Vitoria's system can be understood as a hybrid avoiding the extremes of unhedged global political power and anarchic self-organization of the commons alike. These are today—in the form of the military-digital complex and libertarian cyber-Utopianism—the two extremes that the political theory of the Internet needs to avoid. Our age of the nomos of the code is always in danger of *in toto* replacement of the law (*nomos*) with the atavistic and more authoritarian code of de facto powers—a replacement that is worse if done by states, corporations and secret services than by smaller actors claiming to be the defendants of the digital commons. In his time, Vitoria opposed totalitarianism in the form of imperial and theocratic tendencies and replaced it by a system of the rule of (natural) law, the commons and republican discursive principles. This is exactly the vital balance that the global political philosophy of the Internet has yet to find.

2 Methodological Preface

Skinner's and Foucault's critiques of the history of ideas as a "reconstructive" discipline[8] are still helpful in avoiding the most dangerous traps of this field. The search for "fathers", known or unknown "predecessors", and the opinions of theorists such as Kant and Hobbes on social democracy, nuclear bombs, cars, the Internet, etc., are at best problematic and nonsensical at worst.

[7]For example: Desantes Guanter 1999.

[8]Skinner 2002, Foucault 1972, Thumfart 2013.

Foucault and Skinner agree: what an author writes or says depends on a specific context and can only be understood within such context. It cannot be decontextualized in order to formulate some general, ahistorical truth, nor can it be read teleologically, starting from later developments in history. This purist, reductionist notion of intellectual history has been embraced by many scholars, inasmuch as it narrows down a discipline that is often too broad and too far removed from actual facts; unfortunately, the history of ideas is neither philology nor neuro-archaeology.

This notion of intellectual history, however, shares the same disadvantages of all purist, and hence essentialist, concepts. How can we ever be sure to have reconstructed the original context of an author? And, what is more difficult: what is the original context of something as intangible as an idea? Is there any possibility of objectively identifying the "actual" context of an idea and the author's intention (Skinner), the "actual" relation between discursive practice and *énoncé* (Foucault, respectively)? And is it not the case that texts—contrary to the spoken word—are meant to be understood by future generations in totally different contexts? Is this unknown, future context not one of the driving forces for writing "for all and none" in any event, to tackle universal problems and hence to write scientifically in the sense of the humanities?

Most of all, Skinner's and Foucault's quests for absolute historical purity are impossible to fulfil. It is not hard to show that both authors failed to fully live up to their incredibly harsh methodological standards, but made conscious and unconscious concessions to the context in which they themselves were writing and thinking.

On the other hand, maybe their method itself is not sufficiently coherent. Because what actually follows from Skinner and Foucault is: if the historian herself, too, is a producer of ideas, then she produces her ideas in a certain context, which however is not necessarily the historical context she is examining, but rather her contemporary one.

In fact, one of Skinner's critics, David Harlan, insists that we need to expand Skinner's method of the historiography of ideas in this sense.[9] It is not enough to keep in mind the context in which ideas have originally been developed. We also must consider the contemporary context, in which we—the historians and their audience—interpret historical ideas. Only in this way can we tackle the extra-contextual, universal intentions of an author, which especially characterize successful writers inasmuch as their ideas are applicable to a number of specific future problems.

As far as this essay is concerned, relating Vitoria to digital networks means giving a meaning to Vitoria that any contemporary reader—surely processing, maybe even accessing Vitoria's text digitally—will in any event have in mind. It is hard to hear of a global *ius communicationis* (right to communicate) today without thinking of digital communication. And possibly, it is dishonest to claim not to do so, since the interpretation of classical texts always depends on our contemporary

[9]Harlan 1989.

context, and openly discussing it makes the interpretative work of future generations much easier.

Additionally—especially in the history of the interpretation of Vitoria—it is not contextualization that is the rule, but rather wild de-contextualization. The history of the study of Vitoria is full of more or less legitimate appropriations, deformations, uses and abuses owing to the changing political contexts of Vitoria scholars. Grotius, Nys, Brown Scott, Schmitt, Walzer[10]: every era of global politics seems to produce its specific reading of Vitoria. Each of these authors has her obvious manipulative vices. Nevertheless, with their different foci and omissions, they have shed light on different aspects of the original source. They have made not only their contemporary realities more accessible by employing Vitoria, but Vitoria's teachings richer by relating his ideas to their respective contemporary reality.

Rather than being an obstacle to the understanding of texts, interesting and justified de-contextualization of an author's writing in this sense can underline the universal aspects in the source, because, once more, and foremost, universality means applicability. This becomes especially clear when Grotius deduces his general principle of the Freedom of the Seas against the Spanish from Vitoria's rather partisan Spanish claims—in a text that was merely a legal opinion dictated by contemporary interests. And, Vitoria, in turn, is guilty of a more or less straightforward de-contextualization of Thomism by his application of it to the New World. This kind of de-contextualization is, at the same time, universalization.

Third and last—and this is the most uncanny reason why it might be justifiable to apply Vitoria in particular to the contemporary context—it could be said that Vitoria's teachings are still recent in aspects, because as with historical medical texts, they describe and try to introduce rules in a subject matter that remains the same: unlike the nation state, the field of global interconnectedness is still full of uncertainties and still developing as it was in Vitoria's time. In this sense, one might say, it is valid to apply Vitoria's teachings to contemporary problems of international relations, because they represent an earlier stage of reasoning on the same subject—like those famous disparate descriptions of one and the same elephant in the room by several blind people. In the same way as being scattered across a room, diverging descriptions of one and the same subject might be scattered over centuries, but nevertheless contribute to a better understanding thereof.

3 Digital Commons

Our partly capitalist, partly state-capitalist and partly socialist world of today is predominantly organized by private, and to a lesser extent public, property. There are commons: the high seas, the air, outer space, the surface of extra-terrestrial planets, the arctic. But these places and substances are remote or unusual in terms

[10]Nys 1894, Brown 2000, Schmitt 1997, Walzer 1997.

of their behaviour. The complete neglect of commons in our society has long been the rule, as was shown in Hardin's landmark essay *The Tragedy of the Commons.*[11]

Whenever property is not public or private, says Hardin, it tends to be destroyed by overuse, because no one is the exclusive owner of it and can limit access to it. To quote an example from economic theory: external costs—for example the destruction of nature and culture, which are mostly de facto, but not de jure commons—are almost never considered in business plans. Otherwise, for example, the whole private car industry would be considered economically unreasonable, since in destroying the environment, its external costs to the commons clearly outweigh its short-term benefits for individuals and states.

When the first experiments in Open Source Software and collaboration in social networks in the Internet reached a larger scale and became known to the broader public in the late 1990s,[12] this was, therefore, nothing short of an economic and political revolution. The collaboration of individuals, who often have never met before, who often live on the other side of the globe and who are disciplined neither by social nor by political coercion, motivated neither by private, nor by public property, questions the basic assumptions of classical economic theory. Even when collaborating on complex projects, it turns out, humans are capable of pursuing other ends than their self-interest. It is because of these empirical revelations that digital networks brought back the idea of commons.

The application of commons to the digital realm must be conceived of as a Renaissance, rather than a discovery. Commons had a strong reality in medieval thought and life before the waves of privatization took place, which characterize the shift to modernity.[13] Especially to Christian thinkers, commons preceded private property ontologically since they represented the *ante peccatum* mode of organizing property. This ontological primacy of the commons, however, did not lead to a complete de-legitimization of private property. The medieval period was a period of strong social inequality, at least in terms of feudal property. But the ontological primacy of the commons led to a strong bias against the idea of a sole legitimacy of property, which, for example, prominently characterizes the opposition of Christian thought towards *usura.*

In international law, the concept of commons is structurally of twofold importance. First of all, international law simply is the only place in modern law where commons, such as the high seas, planets or the arctic actually need to be considered. Second—and this is more important to this essay—only commons can prepare the ground for solving the principle problem of international law—the *homo homini lupus* in the state of nature, the anything goes in the realm of sovereign powers. Because of commons, the realm between sovereign powers is not "gapless"[14] or a

[11]Hardin 1968.

[12]Good introductory texts on these phenomena are: Benkler 2006, Lessig 2005, Shirky 2010.

[13]For example: Wallerstein 1974.

[14]Hildebrandt 2013, 206.

mere vacuum without laws. Commons provide a common, third ground—or at least a common battlefield of diverging interests—that can be used to mediate between sovereign powers.

Especially for Vitoria—who teaches before the classical notion of sovereignty by Bodin was developed and whose teachings bear strong medieval, pre-state traces—the notion of commons is the central concept that holds together his system of international relations. Whilst the *res publica totius orbis* (republic of the whole world) is mainly a metaphor that Vitoria employs in one episode of the *De Potestate Civili*, the notion of commons is systematically central to his thought in *De Indis*, which is widely considered the first lecture on modern international law.

He repeatedly employs it in order to make the point that the undivided state of an interconnected world is more natural than the divided one and therefore ontologically and juridically precedes the latter as a stronger claim: "*A principio orbis* (…) *omnia essent communia*"[15]—"In the beginning of the world (…) all things were held in common".[16]

In this way, the commons are also the base of Vitoria's strongest just title in favour of conquest, the *ius communicationis*. Vitoria says that the Spaniards cannot conquer the Americas because of papist or imperial power over the world (*dominium orbis*), but only as a retaliation, if the Amerindians ban or expel the Spaniards from their right to travel the commons, the seas and rivers, and to be subsequently welcomed as guests.[17]

Whilst his contemporaries tried to justify the Conquest by using papal or imperial claims, Vitoria employed the seemingly "soft" and "open" notion of the commons to achieve the same goal. The questions that lie at hand—whether Vitoria is maybe misunderstood, maybe a prototype of "benevolent colonialism" or maybe himself a victim of misinformation or ideological euphemization—are beyond the scope of this essay.

What makes Vitoria's teaching so interesting to the contemporary—at first rather descriptive than normative—Renaissance of the commons in the digital world is that—in spite of the theological underpinnings of his legitimization of the Conquest via the commons—it bears traces of a minimal normative claim that stems directly from a mere description. Unlike modern man—especially after Bentham and Kant—Vitoria is convinced that nature itself has an objective, normative dimension, starting from the notion of a non-anthropomorphic creator-god and his intentions for his creation: "*Omnia, quae caelo continentur, alicuius usus et finis gratia stetisse fierique omnia atque ita fieri necesse propter finem, unde ratio et necessitas rerum accipienda est*"[18]—*Everything under the sky has been made for some purpose and use. And everything happens and necessarily happens for a purpose. And*

[15]de Vitoria 1997 (*De Indis*), III, Primus titulus, 1.

[16]de Vitoria 2010, 278.

[17]de Vitoria 1997 (*De Indis*), III, Primus titulus, 5.

[18]de Vitoria 1995 (*De potestate civili*), 2.

this must be the beginning of the understanding of the essence (ratio) and necessity of every thing.[19]

The descriptive—possibly phenomenological in a Husserlian sense—analysis that follows from this theological and teleological assumption, and which we can witness in many places in Vitoria's teachings, is therefore often simply directed at identifying a *telos* inherent to objects that one can understand whilst accepting a creator-god—but also without such acceptance. It is, for example, completely understandable to secular common sense that the air and the seas are commons, since they cannot—not today and even less so in Vitoria's times—actually be appropriated or controlled by a private or public owner (an argument that we find later at Grotius, and much later at Schmitt.[20])

In order to turn this into more than a capitulation of legal philosophy vis-à-vis the status quo, it must be noted that Vitoria does not restrict the normative implications of nature to human beings. This, for example, is also the case in relation to a general tendency towards *conservatio sui*, which can be found in all living creatures and which is the basic principle of Vitoria's natural law.[21] In one passage of the commentary on the *Summa*, Vitoria even ascribes *ius naturale* to stones and fire. He writes that it is *ius naturale* that fire burns and not stones: "*Patet, quia ius naturale est ignem ascendere et comburere, sed hoc non est commune omnibus animantibus, quia non lapidi*".[22]

Although this might be either a *reductio ad absurdum*, or an episodic confusion by Vitoria or the editors, Vitoria discusses the same question in *De Indis* when talking about the *dominium* of creatures and objects without reason, where he comes to the opposite conclusion: the sun and a wolf, for example, cannot have rights, he says there, because they cannot suffer injuries in the legal sense: "*Creaturae irrationales* (…) *non possunt pati inuriam. Ergo non habent ius*"[23]—"(…) *Irrational creatures cannot be victims of an injustice, and therefore cannot have legal rights*".[24] However, Vitoria posed the question after the *dominium* of non-reasonable beings with full sincerity, since this was the central question of *De Indis.* To him, it is not the nonsensical question that it is to subject-oriented contemporary philosophy.

With his non-anthropocentric, object-oriented, teleological tendency in mind, one must re-read Vitoria's definition of the commons as "air, flowing waters, the sea, bays": "*Iure naturali communia sunt omnium aer et aqua profluens et mare,*

---

[19]Own translation. As an exception, the English translation by Pagden is not adequate at this place: "Every atom exists for some use or purpose" is not contained in the Latin version, but maybe he is working from another manuscript. de Vitoria 2010, 6. Pagden also entirely omits the epistemological point that this purpose must be the beginning of our understanding, which de Vitoria 1995 mentions.

[20]Hildebrandt, Mireille 2013, 214.

[21]de Vitoria 1995 (*De homicidio*), 1.

[22]de Vitoria 1928 (*In IIa-IIae*) q. 57, a. 3. There is no English translation available.

[23]de Vitoria 1997 (*De Indis*), I, 12,1.

[24]de Vitoria 2010, 248.

item flumina et portus. Atque naves iure gentium undecumque licet applicare, et eadem ratione viae publicae. Ergo neminem licet ab illis prohibere"[25]—"(…) *By natural law running water and the open sea, rivers, and ports are the common property of all, and by the law of nations ships from any country may lawfully put in anywhere*".[26]

Vitoria compares those substances, landscapes and places to public roads (*viae publicae*) inasmuch as it is their *telos* to enable traffic among people. Thus, it is not only because of a sociable human nature—or the uncontrollability thereof—that *air, flowing waters, the sea, bays* are commons, but because of the very ephemeral and moving nature of the substances air, flowing waters, the sea, which shows their teleological inclination: to enable traffic, movement, communication of all sorts and kinds—of animals, meteorological phenomena, currents, viruses and also of humans.

Whilst these non-anthropocentric aspects of Vitoria's thought used to be put aside by many historians of ideas as typically medieval and therefore uninteresting, they are helpful today in terms of environmental thought—but also in terms of the philosophy of technology. If technology really is an independent evolutionary force, as Simondon and Stiegler suggest,[27] respectively, "the Seventh Kingdom of Life on Earth" as Kelly writes,[28] then we are doing well to consider the inclinations of technology when conceiving of legal frameworks for technology.

For the normative dimension of positive law cannot survive very long if it is totally divorced from the logics that are inherent to those processes and objects which it should regulate. And, in this sense, it does not matter whether objects are rational, natural or unnatural—or if there is a creator-god or not—for objects to have a normative, super-positivist dimension.

Even if their subject matter is technology, and not nature in the—arguably anyway nonsensical—essentialist sense, lines of thought which are very popular today, such as "information wants to be free", must be taken seriously as a renaissance of natural law. They attribute a normative value to non-human entities, such as Vitoria did, but to tendencies inherent to technology.

Examining the evolution of technology—which is much clearer than the doubtful evolution of culture—one can easily see that technology is moving steadily forward along the lines of densification, complexity, diversification, acceleration, disruption and transborder movements—as already becomes clear during Vitoria's times, in which, for example, Muslims and Christians wage war against one another, but cannot resist copying their technologies, as if driven by a non-human actor that wants to spread its influence, complexity and power, regardless of human borders and human ideologies.

[25]de Vitoria 1997 (*De Indis*), III, Primus titulus, 1.

[26]de Vitoria 2010, 279.

[27]Simondon 2011, Stiegler 1998.

[28]Kelly 2010.

It might sound like science fiction, but such a renaissance of object-oriented natural law thinking is a necessary correction of legal positivism, since normative concepts cannot persist in contrast to technological reality. The best example for a clash between technological and legal reality is the fact that before the popularization of civil air traffic in the beginning of the twentieth century, the space above private property was legally conceived of as extending infinitely above it. Quickly, this closed conception was changed because it was in sharp contradiction to the very nature of aeronautical technology. Airplanes were given the right to cross airspace above private territories.[29]

In a similar way, the notion of intellectual property is in a deep crisis today. Intellectual property in its contemporary form criminalizes broad masses of Internet users. By doing so, it both undermines the credibility of the rule of law and, de facto, creates a continuous global state of exception, which enables, for example, totalitarian regimes to imprison dissidents because of copyright infringements.[30] Since most technological progress is produced outside of the private economy, intellectual property also serves as an obstacle to progress in sciences rather than as its promoter, which it was intended to be.[31]

Furthermore, those companies and secret services who actually seek to have power over the Internet—due to the inherent totalitarian aspects of their claims to control a world with material foundations beyond unilateral control—seem in danger of claiming unlimited, uncontrolled power, which democracies cannot allow institutions to have. In the age of the nomos of the code, there is always a danger of fulfilment of tautological destiny, of the age becoming the age of absolute, unhedged power, in which an authoritarian code, issued by a de facto power, replaces the law *in toto*. In this sense, the code is the total, yet de-politicized and technocratic nomos, which—unlike the political or legal nomos[32]—has no relation to a specific territory and its borders.

Reinterpreting Vitoria's notion of the commons, it is obvious that private property and particular political interests cannot trump common progress and common interests, especially if the inclination towards the commons is written in the very essence of the objects that should be regulated by property laws. Due to the Internet's de-centralized mode of organization and its technological accessibility a priori, one can conclude that closed visions in a political or legal sense are in contradiction to the technological essence of the Internet: its a priori neutrality, its lack of a centre in the functioning of TCP/IP, its nature as an enabler of open collaboration and communication and as a means to distribute a practically infinite amount of copies without, or with practically no, loss of quality.[33] Just as the essence of air travel contradicts the notion of private real estate extending endlessly

---

[29]Lessig 2005.

[30]Levy 2010.

[31]Lessig 2005.

[32]Schmitt 2006.

[33]MacKinnon 2013.

into the sky, the de-centralized essence of the Internet contradicts attempts to control it by companies and governments.

Of course, it is possible to neglect this incongruence. Being merely *ius naturale* and not positive law, this incongruence does not represent a demand by an institution endowed with punitive or coercive power, but, rather, a description. This means that it is stronger than positive law, which can be cheated. If this systemic incongruence is neglected, no court will issue a verdict, but severe problems will arise: an endless amount of copyright infringement cases, the criminalization of large parts of the population, a deceleration of progress, and governments and enterprises out of control.

Facing questions concerning the digital realm, we therefore actually need to "reinvent natural law theory", albeit in a systematic and not merely utopian way.[34] Only the natural law tradition with its non-anthropocentric mode of normative and super-positivist analysis can provide orientation in a world that is more borderless than ever, further from the legal restrictions of private and public property than ever and, at the same time, further from the democratic control of state power than ever.

Clearly, cyber-heroes such as Edward Snowden, Chelsea Manning and Julian Assange already act in their "private just wars" with the same kind of absolute and intuitively true, yet technically illegal, legitimacy that only the natural law tradition can provide, and more will be said about this below. In the same way, courts taking on Google and Facebook seem to represent an uprising of justice in opposition to de facto world super powers, with a clarity not seen before. Concerning the massive crowd of everyday life users that frequently do technically illegal things in the Internet, we are facing a crisis of legitimacy and a voting with the feet comparable only to mass disobedience in Gandhi's India.

From a perspective of the philosophy of international law, one needs to welcome these irritations and the contemporary debates, since these debates—however they may be decided—produce a common ground between sovereign nations on which —but not against which—a new kind of democratically legitimized global rule of law beyond private property can be established, such as the discovery of the uncontrollable world oceans led Vitoria and his contemporaries to the formulation of the principles of international law as an adjustment to the openness of the spaces that were discovered.

4 Ius Communication Is as a Human Right to Communicate

It is curious that Vitoria mentions that—according to natural law—man cannot possibly have the intention to abolish the right to communicate—the *ius communicationis*—to travel, to discourse, to visit other nations, in other words: to use the

[34]Hildebrandt 2013, 197.

commons in the way they are intended to be used.[35] One reason why this is self-evident to Vitoria (and not to us) lies in the connection between commons, communication and the ontology of humanity according to Vitoria. Commons are so important to Vitoria because they are directly connected to the "hospitable nature" of humans—albeit "hospitality" is a weak term for the huge role that human interrelations play in Vitoria's thought. Here, too, we need to dare to take on a non-anthropocentric perspective.

The *ius communicationis* is central to *De Indis*, because it is central to Vitoria's strictly non-biologist, Artistotelian-Thomistic, communitarian ontology of humanity as an entity that constitutes itself in and only in communicative action, with *communicatio* meaning many different things for Vitoria in addition to travel, eating together, the exchange of ideas and trade.

The ontological strength of Vitoria's communicative communitarianism cannot be stressed enough. Vitoria says for example: even if there was "wisdom without speech" (*sapientia* […] *sine sermone*), such a truth would be of no value, because it would be "unedifying and unsociable" (*ingrata et insociabilis esset ipsa sapientia*).[36]

Furthermore, Vitoria's teachings lead to the conclusion that an exclusion from human *communicatio* also signifies an exclusion from the essence of humanity, i.e., non-humanity, which corresponds to the formula "*Et si non est civis non est homo*" that the Dominican Remigio dei Girolami derived earlier from similar exclusive statements in Aristotle: "*Et si non est civis non est homo, quia homo est naturaliter animal civile, secundum Philosophum in VIII Ethicorum et in I Phisicorum*"[37]—*If he is not a citizen, he is not a human being, because man is a political animal.*

Vitoria must be construed as follows: the *ius communicationis* not only describes a sufficient condition for humanity, but a necessary condition. That is exactly where its strong normative significance finds its origin.

There are at least four passages in Vitoria's teachings in which an exclusive understanding of the *ius communicationis* can be exemplified:

(a) Vitoria's agreement with Aristotle's claim that a human being outside of a political community is either an animal or a god.[38]
(b) Vitoria's deduction of the *dominium* of the Amerindians from their specific politics, i.e. in Thomistic terms their organization of *communicatio*. (Thomas: "*Civitas est quaedam communicatio*".[39]): "*Habent ordinem aliquem in suis rebus, postquam habent civitates, quae ordine constant, et habent matrimonia distincta, magistratus, dominos, leges, opificia, commutationes, quae omnia*

[35]de Vitoria 1997 (*De Indis*), III, Primus titulus, 1: "*Nunquam* (…) *fuit intentio gentium per illam divisionem* (*rerum*) *tollere hominum invicem communicationem*".
[36]de Vitoria 1995 (*De potestate civili*), 4.
[37]Girolami (*De bono communi*), IX.
[38]de Vitoria 1995 (*De potestate civili*), 5.
[39]Aquinas (*Sententia Politicorum*), II, 1, 6.

requirunt usum rationis"[40]—"(…) They have some order in their affairs. They have properly organized cities, proper marriages, magistrates and overlords, laws, industries, and commerce, all of which require the use of reason".[41]

(c) Vitoria's argument in favour of *ius soli* because a human being that is born without being part of a political community makes no sense to him.

> *Civis dicatur et sit, qui natus est in civitate. Et confirmatur, quia cum homo sit animal civile, talis natus in una civitate non est civis alterius civitatis. Si enim non esset civis illius, non esset civis alicuius civitatis, pero quod impediretur a iure naturali et gentium.*[42]—(…) The law of nations defines a 'citizen' as a man born in a community. The confirmation is that man is a civil animal, but a man born in one community is not citizen of another community; therefore, if he is not a citizen of the first community, he will not be citizen of any community, and this would be inequitable by the law of nature and of nations.[43]

(d) Vitoria's repeated assertions that an individual is similar to a member of the bigger body of a political community and can even be killed if it is in the interest of the larger body.[44]

Today, in our age of digital networks, the non-biologist, inclusive and exclusive aspects of the *ius communicationis* are useful because:

(a) They help us to understand the catastrophic implications of a digital divide between rich and poor. If, for example, "Cognitive Enhancement" via wearable technology connected to the Web such as *Google Glass* and crowdsourced devices such as *Ushahidi* really alter the intellectual capacities of humans in a dramatic way, as some claim,[45] then the divide in access to means of communication could break up the very physical coherency of the species. In a more practical sense, i.e., if politics is only *communicatio*, then having no Internet access means not being able to freely participate in discourse, therefore not being a citizen in a Habermasian sense, and to Vitoria even, therefore not being human in the sense of the political animal. Thus, obviously, a *ius communicationis* that is understood in its exclusive aspects could be of particular use in legitimizing a contemporary human right to Internet access.

(b) Also, the vast openness of the term *communicatio*—which contains a lot of different things for Vitoria in addition to travel, eating together, the exchange of ideas and trade—is useful in the digital age. Communication has become a meta-activity that can have private, scientific, military, political or other implications ranging from the production of physical objects to their transport and their destruction in cyber-warfare. Today, the right to communicate is a super-right with implications as rich and diverse as Vitoria's *ius communicationis.*

---

[40] de Vitoria 1997 (*De Indis*), I, Tertia Propositio, 15.

[41] de Vitoria 2010, 250.

[42] de Vitoria 1997 (*De Indis*), III, 4.

[43] de Vitoria 2010, 281.

[44] de Vitoria 1995 (*De homicidio*), 18.

[45] Buchanan 2011.

(c) In the digital age—as with Vitoria and the Amerindians—we are once again confronted with beings on our epistemological frontiers whose humanity is in question. In its non-biologist nature, the *ius communicationis* opens up the possibility of non-human or post-human agents being granted the moral and juridical status of humans with respect to their rights and their responsibilities within the *res publica totius orbis*. In fact, the Turing Test, the most popular test to detect artificial intelligence, is based on the idea that a machine is intelligent if it can communicate in a way that is indistinguishable from a human being.
(d) Even the eschatological aspects of the *ius communicationis* make sense at the present time, i.e. the *ordinatio ad unum* of *communicatio*, which paradoxically legitimizes open *communicatio,* because it is a means to global conversion to Christianity and, thus, to the end of history in an unified belief,[46] which is alien to modernity, but crucial to Vitoria. Spontaneous processes of communication have been found to produce strong accumulative tendencies in the so-called heavy tailed distributions, as the enormous concentration of the digital market shows.[47] Similar to the eschatological aspects of the *ius communicationis*, those accumulative tendencies make the *ius communicationis* even more important, because they ultimately will not only produce huge oligopolies such as Facebook and Google, but they might be the breeding ground for the emergence of the singularity: an autonomous artificial intelligence as the highest form of digital accumulation. And if, for example, common aspects of global communication are restricted in favour of proprietary aspects, then the resulting accumulative tendencies might have anti-human, inhumane aspects. Eschatology in general is very helpful for object-oriented thought since it is based on the idea that a certain environment produces an external, completely different effect that is in terms of quality independent from the environment. Understanding technological emergence means understanding the importance of creating the kind of technological ecology that produces wanted singularities and avoids unwanted ones.

5 Just Cyber-wars

Similar to what Schmitt called the age of police-bombing and the age of humanitarian interventions that started in the Nineties, our present age of "the Nomos of the Code" is, once more, a non-Westphalian order. In fact, the legal problems related to

---

[46]de Vitoria 1997 (*De Indis*), III, II, Articulus II (IX) *Utrum cum infidelibus possit communicari*: "*Non est dubium quin converteremus ad fidem Christi maiorem partem saracenorum, si cum eius haberemus familiaritatem, quia in secta sua non habent nisi meras fabulas et meras nugas*".
[47]Shirky 2003.

cyber-wars are even more complex than the post-territorial problems of the ages before.

(a) In many cases, cyber-attacks cannot be clearly ascribed to a single attacker, because they are usually directed as false flag operations via other agents, for example by using botnets.
(b) Often, instances of cyber-attacks are not verifiable by the public because they target confidential material.
(c) Differences between cyber-war (international), cyber-criminality (private), cyber-intrusions (aimed at digital networks), cyber-attacks (aimed at infrastructure) are unclear, especially because of (a) and (b).
(d) Another major problem connected to all of those points is to find an adequate response to cyber-attacks, which has led several contemporary theorists of cyber-war to the idea of *bellum iustum.*[48]

The main problem of all of those points is of course the problem of all theories of war: de facto, there is no international sovereign to regulate the actions of sovereign states. A reinterpretation of Vitoria's idea of the *bellum iustum* can be helpful in this area, because it hedges the sphere of action of political power in the international sphere and subordinates it to the global common good.

(a) Concerning *ius ad bellum*, the *ius communicationis* allows global digital commons to be classified as a good that can be defended with just, possibly also private, cyber-wars. Here, it is the intention that makes the difference between war and attack. A just private cyber-war is how one could defend the actions of Snowden. In terms of Grotius's re-reading of Vitoria, Snowden has led a *bellum iustum privatum* to protect the freedom of the digital global commons against U.S. attacks.
(b) Concerning *ius ad bellum*, one could formulate a right to invade a foreign state to transform it into what Vitoria calls in *De Indis* a *res publica legitima et ordinata*,[49] which participates in an orderly form in the digital commons. This seems to provide a fair justification to—digitally or even non-digitally—invade countries that willingly or unwillingly act as safe havens for cyber-criminals (such as allegedly Russia and China). This eliminates one of the biggest problems of the difficulties with the distinction between cyber-criminality and cyber-warfare. Extra-territorial jurisdiction could in some ways—depending on the specific relation between two states—be enforced.[50] As in the Snowden case, a justification for this could be a *bellum iustum*—in this case led by a state —whose aim is to defend the global digital commons.
(c) Concerning *ius ad bellum*, in spite of the often confidential nature of cyber-intrusions, possibilities of verification by the public must be granted, because such a public discussion is one of Vitoria's conditions of *bellum iustum*

[48]Giesen 2014, Solis 2014, Hildebrandt 2013.
[49]de Vitoria 1997 (*De indis*), III, 7, 17.
[50]Hildebrandt 2013.

elaborated in *De Iure Belli.*[51] If there is no possibility to prove cyber-attacks to the public, then a just defensive war cannot be pursued. National common sense serves here as the representative and legitimate custodian of the global commons (which would make sense, for example, from a Kantian perspective, according to which all discourse is a priori universalization).

(d) The *ius in bello* limits just wars to a great extent, inasmuch as Vitoria demands most of all proportionality. The rule of proportionality could also provide a legal framework to limit the possible responses to acts of cyber-war, which can at the present time—according to NATO—also include conventional warfare to an unclear extent. The NATO Wales Summit Declaration from 2014 reads: "We affirm that cyber defence is part of NATO's core task of collective defence. A decision as to when a cyber attack would lead to the invocation of Article 5 would be taken by the North Atlantic Council on a case-by-case basis".[52] As a general rule, retaliation for acts of cyber-war should only be proportional to the amount of injury that the attacked party actually suffered, whether that party received it digitally or non-digitally.

(e) Concerning *ius in bello*, the distinction between civilians and combatants, which Vitoria emphasizes, and which is especially blurry in cyber-warfare, needs to be upheld in a *bellum iustum.* Measures such as Prism by the US military eradicate the distinction between civilians and combatants,[53] innocents and suspects. Of course, in fact, the demand to keep up this distinction is especially important because the intrusions by the US government in the case of Prism were deliberately used to commit economic espionage, which undermines trust in the global economy and which is, in its broadest sense, a common crucial to international relations.

(f) Concerning *ius post bellum*[54]—and similar to what Vitoria says about the treatment of a defeated nation—one could argue that legal responses to cyber-attacks and cyber-wars cannot irreversibly limit the accessibility of the global digital commons as is the case in most contemporary attempts to generate cyber-security. Rather, digital commons need to stay accessible also after a possible just war response to an attack and the destruction of commons must be kept to a minimum, because, at least according to Vitoria, commons ontologically precede the legitimate titles of just wars: "*Parta victoria et completo bello oportet moderate et modestia (…) victoria uti. Oportet victorem existimare se iudicem sedere inter duas res publicas. Alteram, quae laesa est, alteram quae iniuriam fecit (…). sine calamitate rei publicae nocentis*"[55]—"*Once the war has been fought and victory won, he must use his victory with moderation and (…)*

[51]de Vitoria 1997 (*De Iure Belli*), IV, 1, 6, 2.

[52]NATO 2014.

[53]de Vitoria 1997 (*De Iure Belli*), IV, 2.

[54]Solis is wrong in ascribing the invention of the *ius post bellum* to Kant. Solis 2014.

[55]de Vitoria 1997 (*De Iure Belli*), Conclusiones.

humility. The victor must think of himself as a judge sitting in judgement between two commonwealths, one the injured party and the other the offender, (…) without causing the utter ruination of the guilty commonwealth".[56]

6 Conclusion

This conclusion addresses general questions, firstly concerning the methodological background of this chapter and the argument that one has to consider both the contemporary and the historical context in order to not only produce sound and transparent intellectual historiography, but also highlight different aspects of historical writings.

At least concerning the teachings of Vitoria, it is clear that an emphasis on non-anthropological aspects of *communicatio* that is directed towards contemporary questions surrounding digital networks can lead to a better understanding of Vitoria's difficult position as a theorist between the subjective (modern) and the objective (medieval) strain of legal philosophy.[57]

Secondly—and this is probably more important—Vitoria does indeed provide some orientation when thinking about various questions in relation to digital networks today, such as digital commons, digital communication as a human right, just cyber-wars. But so also probably do Kant, Hegel, Hobbes and virtually any historical theorist of international relations. One can, however, make the point that Vitoria's significance goes beyond this. Since he is one of the authors—indeed *the* author par excellence—with regard to formulating a global "nomos" in the Schmittian sense, holding his texts next to our contemporary reality tells us also a lot about general questions. What is the "nomos of the code"? What are the characteristics of this age? What are its dangers?

It is best to answer these questions by reference to Vitoria's teachings and the historical genealogy they have founded. One of the most startling ideas in the teachings of Vitoria is the instantaneous turn from the idea of an all-encompassing global communicative community to a justification of the Conquest. Since the criticism by Schmitt, Koskenniemi, Anghie,[58] this turn has been noted as partly surprising, partly anachronistic, partly cunning. It makes Vitoria an essential reading for many following justifications of colonial conquest, in which the ideas of international community and humanism, exploitation and war form a dangerous amalgam that some say discredits the concept of European universalism as a whole.

In Vitoria's time, the seamlessness with which peaceful communication leads to violent conquest might be an indicator of the ideological nature of his thought.

---

[56]de Vitoria 2010, 327.

[57]Brett 2003.

[58]Schmitt 2006, Koskenniemi 2010, Anghie 2004.

According to Marx, ideology always depicts the world "upside down"[59] and can be identified by the kitsch nature and detachedness of its concepts from reality—such as imagining heavily armed Spaniards as exercising their right to hospitality and to "*communicatio*"—a narrative as idealized and absurdly far from reality as Don Quixote's knightly tales from the same period. The partly ideological, sometimes clearly ironic or simply partly uninformed, nature of these incongruences between reality and thought in Vitoria's teachings has rarely been discussed. However: in spite—or because?—of the unrealistic nature of these claims, Vitoria's demands of *communicatio* and global responsibility were the blueprint for the realities of open door policies and humanitarian interventions until today.

We are now, however, living in a world in which a simple intertwining of peaceful communication and war does make much more sense than it did in the golden age. Since—of all people[60]—Hilary Clinton's 2010 speech at the *Newseum*, the promotion of "Internet Freedom" is an official doctrine of US foreign policy.[61] Since Snowden, however, almost all citizens of the world have learned that "Internet Freedom" not only allows peaceful citizens to use the large databases of Google and Facebook, but, in turn, makes them part of those databases, which are available to the NSA de facto at any given time without a warrant, which is why some speak of a military-digital complex.[62]

This new digital imperialism is increasingly being understood as such. As I am writing this, the European Court of Justice has issued an opinion against passing EU citizens' data to US authorities, which is a first step towards regaining data sovereignty.[63] China's Internet regulations, too, can be interpreted not only as totalitarian coercion, but also as a restitution of data sovereignty.

But as long as such exceptions are not the rule, it can be said that we are once more living in the days of *conquista* and *koophandel met force* (commerce with force) that characterized the golden age of discovery. Through the gateway of digital communication, everything is up for grabs. The age of the nomos of the code is always in danger of *in toto* replacement of the law (nomos) by the atavistic and more authoritarian code of de facto powers, which is a priori without that close relationship to borders and territories that characterize the political or legal nomos.

Rather than being an uncanny coincidence in history, the fact that Vitoria's idea of *communicatio*—in all its problematic ambiguity—turned into reality might point to the fact that "the nomos of the code" signifies a tautological point in which modern occidental history has reached its *telos*. Was not the unified global discourse that we have today at least the ideological aim of Western imperialism, in both its Enlightenment and its Christian version? And does it not become

[59]Marx 1975.

[60]Clinton protected her own e-mails to an illegal extent.

[61]Morozov 2011.

[62]Brito and Watkins 2011.

[63]Kelion 2015.

increasingly clear that this aim is not problematic merely because it served as a euphemism for colonialism, but problematic in itself?

The idea of *communicatio* as an aim in itself—one which, by the way, all Kantianisms in general share—is probably the dominant idea of the age of the nomos of the code, one that has been criticized as "Cyber-Utopianism", "Californian Ideology" or "Cyber-Maoism"[64] and that has been characterized for example by Hildebrandt as being "based on the idea that a free Internet will automatically bring salvation (…)."[65]

Only when we relate this idea again to one of its most important origins in terms of global politics—to Vitoria's *De Indis*—do we see why this idea of communication as an aim in itself is so erratic. During the course of time, something like a "*Kommunikationsvergessenheit*" happened, a forgetfulness of communication, to Heideggerize this. Unlike in Vitoria's time, today, the primacy of communication is not understood within the intellectual context it was originally developed.

With Vitoria, we do not have the partly toxic mixture between consumer individualism, post-political executive forces and total communication that is characteristic of the age of the nomos of the code, but the notion of global communication is connected to a systematic complex of different non-subjective levels of the common good. This nexus binds *communicatio*, the common good and global communication in a way that is not even communitarian, but non-anthropocentric, in a sense that neither the individual, nor the state stand in the centre of Vitoria's conception, but rather the global common of communication itself.

It is the normative purpose of any law—especially international law—to safeguard this common good beyond anarcho-libertarian and totalitarian conceptions alike. In a more descriptive way, by definition, international agreements can only be forged on the basis of debate and the institutional processes concerning global commons, natural and non-natural in an essentialist sense. Because today they materially and therefore also ontologically depend on the digital global commons, international agreements—by virtue of natural law—cannot coherently include strict laws on cyber-security, cyber-vigilance or copyright that threaten the digital commons in their very existence. Rather, institutional solutions have to be found, which guarantee the openness of the digital commons in spite of totalitarian aspirations.

Here, the Vitorian perspective appears to be in line with the standpoint of Internet theorist Jodi Dean[66]: the Internet seems, especially in its openness, to be an "institution zero" of future global solutions, a birthplace and an environment for institutional solutions that is, however, not directly institutionalized itself and should not be institutionalized, so that it can fulfil its function of being a kind of catalyst and breeding ground for institutions and—at the same time—a counterweight to them. It is a misunderstanding of Vitoria's teachings to assume that the

---

[64]Barbrook and Cameron 1995, Lanier 2010.

[65]Hildebrandt 2013.

[66]Dean 2003.

res publica totius orbis is per se organized in a manner similar to that of an exclusively intergovernmental institution such as the UN. Rather, it consists of the direct and informal political participation of citizens who—"*expresserunt consensum* [...] *potius factis quam verbis*"—"express consent rather in deeds than in words".[67]

References

Anghie A (2004) Imperialism, sovereignty, and the making of international law. Cambridge University Press, Cambridge

Aquinas. Sententia Politicorum, II, 1, 6. http://www.corpusthomisticum.org/cpo.html. Accessed 30 July 2016

Barbrook R, Cameron A (1995) The Californian Ideology. http://www.hrc.wmin.ac.uk/theory-californianideology-main.html. Accessed 25 Sept 2015

Brown SJ (2000) The Spanish origin of international law. Francisco de Vitoria and his Law of Nations. The Lawbook Exchange, New Jersey

Brett AS (2003) Liberty, right and nature. Individual rights in later scholastic thought. Cambridge University Press, Cambridge

Benkler Y (2006) The wealth of networks. Yale University Press, New Haven

Buchanan A (2011) Better than human. The promise and perils of enhancing ourselves. Oxford University Press, Oxford

Brito RDJ, Watkins T (2011) Loving the cyber bomb? the dangers of threat inflation in cybersecurity policy. Working Paper Mercatus Center at George Mason University 11–24, 1–34

Bratton B (2014) The black stack. http://www.e-flux.com/journal/the-black-stack/. Accessed 25 Sept 2015

de Girolami R "De bono communi", IX. http://www.e-theca.net/emiliopanella/remigio2/8540.htm. Accessed 30 July 2016

de Vitoria F (1928) Los manuscriptos del Maestro Fray Francisco de Vitoria. Edited by Beltran de Heredia. Tipgrafia Moderna, Valencia

de Vitoria F (1995) Vorlesungen I. Völkerrecht, Politik, Kirche. Latin and German. Edited by Ulrich Horst u.a. Kohlhammer, Stuttgart

de Vitoria F (1997) Vorlesungen II. Völkerrecht, Politik, Kirche. Latin and German. Edited by Ulrich Horst u.a. Kohlhammer, Stuttgart

Desantes Guanter JM (1999) Francisco de Vitoria, precursor del derecho de la información. Fundación de la Comunicación Social, Madrid

Dean J (2003) Why the net is not a public sphere. Constellations 10:95–112

de Vitoria F (2010) Political Writings. English. Edited and translated by Pagden A, Larwence J. Cambridge UP, Cambridge

Foucault M (1972) The archaeology of knowledge. Pantheon Books, London

Giesen Klaus-Gerd (2014) Justice in Cyberwar. Ethic@—An Int J Moral Philos 13(27): 1677–2954

Hardin G (1968) The tragedy of the commons. Science 162:1243–1248

Harlan D (1989) Intellectual history and the return of literature. Am Hist Rev 94(3):581–609

Hildebrandt M (2013) Extraterritorial Jurisdiction to enforce in Cyberspace? Bodin, Schmitt, Grotius, in Cyberspace. Univ Toronto Law J 63(2):196–224

Kelly K (2010) What technology wants. Penguin Books, New York

---

[67]de Vitoria 1928 *In IIa-IIae*, q. 62.

Koskenniemi M (2010) The gentle civilizer of nations. Cambridge University Press, Cambridge
Kelion L (2015) "Facebook privacy campaign advances after EU court opinion", BBC News, 9/23/2015. http://www.bbc.com/news/technology-34336111. Accessed 24 Sept 2015
Lessig L (1999) Code, and other laws of cyberspace. Basic Books, New York
Lessig L (2005) Free culture. Penguin, New York
Levy CJ (2010) "Russia uses microsoft to suppress dissent", New York Times, 9/11/2010. http://www.nytimes.com/2010/09/12/world/europe/12raids.html?_r=0. Accessed 25 Sept 2015
Lanier J (2010) You are not a Gadget. Knopf, New York
Marx K (1975) The German Ideology. Lawrence and Wishart, London
MacKinnon R (2013) Consent of the networked: the worldwide struggle for internet freedom. Basic Books, New York
Morozov E (2011) The net delusion. PublicAffairs, New York
Nys E (1894) Les origines du droit international. A. Castaigne, Bruxelles
NATO (2014) Summit Declaration 2014. http://www.nato.int/cps/en/natohq/official_texts_112964.htm. Accessed 2 July 2016
Stiegler B (1998) Technics and time. Stanford University Press, Stanford
Skinner Q (2002) Visions of politics. Regarding method, vol 1. Cambridge University Press, Cambridge
Shirky C (2003) "Power Laws, Weblogs, and Inequality", First published February 8, 2003 on the Networks, Economics, and Culture mailing list. http://www.shirky.com/writings/powerlaw_weblog.html. Accessed 2 July 2016
Schmitt C (2006) The Nomos of the Earth. Telos, New York
Shirky C (2010) Cognitive Surplus. Penguin, New York
Simondon G (2011) The essence of technicity. Deleuze Studies 5:406–424
Solis GD (2014) Cyber warfare. Mil Law Rev 219:1–52
Thumfart J (2013) Archäologie—Ideengeschichte—Topik. Zur Gegenüberstellung der Methoden Foucaults und Skinners. In: Busen A, Weiß A (eds) Ansätze und Methoden zur Erforschung politischer Ideen. Nomos, Berlin, pp 127–148
Wallerstein I (1974) The modern world system I: capitalist agriculture and the origins of the european world economy in the sixteenth century. University of California Press, New York
Walzer M (1997) Just and unjust wars: a moral argument with historical illustrations. Basic Books, Philadelphia

CPSIA information can be obtained
at www.ICGtesting.com
Printed in the USA
BVOW06*1658090917
494450BV00012B/83/P

9 783319 629971